D1464212

PENGUIN  CLASSICS

# WILLIAM SHAKESPEARE: THE NARRATIVE POEMS

170   240

# WILLIAM SHAKESPEARE

## THE
# NARRATIVE POEMS

EDITED BY
MAURICE EVANS

| NORWICH CITY COLLEGE LIBRARY | | |
|---|---|---|
| Stock No. | 170240 | |
| Class | 821·3 SHA | |
| Cat. | Proc. | |

PENGUIN BOOKS

## PENGUIN BOOKS

Published by the Penguin Group
Penguin Books Ltd, 27 Wrights Lane, London W8 5TZ, England
Penguin Putnam Inc., 375 Hudson Street, New York, New York 10014, USA
Penguin Books Australia Ltd, Ringwood, Victoria, Australia
Penguin Books Canada Ltd, 10 Alcorn Avenue, Toronto, Ontario, Canada M4V 3B2
Penguin Books (NZ) Ltd, 182–190 Wairau Road, Auckland 10, New Zealand

Penguin Books Ltd, Registered Offices: Harmondsworth, Middlesex, England

This edition first published in Penguin Books 1989
5 7 9 10 8 6

This edition copyright © Penguin Books, 1989
Introduction and notes © Maurice Evans, 1989
All rights reserved

Printed in England by Clays Ltd, St Ives plc
Set in Bembo (Linotron 202)

Except in the United States of America, this book is sold subject
to the condition that it shall not, by way of trade or otherwise, be lent,
re-sold, hired out, or otherwise circulated without the publisher's
prior consent in any form of binding or cover other than that in
which it is published and without a similar condition including this
condition being imposed on the subsequent purchaser

# CONTENTS

# INTRODUCTION

## THE NARRATIVE POEMS

*Venus and Adonis* (1593) and *The Rape of Lucrece* (1594) were both dedicated to Henry Wriothesley, third Earl of Southampton, who was an influential and discriminating patron of the arts. The public theatres were closed on account of the plague from the middle of 1592 until early 1594, so Shakespeare may have been driven to write and publish his poems 'to take advantage of all idle hours', as he puts it in his dedication to *Venus*, in order to keep the wolf from the door. That he succeeded in this aim is proved by the sixteen editions of *Venus* and eight of *Lucrece*, as well as by the many imitations and innumerable literary references which appeared before 1640: both poems were very widely read, although neither was included in the First Folio. After the middle of the seventeenth century, however, their popularity declined sharply; and, although by 1790 Edmond Malone had established them finally in the Shakespearian canon, they have generally been treated as the poor relations, included in the collected works only for the sake of completeness or for any light which they might throw upon the plays. Even during the last thirty years, which have produced much good criticism and a number of important editions, the interest in the poems has been primarily academic, and they have never regained the truly popular appeal which they had in Shakespeare's life-time, and which the plays and sonnets still retain.

In the dedication to *Venus*, Shakespeare describes the poem as 'the first heir of my invention', although by this time he was already established as a major dramatist. His description is generally taken to mean that he looked on *Venus* as his first genuine 'literary' creation because it was a poem and not a play. In the early 1590s, the drama of the public theatres was not yet taken seriously as an art form, and Sidney's scathing attack on it some ten years earlier in his *An Apology for Poetry* was still indicative of the accepted literary hierarchy of the period. In recommending himself to a young humanist patron, therefore, Shakespeare inevitably offered poems rather than plays; and the fact that he prefaced *Venus* with a Latin motto taken from Ovid's *Amores* underlines the point:

> *Vilia miretur vulgus; mihi flavus Apollo*
> *Pocula Castalia plena ministret aqua.*

(I, xv)

> Let base-conceited wits admire vile things:
> Fair Phoebus lead me to the Muse's springs.

(Marlowe's translation)

In this, Shakespeare is insisting that his poem is serious 'highbrow' literature and not designed for the ears of the groundlings.

Some of the pressures which helped to shape Shakespeare's literary intention in this way have been investigated by M. C. Bradbrook in her account of the social purpose of *Venus*. In September 1592, seven months before the publication of Shakespeare's poem, *Greenes Groats-Worth of Witte* had been registered, containing its notorious attack on the '"upstart Crow", beautified with our feathers, that with his *Tygers hart wrapt in a Players hyde*, supposes he is as well able to bombast out a blanke verse as the best of you: and . . . is in his owne conceit the onely Shake-scene in a countrey'. It is clear that Greene was attacking Shakespeare in particular, but through him also the whole acting and dramatic profession, equating them with the lowest and most scurrilous types of ántic and mime. His prime motive was, no doubt, envy of a writer more successful than himself, but beyond this he voices the contempt and the uneasiness of the University Wit in the presence of the new, popular and relatively unlettered medium which was challenging the established literary kinds. The fact that

Greene had written for the popular stage makes this sneer of the University Wit at a non-university writer peculiarly hypocritical. It would seem that Shakespeare answered this attack with his poems which were designed to beat the opposition at its own game. *Venus* and *Lucrece* exhibit a range of poetic skills which equalled anything else in the period and proved incontrovertibly that a playwright could also be a poet and, indeed, a popular one.

This assumption explains a good deal about the nature and quality of the poems. At one level at least the two are essentially 'display' poems which demonstrate an extraordinary mastery of poetic rhetoric and a knowledge of all the fashionable poetic narrative modes of the period. To this fact they owe both their contemporary popularity and their subsequent decline, for they were tailored most precisely to what are specifically Elizabethan standards of excellence and have, in consequence, become the most dated of Shakespeare's works in later periods. The two poems differ greatly in theme and method, and it will be profitable to consider them separately; but it should be said of both that the problems they present to a modern reader stem from a change of taste rather than from any failure in the poems themselves. It is important to recognize too that the common tendency to consider them exclusively in relation to the plays, especially in the case of *Lucrece*, has often led to judgements based on inappropriate dramatic criteria. These are narrative poems with their own conventions and decorum, and they belong more properly with other narrative works of the time such as Sidney's *Arcadia* or even Spenser's *Faerie Queene* rather than with Shakespeare's own plays. The relationship between *Venus*, in particular, and Books II and III of *The Faerie Queene*, published in 1590, is, as we shall see, a very close one. I shall discuss the poems primarily, therefore, in relationship to Elizabethan narrative and poetry.

# VENUS AND ADONIS

I

*Venus* is a very literary poem, both in language and in kind. For his literary genre Shakespeare turned to the new and fashionable models of Ovidian verse which had been encouraged by Arthur Golding's translation of the *Metamorphoses* (1567), and subsequently by the range of Marlowe's Ovidian translations and poems in the 1580s and early 1590s which were widely known in manuscript. His immediate model was probably Thomas Lodge's *Scillaes Metamorphosis* of 1589, but he knew and may have been influenced by Marlowe's *Hero and Leander*, written about the same time as *Venus* although not published until 1598. He may also have known a short poem in Latin called 'Narcissus', which, like *Venus* was dedicated to Southampton and published in 1591. Its author, John Clapham, was one of Lord Burleigh's secretaries, and his poem, as G. P. V. Akrigg suggests, may be concerned with contemporary events with which Shakespeare was also familiar. Southampton was a ward of Burleigh and from 1590 onwards was under pressure from his guardian to marry the Lady Elizabeth Vere, Burleigh's granddaughter – a pressure which he resisted, even though in 1592 he had to pay Burleigh £5,000 for refusing to comply with his wishes. It looks as if Clapham's poem was designed to curry favour with Burleigh by making a delicate plea to Southampton to marry in the normal dynastic way.

The poem offers a traditional interpretation of the Ovidian story in terms of self-love. Narcissus enters Cupid's palace and receives from the god both time-honoured advice on how to woo a woman and a warning about the dangers of self-love.

4

On leaving, he mounts his horse of Blind Desire, which runs away with him and eventually throws its rider besides the stream of Philautia, or Self-Love, from which he drinks and by which he is so changed that he can no longer recognize his own reflection in the water. He falls in love with it, therefore, and when night blots out the image, he voices his grief with a lament which, as in Ovid, is repeated by the watching nymph Echo. In the morning he dies of his grief, and Venus, taking pity on him, transforms him into the flower which bears his name. 'Narcissus' is an undistinguished, cliché-ridden poem which had little to offer Shakespeare except, perhaps, the conception of the unruly steed which Shakespeare put to a subtler and more organic use in his own poem. The theme of self-love, however, coupled with the dedication to Southampton, links it with Shakespeare's study of a Narcissistic Adonis and also, of course, with the first sixteen of his sonnets, which imply that the young man suffered from the same disease. It seems likely that *Venus* was initially a topical and 'in' poem, although based on a different myth and given a universal application.

## II

In *Venus* Shakespeare drew upon two separate Ovidian traditions. The one, that of the *Metamorphoses*, dealt in mythology which had acquired a strong dimension of moral allegory from the Middle Ages: the other, that of the *Amores*, was erotic, mainly comic and wholly concerned with the behaviour of human beings. Marlowe had translated the work, and Donne was to imitate it in his early *Songs and Sonets* and *Elegies*, earning thereby the compliment from Thomas Carew that he had silenced the 'tales o' th' *Metamorphoses*' and banished the 'traine of gods and goddesses' from 'nobler Poems'. Shakespeare's *Venus* is an attempt to combine both traditions without muting either, and the combination of myth with dramatic realism has worried modern critics. The Elizabethans were more flexible readers than we are, able to accept simultaneously, and yet enjoy separately, the levels of allegorical myth and naturalistic narrative. The popularity of *The Faerie Queene*, for example, suggests that they could read it both as a complex allegory and as a romantic tale at the same time. We are less adept at this kind of dualism and expect a work to be one thing or the other. When, for example, Venus boasts that her flesh is soft and plump and shows that her arm is powerful enough to hold Adonis down, yet at the same time her foot leaves no print on the sand and even a primrose is strong enough to support her, we are more likely to think of Gilbert's literal and solid Fairy Queen in *Iolanthe* than to kindle to the idea that love can be both heavy and light.

> Love is a spirit all compact of fire,
> Not gross to sink, but light, and will aspire.
>
> (149–50)

says Venus, explaining her own allegory. Similarly we find it easier to accept the idea of physical lust when it is defined in intellectual terms in Shakespeare's Sonnet 129 than when it is embodied in Venus, whose 'face doth reek and smoke, her blood doth boil' (555). For the one-dimensional reader, which most of us are, the literal and the allegorical dimensions within the poem tend to fight and exclude each other rather than coexist peacefully. It was not a problem that Shakespeare had to face in any serious degree, but he was aware of it and occasionally plays off the abstract idea against the concrete figure which clothes it. This is the case in the passage previously cited about the primroses which uphold Venus: 'These forceless flowers like sturdy trees support me' (152). The comparison to 'sturdy trees' blots out the image of fragile primroses, and hints that although love itself may be light and aspiring, Venus herself is certainly not. Much of the comedy of *Venus*, indeed, comes from Shakespeare's ability to exploit the tensions between the two Ovidian modes of allegory and naturalism.

   Ovid, of course, was no new discovery: he had long been the saint of love poets, as he was for Chaucer, and he was still familiar under such medieval guises as the *Ovide Moralisé* or the poetry of Courtly Love. But the sudden explosion of Ovidian verse in the late sixteenth century represented a characteristic humanist return to the original Ovid, a frankly erotic Ovid who provided a counter-blast to the current fashion of Petrarchan idealism. In choosing the Ovidian mode, Shakespeare was using and extending a genre which was not yet too strictly bound by the conventions of established form, and which offered opportunities both for erotic pleasure and for serious meaning, as well as encouraging the enjoyment of mythology for its own sake. Such a combination was guaranteed to appeal to the young humanist Southampton.

The language of *Venus* is highly allusive, as T. W. Baldwin shows, not only in such traditional set-pieces as the description of the boar or of Adonis' horse, which follow well-known patterns originating in Ovid and Virgil, but in the very texture of the narrative verse, which is studded with familiar topoi and literary commonplaces. The language of poetry has always been literary, whether building upon what has gone before or reacting against it; but the heightened literary consciousness of the Renaissance was aware to an unusual degree of the heritage available to it and ready to be redeployed. From the opening description of the sun 'with purple-coloured face' – a passage which, as Baldwin says, has Spenser, Ovid and the Bible among its literary god-fathers – the poem goes on its way with phrases and images which would raise an echo in every educated Elizabethan bosom. 'Rose-cheeked Adonis'(3) or 'the gentle lark' mounting on high from his moist cabinet (853) or the comparison of repressed speech to 'An oven that is stopped, or river stayed' (331) are all permutations of familiar material. Allusiveness of this kind is scarcely a conscious process since topoi are the very medium of such poetry, and Shakespeare incorporates them as naturally as breathing. They give a resonance to the poem which is the most difficult quality for a modern reader with his different cultural background to appreciate.

What is more easily recognized is Shakespeare's exploitation of contemporary poetic styles. Renaissance literary decorum dictated that love should have a poetical language of its own, not only in such obvious forms of love poetry as the Petrarchan sonnet but even in the drama, where the characters are apt to change style and adopt the rhetoric of love whenever the action embraces it. As the goddess of love, Venus inevitably uses the whole familiar battery of sonnet images, hyperboles and conceits as the trade-mark of her role in myth. The fire-darting eyes (196), the sighs which emulate the wind (189), the pretty dimples where Cupid hides himself (242), the Ovidian banquet of the senses (445), love as a matter of law (334) or of sale and debt (511), love as war (355) – all these and countless more are the medium of her wooing. And in a poem where the hunt plays so important a part, whether the soft hunt of love or the hard hunt of the boar, the old and hackneyed hart/heart, deer/dear conceit is inevitably there, though brilliantly extended by Shakespeare into a whole cosmography of the human body almost as elaborate as that in Donne's nineteenth elegy, 'To His Mistris Going to Bed':

'Fondling,' she saith, 'since I have hemmed thee here
Within the circuit of this ivory pale,
I'll be a park, and thou shalt be my deer;
Feed where thou wilt, on mountain or in dale;
   Graze on my lips, and if those hills be dry,
   Stray lower, where the pleasant fountains lie.

'Within this limit is relief enough,
Sweet bottom-grass and high delightful plain,
Round rising hillocks, brakes obscure and rough . . .'

(229–37)

These are all very familiar materials in the period, but the use to which Shakespeare puts them is a new one. Sonnet conceits and pleas for love or pity of this kind are normally offered by the lover to his obdurate mistress; but it is typical of Shakespeare that he stands the convention on its head and makes Venus play the part of the male lover. In one way, of course, this is proper, since it is love itself which makes the advances, whatever the sex; but here love is embodied in so conventionally feminine a form that the use of a traditionally male language comes as a shock. It is Adonis, not the goddess, who is the besieged fort:

Remove your siege from my unyielding heart;
To love's alarms it will not ope the gate.

(423-4)

The expected pattern is that of Spenser's male lover vainly encouraging his defeated troops back to the siege:

Retourne agayne my forces late dismayd
Unto the siege by you abandon'd quite,

(*Amoretti*, XIV)

or of Sidney's Astrophel lamenting that Stella's heart

. . . is such a Cittadell,
So fortified with wit, stor'd with disdain,
That to win it is all the skill and paine.

(*Astrophel and Stella*, XII)

A poetry reader of the 1590s would have been quick to recognize the inversion and have found *Venus* witty and provocative because of it. In contrast to the Petrarchan tradition, Ovid's *Metamorphoses* is full of aggressively passionate women who, like Shakespeare's Venus, do all the wooing. The stories of Echo with Narcissus or Salmacis with Hermaphroditus – both of them providing source material for Shakespeare – or of Myrrha, the ill-fated mother of Adonis himself, all have heroines whose behaviour anticipates that of Venus. Shakespeare's poem uses the language of the Petrarchan sonnet to express Ovidian themes, and the mixture is a piquant one.

III

In any narrative poem by Shakespeare we should expect to find a strong dramatic dimension; and the story of Venus and Adonis is told mainly through dramatic dialogue which sets the scene and invites the audience to visualize the action as well as listen to the words:

What see'st thou in the ground? hold up thy head,
Look in mine eyeballs, there thy beauty lies;

(118-9)

Lie quietly and hear a little more;
Nay, do not struggle, for thou shalt not rise.

(709–10)

Shakespeare is not, however, simply following his natural bent as a dramatist but is writing according to the normal Renaissance theory of narrative poetry which derived from a blend of Aristotle's *Poetics* and Horace's *Ars Poetica*. Aristotle's *mimesis* (imitation), in terms of which he defined poetry, was taken to imply visual representation; and this, when crossed with Horace's famous phrase '*ut pictura poesis*' ('Poetry is like painting'), led to the common Renaissance definition of poetry as a 'Speaking Picture' which Sidney, for example, propounds in his *An Apology for Poetry* (p. 101). The strongly pictorial emphasis of Renaissance poetic theory is reflected in the large number of rhetorical figures in the contemporary handbooks of poetry, the function of which is to help the poet present his characters, places, occasions and actions in visual form. George Puttenham's *Arte of English Poesie* (1589) defines a whole battery of them – for example, '*Hypotiposis* or the counterfait representation', which enables the poet to 'set foorth many things, in such sort as it should appeare they were truly before our eyes' (p. 238). Narrative poetry in particular needs such devices, since it has to present actions without the help of actors to flesh them out; and for this reason *Venus* abounds in visual description throughout, and not merely in such set-pieces as the account of Adonis' horse or the hunting of the hare.

An even more important aspect of narrative is that it implies a narrator; and we are always conscious of his presence in *Venus*, telling the story, describing the scene, commenting on the action or inviting the reader to take notice: 'Look when a painter would surpass the life / In limning out a well-proportioned steed' (289); 'Look what a horse should have he did not lack' (299). The narrator draws attention both to the scene and to the skill of his own verbal picture; he comments with kindly detachment on the characters – 'poor fool', 'good queen' – and he presents his whole account of them as a narrative artefact in conceited language which continually directs attention to the art of the story-teller – for example, the ingenious euphemisms by which Adonis' mouth or Venus' tongue and eyes are described: 'Once more the engine of her thoughts began' (367); 'Once more the ruby-coloured portal opened, / Which to his speech did honey passage yield' (451–2); 'Her two blue windows faintly she upheaveth' (482). The interest is transferred from the story itself to the way in which it is told, and the reader, in consequence, is kept at a distance from the action, made to observe rather than to participate. By this means the eroticism of the poem is transmuted into witty verbal display which rescues it from pornography, as Coleridge recognized; and similarly the pain of grief is undercut by the obtrusive art which describes it, just as in the *Arcadia* Sidney turns the most heart-rending scenes into picturesque tableaux. The sorrowing Venus is described in language which arouses admiration of its virtuosity rather than pity or fear at what is told:

> O, how her eyes and tears did lend and borrow!
> Her eye seen in the tears, tears in her eye;
> Both crystals, where they viewed each other's sorrow,
> Sorrow that friendly sighs sought still to dry;
> But like a stormy day, now wind, now rain,
> Sighs dry her cheeks, tears make them wet again.
>
> (961–6)

The more intense and potentially tragic the occasion, the greater is the display of the art by which the reader is distanced from it. At the same time the moments of most tragic action are played down so that nothing is strong enough to break through the surface embroidery: the discovery of Adonis' dead body seems almost incidental and is described in a mere couple of lines

> And in her haste unfortunately spies
> The foul boar's conquest on her fair delight;
>
> (1029–30)

and immediately the reader is moved on and distracted by the quaint and charming comparison of Venus' eyes, turned away from the tragic sight, to the snail, 'whose tender horns being hit, / Shrinks backward in his shelley cave with Pain' (1033–4). In this way style prevents tragic material from producing full tragedy; and for the same reason the comic scenes are not comedy in the Shakespearian sense of the term. Shakespeare's tragedies and comedies alike normally seek to involve the audience in the feelings they portray, but *Venus* and, as we shall see later, *Lucrece* also keep the reader at arm's length; as the critic Walter Raleigh describes Shakespeare's method in the poems, 'He handles life from a distance, at two removes, and all the emotions awakened by the poem are emotions felt in the presence of art, not those suggested by life.'

IV

The unashamed artifice of *Venus* has provoked a surprising diversity of interpretations by posing such questions as whether it is tragic or comic, whether genuinely erotic or a satire on erotic poetry. A deeper reason for its ambiguity, however, lies in the variety of allegorical interpretations which the poem encourages without committing itself finally to any of them: indeed, Shakespeare seems to set up allegories and invoke myths only to parody them, or at least to divorce them from their traditional and expected meanings. For example, the choice of Adonis between the soft chase of love and the hard chase of the boar recalls the famous choice of Hercules between the paths of pleasure and of labour – except that Adonis is clearly no figure of Hercules; and, similarly, his debate with Venus parallels and yet parodies that between Venus and the chaste huntress Diana in *The Faerie Queene* (III, vi). On the moral level, the boar carried traditional associations of virility and lust: the image of Venus riding on a boar was a familiar medieval emblem, and in *The Faerie Queene* Lust himself has 'Huge great teeth, like to a tusked boar'. The death of Adonis was commonly taken as an allegory of lust's destructive power; and Shakespeare's introduction of an overtly lustful

Venus into the myth of the death-dealing boar invites the reader to expect the conventional moral. But the expectation is disappointed: whatever Adonis may be punished for, it is certainly not lust. Shakespeare's Adonis differs from all other versions in that he is uniquely resistant to Venus' charms: even Ovid's Adonis was not opposed to love but simply preferred hunting.

In another context, the poem is full of references to love and beauty, and these were a central preoccupation of Renaissance Platonism. When Shakespeare makes Venus declare of Adonis, 'For he being dead, with him is Beauty slain, / And, Beauty dead, black Chaos comes again' (1019–20), he is putting into her mouth the fashionable jargon of contemporary Platonism which defined love as the desire for beauty, and beauty as the divine form within the material creation. In such terms, the death of Adonis becomes a tragedy of truly cosmic significance, so that critics have been tempted to place him at the centre of the poem as the embodiment of high tragic idealism. But Shakespeare's portrait of the young man undercuts such an interpretation and refutes Venus' claim. Adonis is drawn as callow, petulant, curiously literal and unpoetic: above all, narcissistic. His first words in the poem

> Fie, no more of love!
> The sun doth burn my face; I must remove.
>
> (185–6)

suggest the kind of self-regarding quality with which beauty would be credited in a Morality Play. The lines would not be out of place in the pageant of the Seven Deadly Sins in Marlowe's *Dr Faustus*. His motives too in resisting Venus have nothing to do with the idealism about love of which he is made the mouthpiece, and in all respects he falls far short of the Platonic conception of beauty. We should note that it is only the sick-thoughted Venus, and not the narrator of the poem, who names and identifies Adonis as beauty. Shakespeare's real concern is not with Platonic allegory but with a theme which he frequently treats in the plays, namely, the blindness of love and its ability to see Helen's beauty in a brow of Egypt.

The most widely known interpretation of the myth of Venus and Adonis in the Renaissance, however, was as an allegory of the annual cycle of the seasons; and it is with this that Shakespeare plays most subtly in his poem. The interpretation goes back at least as far as Macrobius' *Saturnalia*, and is still there in Boccaccio's *Genealogia Deorum*, which was a major source of allegory for the Renaissance. It was popularized by Renaissance iconographers such as Cartari and Natalis Comes, and can be found, for example, in Abraham Fraunce's *The Third Part of the Countesse of Pembrokes Yvychurch*, published two years before *Venus*. In this tradition, Adonis signifies the sun, Venus the earth and the boar, winter, which destroys their fruitful conjunction. Spenser clearly had this in mind in his own version of the myth in *The Faerie Queene* (III, vi). His ideal Garden of Adonis, in specific contrast to the normal allegory, is a garden of eternal summer and unending fruitfulness, where Venus reaps 'sweet pleasure of the wanton boy', and where the boar of winter has no place but is shut away under the hill.

Shakespeare keeps closer to the traditional allegory of summer and winter. A. Fowler and C. Butler, for example, have uncovered by their analysis of number symbolism in the poem an elaborate sequence of references to the passage of the seasons which is supported by the extensive imagery of summer, winter and fading flowers throughout. As A. C. Hamilton has pointed out, Venus offers herself as a figure of the fruitful earth, and Adonis enters the poem like the sun-god: his first appearance as 'Rose-cheeked Adonis' coincides with the rising sun 'with purple-coloured face', and his death by the boar follows the traditional winter pattern.

Even as he suggests it, however, Shakespeare qualifies and in some ways appears to make fun of the interpretation which we have been encouraged to expect. Venus is more interested in pleasure than in procreation, and Adonis dislikes the sun and wears his bonnet to protect himself from it. He chooses the sterile chase of the boar in preference to the kiss of Venus just as, when faced with the natural behaviour of his horse, his only thought is 'how to get my palfrey from the mare' (384). His defence of his own values against those of Venus is couched, ironically, in imagery which reverses the traditional pattern, associating the amorous desires of Venus with winter and his own sexless conception of love with the spring:

> Love's gentle spring doth always fresh remain,
> Lust's winter comes ere summer half be done;
>
> (801–2)

At this point, Shakespeare is playing off the moral tradition of interpretation against that of the changing seasons.

Although in *Venus* Shakespeare is characteristically iconoclastic in his treatment of traditional myths, the poem is not just a game with the reader. Its essential seriousness lies in the debate between Venus and Adonis, which is more a clash of abstract ideas than the expression of the characters themselves, and to which the death of Adonis provides a logical conclusion. The debate is about the nature of love, and Shakespeare's concern with sexual matters in the poem is typical of the period, which had become less confident in its sexual certainties and very prone to theorize about them. Sex had presented no especial problem to Chaucer, for whom the animal, the human and the spiritual still had their accepted places and roles in a great and all-embracing hierarchy. Much of this had been lost by the end of the sixteenth century, however, and the revival of Platonism in particular had created a new pressure to idealize sexual love and to deplore its animal qualities or at least to make them respectable. For Sidney, in *Astrophel and Stella* and the *Old Arcadia*, the sexual appetite seems uncontrollable, and he shows, rather ruefully, the havoc which it wreaks upon even the most princely idealism. Spenser, the most traditional poet of the period, takes up two Books of *The Faerie Queene* to re-establish, in Book III, the basic function of sex as procreation and, in Book IV, the rules and conventions by which it may be rendered safe and civilized. Donne's *Ecstasie*, in another key, is an attempt to reconcile at the level of personal feeling the conflict between the physical and spiritual components of love. At the extreme end of the spectrum, the

Platonists seek to transcend the physical altogether, with the help of such images as Marsilio Ficino's ladder of love, by whose aid the lover may ascend from the sensual pleasures of particular human beauty to the higher delights of intellectual beauty, and ultimately to a communion with the divine Idea of beauty itself.

These are all variations on the time-honoured theme of reason in conflict with passion, and Shakespeare was as much concerned with it as his contemporaries. The intensity of his response, however, makes him place the emphasis upon the dilemma of the human being torn between the demands of a sexual appetite which is essentially lustful and the equally insistent demands of the idealism and altruism which are also a necessary part of love. Venus is the central figure in Shakespeare's handling of the myth. She is the Venus *vulgaris* of the Renaissance, the Venus of the world, the flesh and procreation; and, although she also possesses qualities which are not in themselves strictly carnal, these, like those of Cleopatra, yet serve to enhance her essentially carnal appeal. As we have seen, she can be light as well as heavy, 'all compact of fire' and able to enchant the ear; but this is all part of her physical charm. She is never in any degree the Venus Urania, the higher spiritual Venus of the Platonists, and has no desire to be so. One of the best known of the Platonic symbols was that of the banquet of the senses, in which the lover, beginning with the pleasures of the lower physical senses, mounts to the higher ones, seeking to achieve through each in turn a knowledge of the divine intellectual beauty at which the physical sensation can only hint. Shakespeare shows Venus enjoying the banquet of the senses which Adonis affords, but her feast is a wholly sensuous one and she approaches it the wrong way round. Beginning with the pleasures of sight, accepted as the noblest and most nearly spiritual of all the senses, she then works downwards through the more purely physical ones of touch, smell and taste (433–50). Her banquet is an anti-Platonic descent of the ladder of love.

Her frank motive in love is physical pleasure, but her justification, in contrast, is the procreation which proceeds from it; and this is not mere hypocrisy. The one wholly unquestioned assertion which the poem makes is that

> By law of nature thou art bound to breed,
> That thine may live when thou thyself art dead;
>
> (171–2)

Here Venus speaks with the voice of Nature herself at the end of the medieval *Roman de la rose*, and equally with that of Spenser in *The Faerie Queene*, where the procreative Garden of Adonis is set at the centre of the whole poem. Her plea for life, together with her lament over the death of Adonis, defines the eternal conflict and invests the poem momentarily with a high and traditional authority.

It is surprising, however, that although Shakespeare insists on the inescapable necessity of the sexual urge, the picture he gives of it is one of calculated ugliness. For Chaucer, the sexual desire and act were full of humour; for Spenser and Donne, full of joy and pleasure; and even in the plays of Middleton and Tourneur the disgust at the sexual act is provoked by its unseemliness in the case of elderly or unnatural lechers rather than by the thing itself. But the image which Shakespeare creates with both Venus and the dark lady of the sonnets is of the almost abstract, raw, animal appetite stripped of all romantic allure. In her greed to enjoy Adonis, Venus is like a hungry eagle, 'sharp by fast', who

> Tires with her beak on feathers, flesh and bone,
> Shaking her wings, devouring all in haste,
> Till either gorge be stuffed or prey be gone;
>
> (56–8)

> And having felt the sweetness of the spoil,
> With blindfold fury she begins to forage;
> Her face doth reek and smoke, her blood doth boil,
> And careless lust stirs up a desperate courage;
>
> (553–6)

Such an urge may be permissible in Adonis' horse with its 'melting buttock', but scarcely in a human being and still less in a goddess. As in the great Sonnet 129 on lust, Shakespeare defines the basic sexual appetite as animal, impersonal and inhuman: it is self-induced and feeds on itself rather than springing from an external source. As Venus shows, it creates the object of its own desire.

It is impossible to tell whether Shakespeare's unflattering picture of the naked sexual instinct springs from his own experience and sensibility, or whether it is his sardonic reaction to contemporary idealized fashions in love and the sentimentalized images of frustrated passion offered by the Petrarchan sonnet. All we can say is that at this stage, here as in *Lucrece* and the sonnets, he seems to have been uniquely obsessed by the thought of lust and to have recognized only this quality in sexual love. He wrote nothing comparable to these studies of the raw, impersonal aspect of sex until *Troilus and Cressida* and the ravings of King Lear, where the vision is the same but the context a more tragic one.

On the other side, Adonis' defence of his own conception of love against that of Venus is not simply the protest of a boy not yet ready for sex; nor is it, as Venus suggests, merely the narcissistic desire to 'live unto himself' which necessarily results in death. Adonis' distinction between love and lust represents an idealism which is as permanent a human need in love as the claims of Venus for sex and procreation. What is unusual, however, is that he finds this idealism totally incompatible with the sexual relationship. Love 'to heaven is fled' (793), he declares, and only sweating lust survives in the world: the one apparently cannot lead to the other or coexist with it. Shakespeare seems to reiterate the point in the curious vision which he gives to Venus when, from seeing the boar as her rival, she recognizes it as her *alter ego*. Her whimsical explanation, derived from the pseudo-Theocritan *Idyl* on the dead Adonis, of how 'the loving swine' killed Adonis by accident, could be a description of how her own importunity destroyed his desires:

> Had I been toothed like him, I must confess,
> With kissing him I should have killed him first;
>
> (1117–8)

As she lies on her back, holding Adonis firmly to her, she sees in her mind's eye

> The picture of an angry chafing boar
> Under whose sharp fangs on his back doth lie
> An image like thyself, all stained with gore;
>
> (662–4)

Her lust destroys his capacity for love, and the image has a more allegorical application to herself than she realizes.

Shakespeare's obsession with the physical aspect of love at this period is unlike that of any other contemporary writer. He does not accept the sexual relationship as naturally as Spenser or Donne; and, although he shows none of the feelings of guilt with which Sidney afflicts his Astrophel, he reveals a kind of fastidiousness about sex, as if he were most repelled by what most attracts him. *Venus* presents love as something necessary but not very nice, and only the humour of the treatment saves it from cynicism and misanthropy.

Shakespeare recognizes the problem, and his description of Venus – 'She's love, she loves, and yet she is not loved' – wittily epitomizes the conflicting responses which love arouses. But his answer is not that of Adonis: love clearly has not fled to heaven but is still there on earth, however ridiculously, 'upon her back, deeply distressed', and that is how we must accept her. For Shakespeare at this period love necessarily involves lust and cannot be separated from it: he sees the sexual relationship in its very essence as a lustful one, and any attempt by Platonist or Puritan to idealize or moralize away the crude animal instinct can lead only to death.

And yet Venus needs her Adonis, for without him love becomes the terrible thing which is described in her final prophecy. This is Shakespeare's conception of the human dilemma which love imposes on the individual; it provokes impulses which are irreconcilable yet equally essential. The same point is made less ambiguously in the sonnets. The need to procreate is defined in the opening sequence, and the incompatible desires which result are expressed through the loves for the young man and the dark lady. The lover must steer his course as best he can between the two loves of comfort and despair; but Shakespeare offers no solution or compromise here or elsewhere. The happy marriages which end the comedies do not reach to the problem because they never analyse the nature of the sexual experience itself, as the poems of Donne, for example, frequently do; and Prospero's advice to Ferdinand about self-control merely evades the issue. The sonnets build no bridge between the love for the dark lady and for the young man, and in the narrative poem, Venus cannot be joined to Adonis.

v

If there is no solution in *Venus*, there is, however, a suggestion of consolation, and that the most traditional one. This is to be found in the concentrated epigrammatic address which Venus makes to the flower at the end of the poem when, having plucked it, she puts it, still dying, into her bosom:

> To grow unto himself was his desire,
>     And so 'tis thine; but know, it is as good
>     To wither in my breast as in his blood.
>
> (1180–82)

It is a curiously diffident claim which Venus makes on behalf of her love, and with reason, for she can offer no answer to personal mortality. The flower will be plucked and wither one way or another, whatever she does, and all she can propose is the vicarious immortality through offspring which, in Spenser's words, makes the world 'eterne in mutabilitie'. Even while it lasts, the love she offers is still far from undiluted happiness, as her parting prophecy makes clear; but between her way and that of the boar, hers is the better option.

Although this is not spelt our explicitly in the poem, it is implied strongly in the fact of the flower itself, and the pattern of supporting imagery throughout. Shakespeare's obsession with the colours of red and white, the white flower and the red, has often been noted. It is so insistent that Hereward T. Price even suggests that it could be the signature tune of the poet fresh from his dramatic triumphs with the Wars of the Roses. The image originates at many removes in the Greek poet Bion's 'Lament for Adonis', and by the Renaissance it had become the accepted heraldry of love poetry, the stock-in-trade of all who deal in love. The ubiquitous application of red and white to Venus and Adonis is enough to establish them both in the realm of literary myth. Throughout his poem Shakespeare plays with these traditional colours of love, weaving them together endlessly in a magnificent display of the rhetoric of love poetry. Sometimes the red and the white reflect the opposition between Venus and Adonis, she red with desire, he pale with anger or fear; at others, the conflict exists within the single colour, 'She red and hot as coals of glowing fire,/ He red for shame, but frosty in desire' (35–6). At times the two unite to produce perfect beauty: 'More white and red than doves or roses are' (10); or they fight among themselves within the same beauty: 'To note the fighting conflict of her hue,/ How white and red each other did destroy!' (345–6). We may have a single powerful colour, as in the description of 'Rose-cheeked Adonis' (3) or of Venus leading Mars 'prisoner in a rose-red chain' (110); in the other register, Venus holding Adonis' hand,

> A lily prisoned in a gaol of snow,
> Or Ivory in an alabaster band;
> So white a friend engirts so white a foe:
>
> (362–4)

The permutations throughout the poem are endless, and though the relationship between the two colours is mainly one of opposition to each other, they can change places even as they grapple together, and sometimes come to a temporary truce.

Hereward T. Price suggests that the warring colours are an expression of Shakespeare's belief in the perpetual conflict at the heart of life and nature itself, and this may be so; but I would suggest a more limited application within the context of the poem. Red and white are the two major concerns of the poem, lust and love, desire and friendship, or whatever one calls them. And what they demonstrate is not only a hostility but also an unbreakable relationship between the two: the colours always wrestle because they are inseparable and interdependent even though incompatible. Only death can unite them, and it is significant that the two colours are taken over by their common enemy, the boar,

> Whose frothy mouth, bepainted all with red,
> Like milk and blood being mingled both together,
>
> (901–2)

and that they subsequently meet in the wound which he gives,

> the wide wound that the boar had trenched
> In his soft flank; whose wonted lily-white
> With purple tears that his wound wept was drenched:
>
> (1052–4)

Death conquers all, and love cannot save the lover; but there is nevertheless a suggestion of hope in the final image of the flower which springs from Adonis and revives once more the vital colours:

> A purple flower sprung up, chequered with white,
> Resembling well his pale cheeks, and the blood
> Which in round drops upon their whiteness stood.
>
> (1168–70)

Adonis, the fairest flower of the field, and the heraldic colours of love all meet in this final elegiac image. The flower is the most traditional of all emblems of transcience and mortality: it is natural that it should be dying, even in Venus' breast. Yet at the same time the image points in two directions: the flower also holds the promise of rebirth with the new spring, as the flowers scattered over Milton's Lycidas are a token both of death and regeneration. In the same way, *Venus* ends on the Janus-like note of traditional elegy. Shakespeare abandons the boar of lust for the boar of winter, and the poem returns to where it began at the first line, in the cycle of the seasons.

I have discussed the framework of ideas at some length because an explicit debate about them forms the centre of the poem; but it must be stressed that *Venus* is by no means simply a poem of ideas. The fact that the argument between Venus and Adonis about love and lust takes place with Venus lying on her back and forcibly holding the unwilling Adonis on top of her introduces a note of irony into the whole discussion which must give us pause in deciding how seriously to take it. It is important to recognize too that Shakespeare does not make his characters mere personifications of the ideas they express: both Venus and Adonis act from motives very different from those which they claim to justify their actions, and the result is to produce a more dramatic interplay without destroying the validity of the arguments themselves. The conceptions of love and lust which are advanced are so time-honoured as to be beyond question, and they stand in their own right, therefore, unaffected by any use that is made of them. In this way the poem exists simultaneously on different levels, as a debate about ideas and as a dramatic clash of personalities, in which the ideas themselves become a part of the drama; and the gap between the two dimensions allows a degree of ambiguity which raises questions rather than imposes solutions.

Above all, *Venus* is a poem with an emotional range from broad comedy to deep pathos at the death of youth: it softens under the graceful veil of poetic myth both its tragedy and the controversial issues which it debates. We should always re-member that it was conceived as poetic entertainment for a sophisticated patron and the cultured, courtly circle of his friends; and that it combines, therefore, the ingredients most calculated to appeal to them: wit, humour, high rhetoric, poetry, myth and a core of ideas about which Shakespeare and his contemporaries alike were deeply concerned.

## NOTE ON THE TEXT

The punctuation and spelling of this text and those of the other poems have been modernized, and archaic forms of words replaced by their modern equivalents: 'rose-cheeked' for 'cheekt' (*Venus*, 3), 'fastened' for 'fastned' (*Venus*, 68), 'battered' for 'battred' (*Venus*, 104), 'mastering' for 'maistring' (*Venus*, 114), 'boisterous' for 'boystrous' (*Venus*, 326). Where, however, the modern form would distort the metre, I have retained that of the Quarto with the addition, where necessary, of an apostrophe to indicate that a syllable has been dropped intentionally: 'new-fall'n' (*Venus*, 354), 'vent'ring' (*Venus*, 567), 'provok'st' (*Venus*, 949). There are no accents to indicate stressed syllables in the Quartos, but I have followed Maxwell and the Oxford Shakespeare in including them to help the modern reader – 'stallèd (*Venus*, 39), 'controllèd' (*Venus*, 270), 'joinèd . . . coinèd' (*PP*, VII) – to maintain the pattern of feminine endings throughout the lyric.

# THE RAPE OF LUCRECE

I

*The Rape of Lucrece* was designed, in Gabriel Harvey's words, 'to please the wiser sort'; and the six editions which it had achieved by 1616 indicate that it was very successful, although less so than *Venus and Adonis*. It is ranked by many modern critics, however, as an interesting failure: for F. T. Prince it falls between the two stools of drama and didactic poetry; for Douglas Bush, its 'Complaints' are too long and too many – 'Declamation roars while passion sleeps'. The comment suggests an unacknowledged desire to read the poem as if it were a play; and for the modern reader, familiar with the whole subsequent range of Shakespeare's drama, such a response is natural, although it is not one which would have seemed inevitable in 1594. The fact too that many of the situations in *Lucrece* are also treated in the plays invokes comparison by which the poem generally suffers. Most obviously, Tarquin reads like a first attempt at Macbeth: both characters undergo similar mental debates before their crime and, unlike all the other tragic figures in Shakespeare, both are fully aware of the consequences of the crime before it is committed. It is no accident that Macbeth goes towards Duncan's chamber 'with Tarquin's ravishing strides'. In such company, Shakespeare's earlier poem finds it difficult to compete.

Nevertheless Tarquin is so remarkable a study of lust that for many readers it splits the poem in half and throws the interest, if not the sympathy, on to the villain at the expense of the wronged Lucrece. We have seen from *Venus* that at this period

Shakespeare was preoccupied with the nature of lust; and in Tarquin he explores the passion more deeply, charting the whole cycle of its progress from the initial desire to the disgust of fulfilment as it is analysed in Sonnet 129: 'Past reason hunted, and no sooner had, / Past reason hated'. In both poems, however, lust is the same thing: like that of Venus, Tarquin's is self-induced and arises within him before he ever sees Lucrece. In Shakespeare's main sources, Livy and Ovid, the affair begins when the Roman noblemen brag about the virtue of their wives and, entering into a wager about it, return to Rome the same night to see how they are behaving in their absence. It is on this first visit that Tarquin sees Lucrece; and, inflamed by her beauty, he returns later with a single servant to accomplish his designs. Shakespeare keeps the sequence in which Collatine brags about Lucrece's chastity but omits the first visit altogether, supplying Tarquin with quite different motives to explain the violence of his passion for someone whom he has not yet seen. Collatine's use of the word 'chaste', for example, acts as a challenge to Tarquin's manhood (8–9), just as the 'boast of Lucrece' sovereignty' (36) challenges his egotism and ambition. The resulting passion has the depersonalized quality of sexual desire devoid of normal human stimulus. Yet Tarquin retains an awareness of the true nature of his passions throughout and some degree of mental detachment from them, so that he never wholly forfeits our sympathy. He is the most comprehensive study of lust which Shakespeare ever attempted.

After Tarquin, Lucrece may seem an anti-climax, but she is, in fact, a much more complex dramatic study than he is. Even her long apostrophes to Night, Opportunity and Time are dramatically justified as the only kind of action of which she is capable at the time – 'This helpless smoke of words', as she herself describes them (1027). In fact, they are not 'helpless', but enable her to survive her initial shock at a horror almost too great to be comprehended, until by the morning she has passed beyond the stage of mere outcry and is able to resolve on a course of considered action. From the first, her inevitable obsession with her own pain makes her apply everything she

sees to herself and find in it new fuel for her grief in which she
freely indulges:

> So she deep drenchèd in a sea of care
> Holds disputation with each thing she views,
> And to herself all sorrow doth compare;
> No object but her passion's strength renews,
>
> (1100–1104)

In this way, the joyful song of the little birds in the morning
reminds her of the more appropriately melancholy song of the
nightingale, which bewails its ravishment with the thorn
against its breast as she herself with the dagger at her own:

> Come, Philomel, that sing'st of ravishment,
> Make thy sad grove in my dishevelled hair.
>
> (1128–9)

It is difficult to believe that Shakespeare is taking her wholly
seriously at this moment.

She finds in the picture of the fall of Troy an ideal reflection
of her own feelings; and, as she studies the tragic figures, she
puts her own words of grief into their mouths, at the same time
taking on herself the outward signs and habit of their sorrow:

> So Lucrece, set a-work, sad tales doth tell
>   To pencilled pensiveness and coloured sorrow:
>   She lends them words, and she their looks doth borrow.
>
> (1496–8)

Hecuba in particular lends herself to this treatment, and
Lucrece 'shapes her sorrow to the beldame's woes', playing her
part and supplying the laments which in the nature of the
medium the painter could not provide:

> The painter was no god to lend her those;
>   And therefore Lucrece swears he did her wrong,
>   To give her so much grief, and not a tongue.
>
> 'Poor instrument,' quoth she, 'without a sound,
> I'll tune thy woes with my lamenting tongue . . .'
>
> (1461–5)

As Lucrece gives voices to the portraits, it could be that Shakespeare is playing with the contemporary definition of poetry as 'Speaking Picture' and, as a dramatist, reminding the reader that a play can do the same thing much better. But whatever Shakespeare's intention, Lucrece's remarkable piece of play-acting is entirely in keeping with her self-conscious mode of grief throughout, with her declamations through the night, and with her carefully stage-managed revelation to Collatine in the morning. She refrains from telling him the whole truth in her letter because she feels that it is more likely to be believed when put over by herself in person:

> she would not blot the letter
> With words, till action might become them better.
>
> To see sad sights moves more than hear them told,
>
> (1322–4)

Even her death, like that of Othello, is dramatically contrived to coincide with the end of a couplet:

> She utters this: 'He, he, fair lords, 'tis he,
> That guides this hand to give this wound to me.'
>
> (1721–2)

I would not go so far as some critics who suggest that Lucrece enjoys her role, but it certainly sustains her; and Shakespeare has turned her into something very different from the uncomplicated heroine of the traditional myth. C. Hulse's suggestion is an attractive one, that she is playing up to the image which history has subsequently given her, and creating the role for herself as the emblem of Roman chastity.

II

In *Lucrece* Shakespeare creates an historical portrait of a Roman matron performing the most archetypal of Roman acts, that of suicide. He was to handle the same situation again in *Julius Caesar* and in *Antony and Cleopatra*, but in neither case with a

comparable emphasis on the ethical questions which this par-
ticular Roman virtue raised in a Christian consciousness. 'If
that be made a theme for disputation,' says Lucrece of her good
name; and, as Don Cameron Allen and others show, her good
name had been a theme for disputation from the time of St
Augustine onwards. Augustine had argued that she should
either have killed herself before the rape or, if she was truly
innocent, not have killed herself afterwards, since by suicide
she destroyed her soul as well as her body. It is the point which
Lucretius, her father, makes in his lament: 'I did give that life /
Which she too early and too late hath spilled' (1800–1801).

In popular mythology and literature she was always
accepted as a virtuous heroine and martyr, but theologians,
even in Shakespeare's day, were less charitable. Shakespeare's
poem does not ignore the difference between Christian and
Roman values, but it never censures Lucrece from a Christian
point of view: indeed, Shakespeare goes out of his way to
negate at least a part of Augustine's criticism by making it clear
that even if she had wanted to, Lucrece could not have killed
herself in time to avoid the rape, since there was no weapon in
her chamber: 'But this no-slaughterhouse no tool imparteth'
(1039). Moreover, the details are so arranged as to emphasize
the essentially Roman nature of her motives: she is not raped by
force but blackmailed into compliance by Tarquin's threat to
destroy her honour and that of her family by killing her slave
and placing him in the bed. She gives in for the sake of honour
and subsequently commits suicide for the same reason. She
feels no personal guilt for the rape, but she is afraid of being
blamed by those without full knowledge of the circumstances;
and she takes great pains, therefore, to tell her story to her
husband in a way designed to forestall criticism. She kills
herself out of a feeling of pollution which, although not her
fault, is a fault in her; and she cannot – as a Christian can
perhaps more easily – separate her soul from her body. If the
latter is polluted, the former is soiled with it, and the only cure
is to wash away the taint from both by death. She dies like
a true Roman, demanding revenge, not pleading Christian
forgiveness.

In the narrator's speech, Shakespeare seems to find it necessary to excuse Lucrece and to comment on the inability of women to resist male strength:

> Not that devoured, but that which doth devour,
> Is worthy blame. O, let it not be held
> Poor women's faults that they are so fulfilled
>    With men's abuses . . .

(1256–9)

More interestingly, however, he makes Lucrece utter a protest which, as A. C. Hamilton points out, has strong Christian overtones. It is sparked off by the picture of Helen of Troy in the painting, but it is clearly intended by Lucrece for herself:

> Why should the private pleasure of some one
> Become the public plague of many moe?
> Let sin alone committed light alone
> Upon his head that hath transgressèd so;
> Let guiltless souls be freed from guilty woe:
>    For one's offence why should so many fall,
>    To plague a private sin in general?

(1478–84)

The lines would certainly have reminded the Elizabethan reader of Original Sin, and have suggested an extra dimension to Lucrece's tragedy, namely, that although she has just had the experience of man's fallen nature, she has no knowledge of its place in the Christian scheme of sin and, more important, of redemption.

It is a curious situation in which the characters appear to refer to both Roman and Christian concepts without any awareness of what they are doing; and I. Donaldson analyses this feature of the poem in his book on the Lucrece legend. He distinguishes between the Roman 'shame' culture and the 'guilt' culture of Christianity, and illustrates how both Tarquin and Lucrece move about in both worlds.

> To live or die which of the twain were better
> When life is shamed and death reproach's debtor.

(1154–5)

Lucrece debates the question with herself, invoking the standards of Roman honour, but continues at once in terms of Christian values:

> 'To kill myself,' quoth she, 'alack what were it
> But with my body my poor soul's pollution?'
>
> (1156–7)

In the next stanza she couples the two together without distinction:

> My body or my soul, which was the dearer,
> When the one pure the other made divine?
> Whose love of either to myself was nearer,
> When both were kept for heaven and Collatine?
>
> (1163–6)

Tarquin stays mainly in the Roman tradition, and his inner debate is between honour and prudence on the one side, and passion on the other: but after the crime he departs, 'a heavy convertite' (743), as Lucrece remains 'a hopeless castaway' (744) – both phrases steeped in Christian association.

It is possible that Shakespeare was not attempting to create an accurate historical picture – there are plenty of anachronisms in his historical and Roman plays – but since he chose what is so essentially a Roman theme, he may have been holding it up in double perspective to his audience, without himself taking sides. As Donaldson says, 'Shakespeare was less interested in arguing a particular case within the poem than in exploring the states of mind from which argumentation springs' (p. 41). The exploration is not in simple dramatic terms because the characters themselves are not aware of the conflict of values in which they are involved; but the presence and weight of unresolved questions in the background helps to explain the frustration which both Lucrece and Tarquin feel in face of the 'smoke of words' by which they are almost smothered, and from which they seek to escape by violent action.

Both Lucrece and Tarquin are interesting dramatic material, and it is not easy to change the natural (and perhaps inevitable) modern dissatisfaction with the poem for not exploiting its potential in exclusively dramatic terms – although one can explain why such a response misses much of what the poem has to offer. But *Lucrece* is not a tragedy any more than *Venus* is a comedy in the strict Renaissance sense of the terms: it is what was called a 'tragical morality', that is to say, a moral narrative on a tragic theme. In this case, as J. W. Lever has shown, the poem combines two traditional genres and an alternative title could be *The Tragedy of Tarquin and the Complaint of Lucrece*.

The first of these genres is tragedy in its medieval sense, as defined, for example, in the Prologue to Chaucer's *Monk's Tale*: it is basically a non-dramatic genre whose identity depends upon its theme, namely, the turning of Fortune's wheel and the fall of a great man. John Lydgate's huge *The Fall of Princes* (1431–8) was still well known as a collection of tragedies in the sixteenth century, and it had been followed up and even exceeded by the enormous anthology of tragedies known as *A Mirrour for Magistrates*, begun in the 1550s and still being added to at the end of the century. The *Mirrour* is a collection of poems, each of which deals with a figure from English history who rose to greatness and subsequently fell; but its tragedies go beyond the medieval pattern in analysing the moral and political reasons for each fall as well as demonstrating the power of Fortune. Furthermore, its 'Tragedies' merge with the medieval 'Complaint' which, as its name implies, is a personal lament. In this tradition the characters come forward, bewail their unhappy fortune, tell their stories and draw the appropriate moral from it. The complaint had a stronger dramatic dimension than the tragedy, since it was spoken by the unhappy victim; and this had been exploited to the full by Samuel Daniel in his very popular 'Complaint of Rosamond', published in 1592, which provided Shakespeare with one of his models for *Lucrece*. The traditional form of verse for these tragic moralities was the seven-line stanza known as rime-royal, which Chaucer used in his *Troilus and Criseyde*, Lydgate in his *Fall of Princes* and which Daniel handed on to Shakespeare.

## IV

In this tradition, Shakespeare uses dramatic material for non-dramatic ends; and, although there is no necessary opposition between the dramatic and the didactic (as the many moral tags in Elizabethan plays demonstrate), its poetic techniques are geared primarily to didacticism, its methods are those of declamation and moral commentary, and the tragic theme is not allowed to arouse the sympathies and emotions of the reader in a way which would be appropriate to tragedy. The most obvious feature of *Lucrece* is the abundance of 'sententiae', or wise saws and moral instances, throughout. There is an ubiquitous narrator – one far more intrusive than the narrator in *Venus* – who comments on the action and encloses every speech and move of the characters in a frame of gnomic sayings. The fact that Lucrece in her innocence has no suspicions concerning Tarquin's visit is embellished with a proverbial comment:

> For unstained thoughts do seldom dream on evil;
> Birds never limed no secret bushes fear:
>
> (87–8)

As Tarquin forces open the door of Lucrece's chamber, we are told that

> The dove sleeps fast that this night–owl will catch;
> Thus treason works ere traitors be espied.
> Who sees the lurking serpent steps aside;
>
> (360–62)

This is the basic pattern of the poem, and, as T. W. Baldwin shows, many of these sententiae are expanded into fully developed moral 'themes' of the kind which formed the basic rhetorical exercise in Elizabethan grammar schools. Every opportunity for a general moral statement is seized and extended as far as it can be taken.

Not only the narrator but the characters themselves traffic in sententiae and moral topoi; and the struggle between the two becomes a battle of language, a conflict of moral saws as much as of people. Tarquin's justification of his passion, 'Small lights are soon blown out; huge fires abide' (647) is countered by Lucrece's assertion of its unworthiness:

> The cedar stoops not to the base shrub's foot,
> But low shrubs wither at the cedar's root.
>
> (664–5)

Even the rape itself is shrouded in the imagery of traditional fable: 'The wolf hath seized his prey, the poor lamb cries' (677). In every case the statement moves from the particular to the general, from the human to the moral drama. Tarquin's wrestling with his conscience is transmuted into the formal pattern of a university *Disputatio* on a moral topic, with the arguments pro and con disposed in their proper order; and the whole tormented sequence develops into a Morality Play, a 'graceless . . . disputation / 'Tween frozen conscience and hot-burning will' (246–7), in which Tarquin plays the role of Youth against 'sad pause' and 'deep regard': 'My part is Youth, and beats these from the stage' (278).

The most elaborate sequence in this battle of rhetorics occurs when Tarquin breaks in upon the sleeping Lucrece. She is described in a great and beautiful set-piece, from which Spenser may have taken more than a hint in his description of Serena among the cannibals, as she lies upon the sacrificial altar in *The Faerie Queene* (VI, viii, 42). The description begins with a decorative and elaborate conceit:

> Her lily hand her rosy cheek lies under,
> Cozening the pillow of a lawful kiss;
> Who therefore angry seems to part in sunder,
> Swelling on either side to want his bliss;
>
> (386)

but it quickly grows into an iconic image which turns Lucrece
into a statue of innocence and virtue upon a tomb, garlanded
with emblematic flowers and expressing mysteries of harmony
and religion beyond normal human comprehension:

> Between whose hills her head entombèd is;
>     Where like a virtuous monument she lies
>     To be admired of lewd unhallowed eyes.
>
> (390–92)

> Her hair like golden threads played with her breath:
> O modest wantons, wanton modesty!
> Showing life's triumph in the map of death,
> And death's dim look in life's mortality:
> Each in her sleep themselves so beautify
>     As if between them twain there were no strife,
>     But that life lived in death and death in life.
>
> (400–406)

An icon such as this exceeds the merely literal, and follows the
convention of emblematic description which Sidney had used
in the revised *Arcadia* and Spenser developed into full allegory.

Tarquin's intrusion into this hallowed scene is heralded by a
very different brand of rhetoric. His entry is presented as an
invasion in terms of the common sonnet rhetoric of Love's
war, used normally, as we have seen, at a flippant level in the
plaints of the unsuccessful lover; but here, for once, the siege is
successful, and the conceit works with a new and shocking
effect in the near-religious context which Shakespeare has
established:

> Anon his beating heart, alarum striking,
>     Gives the hot charge, and bids them do their liking.

> His drumming heart cheers up his burning eye,
> His eye commends the leading to his hand;
> His hand, as proud of such a dignity,
> Smoking with pride, marched on to make his stand
> On her bare breast, the heart of all her land;
>
> (433–9)

It is especially ironic that he comes to scale her 'never-conquered fort' under Lucrece's own colours of red and white, which are established as her heraldic colours at the beginning of the poem:

> This heraldry in Lucrece' face was seen,
> Argued by beauty's red and virtue's white;
>
> (64–5)

Here, under Tarquin's attack, they have developed into the red blush of shame and the white of virtuous fear which he claims must bear the responsibility for the violence of his passion:

> Under that colour am I come to scale
> Thy never-conquered fort: the fault is thine,
> For those thine eyes betray thee unto mine.
>
> (481–3)

The same imagery of red and white is extended even further at a later point in the poem, in connection with the picture of Sinon in the painting of Troy. In Lucrece, the red and the white are always distinct from each other, but in harmony and able to change places: 'Of either's colour was the other queen, . . . / That oft they interchange each other's seat' (66–70). In this 'silent war of lilies and of roses', which takes place in Lucrece's 'fair face's field' (71), Tarquin is trapped and disarmed, his 'traitor eye' vanquished when he sees the two, and he is forced to dissemble. Sinon, in contrast, makes no distinction of colour in his face, and the two are fused into a neutral tone:

> Cheeks neither red nor pale, but mingled so
> That blushing red no guilty instance gave,
> Nor ashy pale the fear that false hearts have.
>
> (1510–12)

Shakespeare has manipulated his colours this time to produce a symbol of treacherous hypocrisy.

As in *Venus*, the overall effect of this elaborate poetic artifice is to distance the reader from the dramatic situation and inhibit the emotional response proper to tragedy: instead we are invited to make a considered moral judgement. Tragedy in

Shakespeare's plays offers a disturbing experience, but *Lucrece* is, if anything, reassuring, because the tragedy is neutralized by its language of proverb and sententiae, which suggests a ubiquitous moral framework strong enough to survive any evil. Not only the narrator and Lucrece but Tarquin himself uses the same language of moral topoi and acknowledges its validity. Oppressed as he is by the weight of so much proverbial wisdom and judgement, it is not surprising that he rails against sententiae and, in doing so, uses an image which is itself a traditional topos:

> Who fears a sentence or an old man's saw
> Shall by a painted cloth be kept in awe.
>
> (244–5)

## V

Just such a painted cloth provides the material for the most interesting and puzzling section of the whole poem, namely, the picture of the fall of Troy which we have seen Lucrece studying so intently while she waits for Collatine to return. The episode offers a breathing space between the two moments of highest drama, the rape and the suicide, and a variation upon the long apostrophes which have preceded it. More important, it establishes the particular tragedy of Lucrece in relation to the wider patterns of history. The fall of Troy provided the Renaissance with one of its most widely used emblems, which served both as a type for any political or civil overthrow and as a symbol of the human body destroyed by the passions. In *Lucrece*, Shakespeare plays down the political aspects of his story and concentrates on the human tragedy, which he links, nevertheless, with the symbol of a more universal disorder. Lucrece immediately identifies herself with Hecuba and seizes on the parallel between Tarquin and the traitor, Sinon, who penetrated the Trojan defences just as Tarquin penetrated her own:

> as Priam did him cherish,
> So did I Tarquin; so my Troy did perish.
>
> (1546–7)

The comparison is made all the more inevitable by the long sequence of siege and battle imagery which Shakespeare uses throughout to describe Tarquin's campaign against Lucrece.

The unexpected feature of the Troy passage, however, is that at this point Shakespeare chooses to digress from the story and discuss in surprising detail how 'this well-painted piece' gains its effect, how 'In scorn of nature art gave lifeless life' with such an effect that 'Many a dry drop seemed a weeping tear' and the painted blood appeared to 'reek' as if it were the real thing (1374–7). He composes a miniature treatise on what he understands mimesis to be in relation to naturalistic art; and his emphasis throughout is on the deceitfulness of appearances and the deception which must occur when art holds up the mirror to nature. Painting depends on illusion: it is an art of feigning, a 'Conceit deceitful' (1423) which gains its effect by throwing the onus of creation on to the viewer, who must be induced to supply out of his own imagination what he thinks would be there in reality but is not and cannot be shown in the picture. Art reminds us of nature but does not represent it. Instead, by a selection of detail, the part is made to suggest the whole, and the viewer makes up what he does not see:

> For much imaginary work was there;
> Conceit deceitful, so compact, so kind,
> That for Achilles' image stood his spear
> Gripped in an armèd hand; himself behind
> Was left unseen, save to the eye of mind:
>   A hand, a foot, a face, a leg, a head,
>   Stood for the whole to be imaginèd.
>
> (1422–8)

Similarly an image which is itself still can suggest movement – it appeared that Nestor's beard 'Wagged up and down, and from his lips did fly / Thin winding breath which purled up to the sky' (1406–7); and figures hidden in the crowd whose scalps alone were visible yet 'To jump up higher seemed, to mock the mind' (1413–4).

This analysis of how a picture communicates is not original, and Shakespeare could have found it in classical textbooks on painting. What is interesting in the context of the poem is that he extends the same principles to the way we interpret those images, once we have reconstituted them visually from the picture. If visualizing a naturalistic picture depends on our assumptions about the reality it represents, to an even greater degree our interpretation of it is coloured by our experience of life and the assumptions about human behaviour which we bring to it. This may seem obvious, but Shakespeare explores this aspect of interpretation in detail, using Lucrece as a sort of guinea-pig to demonstrate his point. She knows the story of Troy and can read the picture visually, but her interpretation of it is governed by her own character and past experience. She is a person innocent to the point of naïvety who has always assumed that appearances do not lie and what the eye sees may be believed, although Shakespeare drops many hints through-out the poem about the uneasy relationship between the eye and the heart. Tarquin's treachery comes to her as a shock and as a revelation which challenges all her basic assumptions. 'Thou art not what thou seems't,' she cries (600). She cannot, however, change her nature, and so rather than rejecting totally her belief in faces, she merely modifies it. Her response is to devise an explanation still based on her own experiences but postulating a difference between the sexes: that women reveal but men can conceal their true natures by their appear-ance. The distinction is spelt out fully by the narrator:

Their smoothness, like a goodly champaign plain,
Lays open all the little worms that creep;
In men, as in a rough-grown grove, remain
Cave-keeping evils that obscurely sleep:
Through crystal walls each little mote will peep.
    Though men can cover crimes with bold stern looks,
    Poor women's faces are their own faults' books.

(1247–53)

In this belief Lucrece assumes that Tarquin 'in his speed looks for the morning light' (745), because he knows that his face will not betray his guilt – although Tarquin himself fears that his crime 'will live engraven in my face' (203) – whereas she 'prays

she never may behold the day' (746), because women 'think
not but that every eye can see / The same disgrace which they
themselves behold' (750–51).

Shakespeare makes it clear that she is wrong in both these
assumptions in the little scene between Lucrece and the mes-
senger whom she sends to Collatine. When he enters, she
blushes, thinking that he must see the signs of her shame in her
looks; and when he blushes in return she assumes that this is the
reason. In fact, her appearance has told him nothing and he
blushes simply because he is bashful (1338–46). Similarly, her
belief that 'women their guilt with weeping will unfold' is
disproved by the fact that all the signs of her long night's
weeping convey nothing of its cause to her maid in the
morning, who weeps with her without the least idea of the
reason. The problem does not lie in the difference between
women and men but in the very ambiguity of appearances
which so rarely indicate the truth within and are open therefore
to subjective interpretations.

Lucrece brings her own individual habits of mind to the
picture, and the difficulties which she experiences in interpret-
ing it enable Shakespeare to deal explicitly with the problems
of communication through art. In the cases where the painted
image speaks with no uncertain voice and where the appear-
ance of the character expresses its inner nature, she is at
home: the unmitigated grief or the boorishness indicated
by the pictures of Hecuba and Ajax respectively cannot be
misinterpreted:

> O what art
> Of physiognomy might one behold!
> The face of either ciphered either's heart;
> Their face their manners most expressly told.

(1394–7)

But with Ulysses we begin to wonder:

> But the mild glance that sly Ulysses lent
> Showed deep regard and smiling government.

(1399–1400)

The word 'sly' suggests that Ulysses does not wear his heart in his face, and that his 'smiling government' might be machiavellian rather than kindly. And with Sinon, the whole problem of interpretation is put squarely in front of us and Lucrece. The naturalistic painter aims to present things as they appear, and he depicts hypocrisy, therefore, not as it is but as it seems, concealed under its cloak of innocence:

> In him the painter laboured with his skill
> To hide deceit and give the harmless show
> An humble gait, calm looks, eyes wailing still,
> A brow unbent that seemed to welcome woe;
>
> (1506–9)

Lucrece's first impulse is to deny the truth of the picture on the grounds that no such innocent appearance could conceal so much guilt:

> Such signs of truth in his plain face she spied
> That she concludes the picture was belied
>
> (1532–3)

But the memory of Tarquin comes into her mind, and she swings to the other extreme with the assertion that all such innocent-seeming faces must necessarily conceal guilt:

> It cannot be, I find,
> But such a face should bear a wicked mind:
>
> (1539–40)

Shakespeare's verse gives an amusing expression of the way she changes her mind in mid sentence and of the difficulties of syntax she encounters because of it. She has, in fact, changed from one extreme of credulity to its opposite, and her wholly subjective interpretation has made her wrong in both cases.

The problem is one peculiar to naturalistic art which is tied to the appearance of things, not their reality, and aims to reproduce life in all its ambiguity. It faces both the painter and the creator of 'Speaking Pictures', the poet, and it is of particular concern to the didactic artist, for whom clarity of meaning and intention is especially essential. The difficulty is that of combining the exemplary with the real and reconciling the demands of verisimilitude with overtly moral statement. The Renaissance took the moral responsibility of the arts very seriously, and there was much discussion and experiment in the period in relation to the most effective modes of didactic rhetoric.

The allegorist in paint or in words has no problems, since his method, by definition, is to reveal the true nature of his subject. Spenser's Ate, the goddess of Discord, is self-defining, with her feet which move in opposite directions and her eyes looking asquint. In contrast, Sidney, whose inclination was towards naturalism, composed his *Apology for Poetry* as a treatise on didactic method, and at once puts his finger on the central difficulty. He dismisses history as a serious vehicle for didacticism because it is 'bound to tell things as things were': the historian's truth to life is of no use to the moralist, since it shows 'doings, some to be liked, some to be misliked. And then how will you discern what to follow but by your own discretion, which you had without reading' (p. 110). He turns to poetry, therefore, which has the freedom of fiction, and can in consequence present images of so idealized a nature that their moral import is unmistakable. The poet, not being tied to 'the particular truth of things', can paint verbal pictures of absolute virtue or total vice: he 'feigns' pure heroes or unambiguous villains, in the one 'each thing to be followed', in the other, 'nothing that is not to be shunned' (p. 110); and these by their natural potency will penetrate the heart of the reader and move him to follow the one and flee the other. The man who carries the image of the all-virtuous Aeneas in the tablets of his memory will, by an inevitable osmosis, become a better man. The trouble with such a theory is that it would cramp the style of any poet who wanted to 'imitate' life, and narrow his range to that of the Heroic poem. We can see Sidney's dissatisfaction with this theory for just this reason in his later writing, especially the revised *Arcadia*, where he is in the process of jettisoning his exemplary heroes in favour of the new character, Amphialus, who is naturalistic, flawed and morally ambiguous.

Sidney's work is the clearest indication of contemporary thought about didactic writing and its problems; and such ideas form the background against which one should consider Shakespeare's only attempt at the genre. Shakespeare shows no sign in his poems or plays that he ever considered dealing in idealized characters or moral absolutes: Venus is more a woman than an allegory. Instead, his method is to redefine the idea of the 'Speaking Picture'. For Sidney, in theory at least, it is a picture in words instead of paint but otherwise the same. For Shakespeare it is a picture with a voice which can instruct in a variety of ways, and his strategy is to educate the ears of the listeners to hear correctly what it has to say. This is the function of the proverbial sayings, the wise saws and moral instances which, as we have seen, envelop every character, episode and situation in *Lucrece*. They are designed to tap the inherited moral reservoir which every Elizabethan reader could be expected to carry within himself, and, by reminding him of the great familiar commonplaces, establish a moral climate which exerts a continuous pressure on his feelings and responses. Rather than advocating specific moral judgements, the method encourages a frame of mind in which it is natural to assess any situation in the light of traditional wisdom and accepted social mores.

This didactic method has the advantage of locating the source of moral judgement outside of the narrative itself, and so enabling Shakespeare to create characters who are real people and not moral stereotypes: they may talk in the language of morality but they behave like ordinary human beings. In this way, deep psychological study can coincide with unflagging and insistent moral assessment. The technique could work only where there is a culture rich in the language and imagery of moral aphorism, and where proverbs are still taken seriously. It can exert little moral pressure for us, though it must have been effective in its time. Shakespeare's faith in its efficacy is shown by the games he plays with it in the poem, the patterns of imagery he establishes, and the application of a single topos in a variety of situations. The familiar Ovidian tag, '*Inopem me copia fecit*' ('Plenty has made me poor'), for example, turns up in all manner of forms: 'poorly rich', 'bankrupt in this poor-rich gain', 'make something nothing by augmenting it', to mention only a few instances, reminding us that lust is self-defeating whatever its object. The hackneyed distinction between appearance and reality is applied in a wide variety of contexts, and runs like a thread through the texture of the poem. It is exemplified as a tragic fact of life in Tarquin and Sinon, and as a source of misunderstanding in most of Lucrece's dealings with the world. In relation to the picture of Troy it is initially of aesthetic interest only, as an explanation of the way in which we look at a certain kind of picture; but Tarquin twists it into a perverted moral assumption with which to attack Lucrece: 'The fault unknown is as a thought unacted' (527). For him, appearance is the reality in moral matters, and sin is only sin when it is seen to be so. Permutations of this kind act both as reminder and as analysis of moral principles: they serve to keep the reader morally alert.

Shakespeare's method also allows him to luxuriate in all the modes of didactic rhetoric without distorting the story-line. At times, indeed, the rhetorical exercise is in excess of the needs of the occasion as, for example, in the sequence which immediately follows the rape, where the morally loaded descriptions of Tarquin and Lucrece are extended into a series of antitheses which are almost self-perpetuating:

> She bears the load of lust he left behind,
> And he the burden of a guilty mind.

> He like a thievish dog creeps sadly thence;
> She like a wearied lamb lies panting there;
> He scowls, and hates himself for his offence;
> She, desperate, with her nails her flesh doth tear.

> (734–8)

There is an element of art for art's sake in such writing, and *Lucrece* is not only a didactic poem but a display of didactic rhetoric. I suspect that this dimension of the poem, as much as its moral and dramatic content, was a source of its popularity. The reader of the 1590s, with his training in rhetoric at school or university, would have appreciated the sure handling of genre, the rhetorical virtuosity and professional skill which the poet exhibits, and would have approved of his ability to construct 'themes' and handle the ratiocinations, the chronographia and all the other elaborate figures of rhetoric which T. W. Baldwin has identified in it. *Lucrece* appealed to the taste which had enjoyed John Lyly's *Euphues* and Sidney's *Arcadia*: it pleased the age to see an English poet handling high rhetoric with all the stops out, and doing it as well as any poet on the Continent or, indeed, among the ancients.

VI

Modern patriotism takes different channels, and only the specialist nowadays is likely to enjoy Shakespeare's performance in *Lucrece* on anything like its own terms. Yet, if much is lost, much also remains. The overall sense of control throughout, the astonishingly brisk and efficient opening which, in three stanzas, puts the reader in possession of all the necessary facts and sets the narrative rolling – these are still impressive achievements. Admittedly, the endless word-play is irritating – 'To shun this blot, she would not blot the letter', 'His kindled duty kindles her mistrust', 'Ere she with blood had stained her stained excuse'. Such mechanical repetition becomes tedious, although under the name of 'Ploche or the Doubler' it was highly recommended as an ornament for poetry in George Puttenham's *The Arte of English Poesie*, published in 1589.

In spite of this, however, the poetry is more varied and more subtle than that of *Venus*. It ranges from the lucidity of Tarquin's self-analysis or of Lucrece's pleas, to ornate rhetoric and extended metaphors of an audacity comparable to that of the Metaphysical poets. The comparison of the ebb and flow of Collatine's feeling to the backward and forward movement of a saw, for example, is as heterogeneous an image as Samuel Johnson could have complained of:

> Even so his sighs, his sorrows, make a saw,
> To push grief on and back the same grief draw.

(1672–3)

And the description of Lucrece's tear-stained face in terms of
cooked and uncooked meat, her eyes scalded with tears yet
looking red and raw, is truly startling: 'Her eyes though sod in
tears, looked red and raw' (1592). The use of a single punning
word to fuse the tenor and the vehicle of a metaphor is as
common in *Lucrece* as in Donne or in Shakespeare's own later
plays. Such a pun is the 'drumming heart' in the military image
used to describe Tarquin's assault (435) or the double meaning
of 'sounds' in both geographical and auditory senses:

> Deep sounds make lesser noise than shallow fords,
> And sorrow ebbs, being blown with wind of words.
>
> (1329–30)

But perhaps the most unexpected characteristic of the style is
its combination of highly elaborate word-play with very con-
centrated epigram. The final couplet of the rime-royal stanza
consistently exploits antithesis to achieve a tone of finality
which is almost Augustan:

> Had doting Priam checked his son's desire,
> Troy had been bright with fame, and not with fire.
>
> (1490–91)

> Thy wretched wife mistook the matter so
> To slay herself, that should have slain her foe.
>
> (1826–7)

> Poor Chastity is rifled of her store,
> And Lust the thief far poorer than before.
>
> (692–3)

In spite of its normal opulent 'oriental' rhetoric, *Lucrece* has
affinities with the more astringent 'attic' style which later
replaced it, and its gnomic tone often anticipates the 'strong
lines' of the seventeenth century.

# 'THE PHOENIX AND TURTLE'

I

'The Phoenix and Turtle' is the most ambiguous of
Shakespeare's poems, and has generated the most controversy.
Its form has invited allegorical readings in terms of both
biography and metaphysics, and the variety of its interpret-
ations ranges from the deep pessimism which W. H. Matchett
finds in it to P. Dronke's argument for a Neo-Platonic opti-
mism. Faced with such ambiguity, many critics, from John
Middleton Murry to F. T. Prince, have placed it in the cate-
gory of 'pure-poetry': that is, poetry not 'about' anything, but
owing its intensity to the remarkable versatility of language
under pressure. Parts of the poem are almost mathematical in
their self-absorption, and the whole seems to stand up as an
artefact in its own right, independent of external reference.
R. A. Underwood's useful survey of the poem gives a full
account of the whole spectrum of interpretations.

A. H. R. Fairchild demonstrated long ago that the poem
belongs to the Court of Love tradition of the bird mass, which
originated in Ovid with Corinna's parrot, and is still familiar in
the popular form of 'Who Killed Cock Robin?' In its long
history, the convention had been handled with varying degrees
of seriousness: in the sixteenth century, flippantly by John
Skelton in *Phyllyp Sparowe*, but in a more genuinely funereal
tone by Matthew Roydon in his *Elegie* on the death of Sidney,
which was included in the late Elizabethan miscellany *The
Phoenix Nest*. It is difficult to assess the kind or degree of
seriousness which Shakespeare brings to it: the invocation to
the birds attending the funeral, with which the poem opens,

has a theatrical, almost mock-heroic quality, 'But thou shriek-
ing harbinger, / Foul precurrer of the fiend'; the central
Anthem which describes the love between the phoenix and the
turtle is a virtuoso struggle with language to define the un-
definable; and the concluding Threnos, which laments the
passing of 'Beauty, truth, and rarity' from the world, does so in
rhythms of such strength that they undercut the melancholy of
its message:

> Truth may seem, but cannot be;
> Beauty brag, but 'tis not she;
> Truth and beauty buried be.

Little is known about the origin of the poem. There is no
agreement about when it was written, but it was published in
1601 as one of the additional poems to Robert Chester's *Loves
Martyr*. Chester's long and frequently absurd allegoric poem is
not worth recognition for its own merits, but it must be
considered because it set the form and provided the subject for
the poems which were published with it. '*Loves Martyr, or
Rosalins Complaint*. Allegorically shadowing the truth of Love
in the constant Fate of the Phoenix and Turtle' – to give it its
full title – included at the end 'Some new compositions, of
severall modern writers whose names are subscribed to their
several workes, upon the first subject: viz., the Phoenix and
Turtle'. The modern writers are John Marston, George
Chapman, Ben Jonson, 'Ignoto', who may be Donne, and
Shakespeare, whose poem comes second in the series. Chester
was a member of the household of Sir John Salusbury of
Lleweni in Denbighshire, on friendly terms with his patron,
with whom he exchanged poetical acrostics and minor con-
ceited verses, and to whom he dedicated his long poem.
Salusbury himself, a distant relation of Queen Elizabeth,
married Ursula Stanley, the illegitimate but acknowledged
daughter of the fourth Earl of Derby, in December 1586. He
was appointed one of the Esquires of the Body of the Queen in
1595, and knighted by her in 1601, the year of the poem's
publication. One of the most puzzling questions is how
Chester, at best a poetaster, or Salusbury, who was no major

figure in the field of literary patronage, managed to induce a number of the most fashionable and distinguished poets of the period to associate themselves with such a curiously old-fashioned work as *Loves Martyr* must have seemed by 1601.

*Loves Martyr* is about the phoenix and the myth of its self-propagation. The Renaissance was very familiar with the traditional lore concerning the mythical bird, its nest of spices in the 'sole Arabian tree', its solitary death in the flames, and the emergence of the new phoenix from the ashes; and its quality of uniqueness made it an obvious metaphor for any kind of special excellence. It was used in relation to religion and, even more extensively, in relation to love: the phoenix was a familiar hyperbole for the Petrarchan mistress and, inevitably, for the Queen herself. Chester's distinction is to have reversed the normal metaphor by transferring the qualities of the woman to the mythical bird. In his poem, Nature goes to Jove with the lament that she has created in the phoenix a creature so perfect that she fears it will never be able to propagate itself in a like degree of perfection by its normal solitary method. Jove, having seen and marvelled at the bird, promises to remedy the matter by providing a fitting mate, and directs Nature to take the Phoenix to Paphos Isle where there will be waiting a male turtle dove, by whose help an even more perfect phoenix will be created. Nature flies with the bird to Paphos, discoursing all the time rather like Chaucer's eagle in the *House of Fame*; and in this way Chester manages to slip in a number of poetic ventures which he must have started at an earlier date. There is a long verse history of King Arthur, for example, which he claims to have included 'being intreated by some honourable friends, not to let slip so good and fit an occasion', as well as a versified account of Nature's works, especially concerning herbs, taken from a popular herbal of the period – although this may be considered relevant to the main line of the poem, since, as W. H. Matchett points out, many of the herbal remedies are to do with propagation. When they arrive at Paphos, they find the turtle dove weeping for the loss of his mate, in performance of his traditional role as the emblem of fidelity; but his grief is quickly dispelled by the ardour of the phoenix, and the two build a funeral pyre into which they ecstatically leap together. Chester has turned the legendary fiery death of the phoenix into an allegory of sexual consummation and ecstasy. This allegorical conclusion is watched by the life-rendering pelican, whose fabled care for its offspring makes it an appropriate spectator for such a scene. The phoenix and the turtle themselves apparently perish in the flames, although Chester's description is slightly ambiguous: 'death's arrest they prove'; but in conclusion an offspring is born out of the ashes, combining the true love and the beauty of its parents as well as the sex of both.

> From the sweet fire of perfumed wood
> Another princely Phoenix upright stood,
> Whose feathers purified did yeald more light
> Than his late buried mother out of sight,
> And in her heart restes a perpetual love
> Sprong from the bosom of the turtle dove.

An allegory of this kind invites biographical interpretation, and the most commonly accepted reading of the poem in such terms is that of Carleton Brown. He argues that Chester wrote *Loves Martyr* in 1586 to celebrate Salusbury's marriage to Ursula Stanley, with Ursula and Salusbury signified by the phoenix and the turtle respectively. He suggests further that the pelican episode was added in the following year when the first child, a daughter, was born. The poem was then laid aside, until it was published in 1601 as a compliment to Salusbury on his receipt of a knighthood, together with the additional poems whose invention, in the words of their dedicatory invocation, was 'to gratulate / An honourable friend'. Ten children had been born of the marriage in the interim, and the eldest had reached maturity and womanhood with the age of fourteen in the same year – a fact to which Marston would seem to be referring in his eulogistic poem:

> What should I call this creature
> Which now is grown into maturitie . . .

This interpretation squares with the facts of Chester's poem, and with all the additional poems except Shakespeare's, which asserts that the phoenix and the turtle died

> Leaving no posterity,
> 'Twas not their infirmity,
> It was married chastity.

(59–61)

A different and surprisingly persistent interpretation of the sequence was advanced initially in a very crude form by Alexander Grosart, who republished the whole work in 1878, but more recently and with much greater subtlety by W. H. Matchett in his study of the 'Phoenix'. According to his reading, the phoenix is Queen Elizabeth, the turtle, Essex, and Paphos Isle, Ireland, where in 1600 Essex was conducting his expedition. The Queen had no heir and was too old to have one, and there was much uneasiness about the succession. The Essex faction hoped that the Queen would marry Essex and make him heir to the throne; and Matchett believes that *Loves Martyr* was written about 1600 as a plea to the Queen to do this. The Irish expedition, however, went wrong, and Essex's ill-fated rebellion put paid to the whole scheme, so the poem, originally intended for Essex, was rededicated at the last minute to Salusbury as a cover-up. Such an interpretation cannot be proved, and there are elements in the poem that resist it: for example, much of the hyperbolic praise of the phoenix seems excessive, even allowing for the convention of extravagant flattery of the Queen in the period. On the other hand it would fit the 'married chastity' of Shakespeare's poem, and would explain how this particular collection of poets came to be involved in the venture, since all were in one way or another sympathetic to the Essex cause. If this were the case, the great Threnos which concludes the 'Phoenix' could be taken, as Matchett takes it, to be Shakespeare's lament over the loss of a great national opportunity at the end of the old Queen's reign.

The trouble with interpreting *Loves Martyr* in this way is that one can find any number of historical episodes in the period which seem to accord equally well with the story-line of

Chester's poem; and R. A. Underwood quotes some even closer parallels which have been suggested as interpretations, in his survey of the 'Phoenix'. In no case is there any evidence of identity, and none of them clarify the meaning or illuminate in any way the unique qualities of Shakespeare's poem. The assumption is always that Shakespeare wrote the 'Phoenix' at the same time as the other additional poems were written, for the publication of *Loves Martyr* in 1601. In his recent book *Shakespeare: The Lost Years*, however, E. A. J. Honigmann puts forward an interesting hypothesis which cannot be ignored. Honigmann has long held the view that Shakespeare began his writing career in the 1580s, some years earlier than the dates normally attributed to his early plays. He accepts the assumption that *Loves Martyr* was written for Salusbury's wedding in 1586, but makes the revolutionary suggestion that the 'Phoenix' was written at the same time, for the same occasion. Ursula Stanley, Salusbury's bride, was sister to Ferdinando Stanley, Lord Strange, who later became the fifth Earl of Derby; and Lord Strange's men formed the nucleus of the later Lord Chamberlain's men, to whom Shakespeare belonged. Honigmann argues that by 1586 Shakespeare was already in Strange's household as one of his players; and in this capacity he would know Ursula Stanley and her new husband, and perhaps even be familiar with the sort of courtly riddles in verse which Chester and Salusbury exchanged with each other, and which are reflected on a larger scale in the allegory of *Loves Martyr*. When Chester produced his long poem for the wedding, therefore, Honigmann suggests that Shakespeare countered with his own brilliant *tour de force* for the occasion. Both poems were laid aside after the wedding; but in 1601, Salusbury seems to have been in political trouble over his violent and irregular activities in connection with his election to Parliament, and in need, therefore, of all the help he could get. For this reason *Loves Martyr* was brought out, together with Shakespeare's poem and any others which friendly poets might be induced to provide – Jonson's 'Ode' which concludes the additional poems, indeed, was not even new and had been used earlier for the Countess of Bedford. The object of this publishing venture was to improve Salusbury's public image by implying that in reality he was as mild as the proverbial dove; and to remind everyone, moreover, that he was married to a noble and very well-connected phoenix.

The theory that the 'Phoenix' is the work of a brilliant young poet showing off his paces and perhaps concerned to outshine such relatively unsophisticated local talents as those of Salusbury and Chester is an appealing one: it would explain the many differences between Shakespeare's poem and the rest of the additional ones, and it illuminates the poem itself. If one finds it difficult to believe that Shakespeare could have written the 'Phoenix' and then gone on to write *Venus* and *Lucrece* with their totally different rhetoric, it should be remembered that these belong to different genres with conventions that had already been established. Shakespeare had a habit of trying his hand at different poetic genres, and his *A Lover's Complaint*, as much as the 'Phoenix', is an isolated venture into a type of poem without counterpart in his works. Certainly there is nothing with which the 'Phoenix' can be compared. In some ways it is an academic poem, handling abstract ideas and implying a knowledge of poetic tradition, but not demanding the experience of life which informs the great plays. Its astonishing 'cleverness' could be within the range of the young Shakespeare.

## II

The 'Phoenix' begins at the point in Chester's poem when the two lovers have been consumed in the fire, and the urn, mentioned in the final verse of the Threnos, contains their cinders. The opening lines immediately raise a problem: the herald who calls the birds to the funeral, 'the bird of loudest lay / On the sole Arabian tree', would seem by his description to be the new phoenix presiding over the funeral of his predecessor, except that we are told that there was 'no posterity'. For this reason, various birds of 'loudest lay' have been suggested, including the nightingale, the crane and even the cock, although he would be an unlikely master of ceremonies for birds of 'chaste wing'. I shall return to the identity of the herald later when I discuss the Threnos. It should be stressed that Shakespeare's choice of mourners is hardly an appropriate one for the amorous death of Chester's loving birds. The tragic and monogamous swan who sings only at the point of death, and the long-lived crow who was popularly supposed to engender by the conjunction of beaks rather than by the normal means, would be out of place in *Loves Martyr*, though fitting in Shakespeare's poem, where the death is a real not a metaphorical one. The 'kingly eagle' does not seem to belong in this company, but Honigmann offers a possible explanation, namely that the Earl of Derby's crest was an eagle carrying a child.

The Anthem, which follows the invocation, is the longest section of the poem; and although its intention is clear, the nature of its theme makes for difficult reading. Shakespeare's subject is the love which existed between the phoenix and the turtle, a love so pure and absolute that it transcended human experience and therefore human language. The commonest method of describing the ineffable is by the use of symbol, as Vaughan, for example, hints at the qualities of divinity; but Shakespeare chooses instead the methods of scholastic logic and uses them as the scholastics defined God by negatives. The experience he describes is the ultimate mystery of union, such as that to which Baldassare Castiglione refers in the final book of *The Courtier*; but whereas the Platonists allowed a ladder for the human ascent from the physical to the wholly spiritual, Shakespeare offers no such access: in his poem the division between the human and the superhuman seems absolute. The language conveys its meaning by making us aware of what it cannot say, and the very inadequacy of its human terms is made the measure of the difference between the two dimensions. Shakespeare draws on the language of the physical senses and the rational concepts which the human mind builds upon them – distance and proximity, difference and identity, unity and multiplicity – but can only apply them to the purpose of defining this transcendent love by presenting them in paradoxes which deny the logic of their essential nature. This love is something which at once preserves and destroys incompatibility, which simultaneously negates and maintains distinction:

> Two distincts, division none:
> Number there in love was slain.
>
> Hearts remote, yet not asunder;
> Distance, and no space was seen . . .
>
> Single nature's double name
> Neither two nor one was called.

It is Donne's 'Phoenix riddle' which his lovers may exemplify without understanding: 'We two being one, are it' ('The Canonization'); but Shakespeare's logic puts it quite outside the range of human experience, since it overturns all the categories of perception and the assumption of reason. The idea of love as a force which drives reason to destroy reason is common enough in the period: as Astrophel says

> For soon as they strake thee with Stella's rays,
> Reason, thou kneeldst, and offerdst straight to prove
> By reason good, good reason her to love.
>
> (*Astrophel and Stella*, X)

Shakespeare is, in fact, playing a popular sonnet game but with an intensity and logic not to be found in any sonnet sequence: as A. Alvarez puts it, 'Relentlessly the constants of reason are stated and then destroyed in exactly the language in which philosophers would have upheld them.'

The love is 'twain' yet possesses the single scholastic 'essence'; the 'distincts' and 'divisions' of logic are turned against each other; the two which are at the same time one destroy the validity of mathematical number. So too distance without separation, identity without sameness, the alchemical 'simple' which is also 'compound' – this methodical destruction by love of all the rational categories and distinctions overwhelms reason herself, and forces her to admit that 'Love hath reason, reason none'. Frequently the oppositions are packed into a single punning word, as in 'Either was the other's mine', for example, where the word 'mine' implies both an external source of richness such as a gold mine, and an internal possession where thine and mine are synonymous. Sometimes the double meanings run parallel to each other, as in the final paradox of the sequence. 'If what part can so remain', where both departing yet remaining, and dividing yet staying together, are implied. This is essentially witty poetry like that of the Metaphysical poets. It is interesting that W. B. Yeats is forced to use a similar technique of paradox to define the indefinable in his poem 'Byzantium', although he juxtaposes material symbols instead of scholastic abstractions. Yeats's 'Dying into a dance, / An agony of trance, / An agony of flame that cannot singe a sleeve' works in the same way for the same purpose.

Shakespeare's Anthem emphasizes the sheerly alien quality, both superhuman and inhuman, of the love of the phoenix and the turtle: it violates the very basis of human reason and expectation. On the few occasions when he attempts to present the impact of such an experience in dramatic terms, the effect on the characters concerned is to produce an incomprehension and panic amounting almost to madness. An example of this is Troilus when he is faced with the sudden transformation of Cressida's fidelity into its opposite, so that she seems faithful and faithless at the same time. 'This is, and is not Cressid,' he cries, and in the presence of mutually exclusive truths, analyses his feelings in terms remarkably close to those of the 'Phoenix':

> . . . O madness of discourse,
> That cause sets up with and against itself;
> Bi-fold authority! where reason can revolt
> Without perdition, and loss assume all reason
> Without revolt: this is, and is not Cressid.
> Within my soul there doth conduce a fight
> Of this strange nature that a thing inseparate
> Divides more wider than the sky and earth;
> And yet the spacious breadth of this division
> Admits no orifice for a point as subtle
> As Ariachne's broken woof to enter . . .
>
> (*Troilus and Cressida*, V, iii, 139–49)

Lear's reaction to his daughters who are no-daughters shows the same bewilderment, though the situation is less explicitly defined. Obviously the contradictions involved in the concept of absolute love are of a different kind from those produced by human dilemmas: yet, as Shakespeare defines them in the 'Phoenix', they present the same problem of assimilation, and their effect on normal human assumptions is equally shattering. This may help us to understand Shakespeare's attitude to human lovers in the last section of the poem.

The concluding Threnos, composed by Reason, sums up the significance of what has happened. With the death of the phoenix and the turtle, beauty-and-truth as a single entity, 'Two distincts, division none', has departed, and what in the absolute exists as simple unity survives in the world only as separate fragments. The sublunary lovers left behind on earth are 'either true or fair' but cannot be both. The birds leave no posterity, for that is born out of the human division which their union transcends; and the 'married chastity' of their state is yet another in the line of paradoxes by which they have been described through the poem, a further fusion of opposites which contradict each other in human terms.

Reason recognizes the tragedy of it all, that truth and beauty have left the world for ever; but no agonizing is demanded; only a wistful sigh in prayer after something which mundane lovers do not and cannot understand. The unhuman splendours of the phoenix and the turtle are outside their comprehension and all they can see is 'these dead birds' capable of arousing pity. If the human lovers could understand what has gone, it is unlikely that they would desire it, in view of the ruthless logic by which its transcendence has been defined and all human attributes stripped away. Human nature can stand very little of such reality. For this reason I question D. Dronke's argument that the phoenix and the turtle leave behind them a vision of perfect love to which all human lovers may aspire. Shakespeare's presentation of such love is hard and logical, lacking the attractive mystery of Vaughan's vision of eternal light, for example. The love of the phoenix and the turtle is described in terms calculated to remove it totally from the human scene; and Shakespeare seems to be casting the same cold eye over the Neo-Platonic ideal of love as, in *Venus*, he brings to bear on the sentimentalization of the sexual instinct. His attitude to love is always down to earth and, while accepting the value of absolutes in their proper place, he recognizes that they are not for human beings and abandons them defiantly, yet with a touch of regret.

If we consider the 'Phoenix' in relation to *Loves Martyr*, it would seem that Shakespeare is challenging and, indeed, debunking Chester's poem, by implication suggesting that the attempt to graft ordinary sexual love on to the phoenix stock is naïve and sentimental nonsense. He therefore dismantles Chester's myth and returns the two birds to their traditional roles. The line 'Death is now the phoenix' nest' is difficult and ambiguous, but the point it is making is the traditional one: the phoenix's nest was always the place of death, but from the cinders arose the new bird which, I think, has been there from the beginning of the poem when it was called to summon the mourners to the funeral. Shakespeare has looked at the new myth from the perspective of the old. As with the phoenix, so too the turtle is placed back in its own kindlier, more Christian tradition to enjoy the eternity of heaven. Chester's myth is rejected and the traditional one restored. It is perhaps relevant that the first of the additional poems to *Loves Martyr*, that by 'Ignoto', follows the same line. The little poem is based on a popular Elizabethan emblem whose 'word' forms the refrain, 'One Phoenix borne, another Phoenix burne'. This would reinforce the suggestion that 'Ignoto' was Donne, for, like Shakespeare, he thought of love in essentially human terms. Neither poet had much use for a relationship which is 'all breathing human passion far above'.

Whether Shakespeare wrote the 'Phoenix' as a very young man or in his maturity is irrelevant to this interpretation of the poem. *Loves Martyr* would have aroused Shakespeare's hostility at any time of his life; but perhaps a young man would be more likely to do something about it.

# THE PASSIONATE PILGRIM

The Passionate Pilgrim is a short poetic miscellany of twenty poems, printed by William Jaggard who, with his son, was later to print the First Folio. There were three editions. The first, published probably in 1599, exists only in an incomplete form and is without a title-page. It is in octavo (Octavo 1) and includes poems I–IV and XVI–XVIII, which are bound up with sheets taken from the second edition to give the complete collection – there being an overlap in the case of XVIII, which is included from both editions. The second edition, also in octavo (Octavo 2) was printed in 1599. Jaggard brought out a third edition, 'newly augmented and corrected', in 1612, but this derives from the earlier editions and has no textual authority.

The Passionate Pilgrim has been traditionally included among Shakespeare's collected works because Jaggard pirated two of Shakespeare's sonnets and three passages from Love's Labour's Lost, together with poems by Richard Barnfield, Bartholomew Griffin and a number of unnamed writers, and issued them all, in the second edition, as The Passionate Pilgrim by W. Shakespeare. The poems by Shakespeare are I (Sonnet 138); II (Sonnet 144); III (LLL, IV, iii, 56–69, Longaville's sonnet); V (LLL, IV, ii, 101–14, Berowne's sonnet); XVI (LLL, IV, iii, 96–115, Dumaine's love poem). We know they were pirated because of a protest made by Thomas Heywood after the publication of the third edition which Jaggard also issued under Shakespeare's name, and augmented with a number of Heywood's poems without acknowledgement. Heywood complained, in his Apologie for Actors (1612), not only of the 'manifest injury' done to himself but also to Shakespeare, who was 'I know much offended with M. Jaggard (that altogether unknowne to him) presumed to make so bold with his name'.

Shakespeare's displeasure may already have made itself felt at an earlier date. The second edition of 1599 inserted between poems XIV and XV a second title-page, 'Sonnets, to Sundry Notes of Musicke', without any ascription to Shakespeare; and it has been argued that this was Jaggard's attempt at pacification by implying that at least not all poems in the collection were by Shakespeare. The fact that four of Shakespeare's poems were sonnets and the fifth a love song provides a clue to Jaggard's motives. Shakespeare's sonnets though not yet published were well known and in circulation among his friends, and Joseph Quincy Adams suggests that Jaggard, by including four sonnets genuinely by him among the first five poems of the miscellany, may have hoped to give the impression that he had penetrated the circle and was releasing the golden hoard to the public. Such practices were not unknown among the hack printers of the period, although Jaggard's venture is unusually blatant in its attempt to increase sales by the illegitimate use of a great name.

The title, *The Passionate Pilgrim*, was presumably chosen by Jaggard himself, and is in the fashion of 'Passionate' titles for love poetry in the period – for example, Thomas Watson's *Passionate Centurie of Love* (1582) and Nicholas Breton's *The Passionate Shepherd* (1604). For the use of the term 'Passion' to describe a love poem, see *Venus*, line 832 and its commentary. For the association between pilgrims and lovers, see the sonnet shared between Romeo and Juliet on their first meeting (I, v, 97–110).

In this edition I have included the sonnets by Shakespeare and the passages from *Love's Labour's Lost*, although their proper place is elsewhere with their complete texts, because they occasionally contain significant variants from the established version. This is particularly true of I (Sonnet 138). I have also included those poems for which no certain author is known, however unlikely it is that they were written by Shakespeare, since these have traditionally been included with

Shakespeare's poems. I have followed the *New Oxford Shakespeare*, however, in leaving out the poems known to be by other authors. These are VIII and XX by Barnfield, XI by Griffin and XIX, which is usually attributed to Marlowe and Ralegh.

A number of the poems in Jaggard's miscellany also appeared in other contemporary collections in forms which give help in the correction of Jaggard's text.

XVI and XVII: *England's Helicon* (1600). A pastoral miscellany.

IV and XI: Folger MS 1.8. A commonplace book, probably compiled between 1620 and 1630.

XVIII: Folger MS 1.112. A small miscellany of verse, known as the Lyson MS.

I, IV, VI, VII, XI and XVIII: Folger MS 2071.7. A commonplace book, compiled by Joseph Hall between 1630 and 1640.

XVII: Harleian MS 6910; and Thomas Weelkes's *Madrigals to 3, 4, 5 and 6 Voyces* (1597).

For a full account of the text, see Joseph Quincy Adams's Folger Shakespeare Library Facsimile and Hyder Edward Rollins's *The Poems: A New Variorum Edition of Shakespeare*.

# 'SHALL I DIE?'

'Shall I Die?' has been known to Shakespearian scholars, though largely ignored by them for almost a century, and the poem only emerged into fame – or notoriety – in 1985 when Gary Taylor launched his claim for it in *The Times Literary Supplement* as a piece of genuine Shakespeare. It exists in two different manuscript collections, the second of which only came to notice during the controversy aroused by Taylor's arguments concerning the first. The two collections are:

(1)  The Rawlinson Poetical MS 160 in the Bodleian Library, Oxford. This is one of the innumerable seventeenth-century miscellanies of poems in manuscript that were assembled by poetry lovers for their private pleasure, and it consists of about 160 poems copied out in a professional hand. It was compiled probably in the 1630s, and the majority of its poems, copies from MS rather than printed sources, belong between 1613 and 1633. Forty-five of its poems are ascribed to specific authors, and the ascriptions to such widely read poets as Jonson, Donne, Herrick and Carew, for example, are accurate, although there are other ascriptions of doubtful validity or demon-strably incorrect. 'Shall I Die?' is ascribed to Shakespeare. (See Peter Beal, *TLS*, 3 January 1986.)

(2)  The Yale MS (Osborn Collection, b 197). This is a miscellany of over 200 poems compiled in 1638–9 by Tobias Alston, a young man whose half brother and cousin were both up at Cambridge with Herrick and who may have supplied him with the texts of his poems. Many

of the poems in the Yale MS are also in the Rawlinson, and the two miscellanies represent the sort of poems being circulated in university circles at this period. The Yale miscellany does not ascribe 'Shall I Die?' to Shakespeare, and includes it without any name. There is a photostat of the Yale MS in the British Library. (See Donald Foster, *TLS*, 24 January 1986.)

The texts of 'Shall I Die?' in both the Rawlinson and the Yale MSS are corrupt but, in some places, correct each other.

Taylor's case is based on two arguments: firstly, that the ascription of the poem to Shakespeare in the Rawlinson MS may be accepted, since the relatively few poems which are ascribed to Shakespeare in the miscellanies of the period are, in fact, by him: secondly, that the stylistic and linguistic parallels between the poem and Shakespeare's early plays are sufficiently numerous and significant to suggest that both came from the same hand (*TLS*, 20 December 1985). The response was immediate, and the debate which followed in the correspondence columns of the *TLS* over the next three months was lively and, for the most part, hostile to Taylor's position. The dependability of ascriptions in the miscellanies was challenged; and the dangers of making comparison between texts were forcibly stated, especially when the sample was so small and the period was one in which the subject as much as the writer dictated the verbal formulae. Taylor had suggested the early 1590s as a likely date for the composition of the poem; and the fact, therefore, that the miscellanies and most of the poems in them were at least thirty years later weighed heavily against his theory. As the most hostile of Taylor's critics put it (*TLS*, 24 January 1986): 'There is nothing about this poem to suggest [Shakespeare's] hand apart from the ascription itself, which appears in a corrupt text, in an unreliable manuscript, copied by an unknown scribe from an unknown source at least twenty years after Shakespeare's death.'

It is not easy to assess the value of the conflicting arguments and contradictory statements advanced in this occasionally acrimonious debate; but I would think that overall, the weight of the evidence is against Taylor's claim. Certainly he has not proved beyond question that 'Shall I Die' is by Shakespeare. But equally it must be stressed that the opposition has not proved that it is not. In the present state of our knowledge neither proof nor disproof is possible, and one can only go on reasonable probabilities. In my own opinion it is possibly, though not probably, by Shakespeare, but it has at least as good a claim to be included in the *Complete Works* as many of the anonymous poems in *The Passionate Pilgrim*. The compilers of miscellanies, though frequently mistaken in their ascriptions, at least were not tempted to drag in Shakespeare's name to increase their sales. The new *Collected Oxford Shakespeare* rightly includes 'Shall I Die?' among its 'Various Poems', although unfortunately without any warning in its brief introduction that it is at best 'doubtful'.

My own largely subjective judgement of the poem is that it is not good enough for Shakespeare. I am not suggesting that Shakespeare invariably wrote well and never had an off day: the point I would make is that 'Shall I Die?' is weak in an area in which, even in his earliest writing, Shakespeare was invariably strong. The poem is an exercise in virtuosity involving an elaborate stanza pattern and a very large number of internal rhymes; and whoever attempted to overcome the problems posed by the form of the poem was not quite good enough for the job. 'Shall I Die?' is often clumsy and over-compressed, with contorted syntax and indifferent rhymes – assuming, of course, that the two versions are not too corrupt to give a reasonable approximation to the poem as originally written. The relatively amateur quality of the poem is to me not to be reconciled with the astonishing verbal virtuosity which Shakespeare shows even in his earliest work. His lapses are rarely in verbal technique, and if he had tried to write such a poem, I think that he would have done it better.

There is nothing else in Shakespeare's work which is strictly comparable to 'Shall I Die?', although as a conventional Petrarchan lover's lament it is balanced by *A Lover's Complaint* in the corresponding feminine genre of the betrayed maiden. All Shakespeare's poems are one-off attempts at different, usually popular, genres; and, having proved that he can do it, he then moves on to something else. 'Shall I Die?' differs from the others only in that it is inferior to them.

Turning briefly to the poem itself: the point was made in the *TLS* correspondence that it is probably a song and, moreover, one in a particular convention of 'Shall I' lyrics common after 1600. Stanley Wells has observed that Shakespeare used the 'Shall I . . .' formula in his Sonnet 18, 'Shall I Compare Thee to a Summer's Day?', possibly written at about the time Taylor thinks the poem was composed. Certainly, the formula was a very common song convention after 1600, and 'Shall I Die?' has affinities with John Dowland's lyric, 'Shall I Sue? Shall I Seek for Grace?' (No. 19, *The Second Book of Songs and Ayres*, 1600), which set the pattern for a number of others written to the same formula: Philip Rosseter's 'Shall I Come if I Swim?' (1601), Robert Jones's 'Shall I Look to Ease My Grief?' (1605), Dowland's later 'Shall I Strive with Words to Move?' (1612), Thomas Campion's 'Shall I Then Hope When Faith is Fled?' (1618), John Attey's 'Shall I Tell You Whom I Love?' (1622), to name only a few out of the larger number cited by Erica Sheen and Jeremy Maule in their letter to the *TLS* (17 January 1986). Beal goes further in suggesting (*TLS*, 3 January 1986) that the poem may have been a song from a play; and since the compilers of miscellanies usually had some reason for attributing a poem to a particular author, it could have been in a play by Shakespeare, although the song need not have been written by Shakespeare himself. There is a background of popular love-song in most of the comedies, and 'Shall I Die?' is just the sort of thing with which Orsino might have indulged himself. It is a very conventional poem, not only in its Petrarchan theme but in its use of other conventions which, even by the early 1590s, were a little old-fashioned. The lover's dream (stanzas 4–9) goes back to the Middle Ages; and the content of the dream is in the form of the traditional icon of the lady's beauty, which begins with the hair and works downwards feature by feature – in this case, only as low as to the breasts. Sidney had done the same thing very much more brilliantly at the end of Book III of the *Old Arcadia*, where Pyrocles describes Philoclea in bed;

and Spenser puts the convention to a variety of allegoric uses in *The Faerie Queene*. When Shakespeare draws on material of this kind in the plays, as in *Love's Labour's Lost* or *Twelfth Night* or *As You Like it*, there is invariably an element of parody in his treatment.

The form in which the poem is printed in this volume is that of the Rawlinson M S. The Yale M S runs the lines together to give half the number of lines of double length.

# THE EPITAPHS

A number of epitaphs have been traditionally attributed to Shakespeare, although in no case is there any direct evidence that he wrote them. They were, for the most part, known earlier, but not ascribed to Shakespeare until the middle of the seventeenth century or even later; and we can see the tradition of their Shakespearian authorship being formed through the unreliable gossip of John Aubrey and being confirmed by Nicholas Rowe, who welcomed all traditional myths in his 'Account of the life of Mr William Shakespeare' with which he prefaced his 1709 edition of the works. The Epitaphs themselves vary in quality and in seriousness, and one would not expect to discover a specifically Shakespearian touch in such a conventional form. Unlike Ben Jonson's Epitaphs, which were literary and intended for publication, those attributed to Shakespeare were either written in jest or were designed to be carved on the tomb-stone. In several cases, indeed, they only exist as inscriptions on the tomb. In all cases they were written about characters with whom Shakespeare is known to have had contact, and for whom he might reasonably be expected to have composed an epitaph. I follow the new *Collected Oxford Shakespeare*, therefore, in including them among the collected poems, although both E. K. Chambers and Samuel Schoenbaum are in some cases sceptical about their authenticity. It would be a pity to exclude, out of a mere scruple, what has been taken for granted by so many for so long as the work of Shakespeare.

# THE POEMS

---

## *VENUS AND ADONIS*

*Vilia miretur vulgus: mihi flavus Apollo*
*Pocula Castalia plena ministret aqua.*

# RIGHT HONOURABLE
# HENRY WRIOTHESLEY,

## EARL OF SOUTHAMPTON, AND BARON
## OF TITCHFIELD

RIGHT HONOURABLE,

I know not how I shall offend in dedicating my unpolished lines to your Lordship, nor how the world will censure me for choosing so strong a prop to support so weak a burden: only, if your Honour seem but pleased, I account my self highly praised, and vow to take advantage of all idle hours, till I have honoured you with some graver labour. But if the first heir of my invention prove deformed, I shall be sorry it had so noble a godfather, and never after ear so barren a land, for fear it yield me still so bad a harvest. I leave it to your honourable survey, and your Honour to your heart's content; which I wish may always answer your own wish, and the world's hopeful expectation.

Your Honour's in all duty,
William Shakespeare

Even as the sun with purple-coloured face
Had ta'en his last leave of the weeping morn,
Rose-cheeked Adonis hied him to the chase;
Hunting he loved, but love he laughed to scorn.
   Sick-thoughted Venus makes amain unto him,     5
   And like a bold-faced suitor 'gins to woo him.

'Thrice fairer than myself,' thus she began,
'The field's chief flower, sweet above compare,
Stain to all nymphs, more lovely than a man,
More white and red than doves or roses are;     10
   Nature that made thee with herself at strife
   Saith that the world hath ending with thy life.

'Vouchsafe, thou wonder, to alight thy steed,
And rein his proud head to the saddle-bow;
If thou wilt deign this favour, for thy meed     15
A thousand honey secrets shalt thou know.
   Here come and sit, where never serpent hisses,
   And being set, I'll smother thee with kisses;

'And yet not cloy thy lips with loathed satiety,
But rather famish them amid their plenty,     20
Making them red and pale with fresh variety;
Ten kisses short as one, one long as twenty.
   A summer's day will seem an hour but short,
   Being wasted in such time-beguiling sport.'

25  With this she seizeth on his sweating palm,
The precedent of pith and livelihood,
And, trembling in her passion, calls it balm,
Earth's sovereign salve to do a goddess good.
    Being so enraged, desire doth lend her force
30      Courageously to pluck him from his horse.

Over one arm the lusty courser's rein,
Under her other was the tender boy,
Who blushed and pouted in a dull disdain,
With leaden appetite, unapt to toy;
35    She red and hot as coals of glowing fire,
    He red for shame, but frosty in desire.

The studded bridle on a ragged bough
Nimbly she fastens – O, how quick is love!
The steed is stallèd up, and even now
40  To tie the rider she begins to prove.
    Backward she pushed him, as she would be thrust,
    And governed him in strength, though not in lust.

So soon was she along as he was down,
Each leaning on their elbows and their hips;
45  Now doth she stroke his cheek, now doth he frown,
And 'gins to chide, but soon she stops his lips,
    And kissing speaks, with lustful language broken,
    'If thou wilt chide, thy lips shall never open.'

He burns with bashful shame; she with her tears
50  Doth quench the maiden burning of his cheeks;
Then with her windy sighs and golden hairs
To fan and blow them dry again she seeks.
    He saith she is immodest, blames her miss;
    What follows more she murders with a kiss.

55  Even as an empty eagle, sharp by fast,
Tires with her beak on feathers, flesh and bone,
Shaking her wings, devouring all in haste,
Till either gorge be stuffed or prey be gone;
    Even so she kissed his brow, his cheek, his chin,
60      And where she ends she doth anew begin.

72

Forced to content, but never to obey,
Panting he lies and breatheth in her face;
She feedeth on the steam as on a prey,
And calls it heavenly moisture, air of grace,
   Wishing her cheeks were gardens full of flowers,     65
   So they were dewed with such distilling showers.

Look how a bird lies tangled in a net,
So fastened in her arms Adonis lies;
Pure shame and awed resistance made him fret,
Which bred more beauty in his angry eyes.     70
   Rain added to a river that is rank
   Perforce will force it overflow the bank.

Still she entreats, and prettily entreats,
For to a pretty ear she tunes her tale:
Still is he sullen, still he lours and frets,     75
'Twixt crimson shame and anger ashy-pale.
   Being red, she loves him best, and being white,
   Her best is bettered with a more delight.

Look how he can, she cannot choose but love;
And by her fair immortal hand she swears     80
From his soft bosom never to remove
Till he take truce with her contending tears
   Which long have rained, making her cheeks all wet;
   And one sweet kiss shall pay this countless debt.

Upon this promise did he raise his chin,     85
Like a dive-dapper peering through a wave,
Who, being looked on, ducks as quickly in;
So offers he to give what she did crave;
   But when her lips were ready for his pay,
   He winks, and turns his lips another way.     90

Never did passenger in summer's heat
More thirst for drink than she for this good turn.
Her help she sees, but help she cannot get;
She bathes in water, yet her fire must burn.
   'O, pity,' 'gan she cry, 'flint-hearted boy!     95
   'Tis but a kiss I beg; why art thou coy?

'I have been wooed, as I entreat thee now,
Even by the stern and direful god of war,
Whose sinewy neck in battle ne'er did bow,
Who conquers where he comes in every jar;
    Yet hath he been my captive and my slave,
    And begged for that which thou unasked shalt have.

'Over my altars hath he hung his lance,
His battered shield, his uncontrollèd crest,
And for my sake hath learned to sport and dance,
To toy, to wanton, dally, smile and jest,
    Scorning his churlish drum and ensign red,
    Making my arms his field, his tent my bed.

'Thus he that overruled I overswayed,
Leading him prisoner in a red-rose chain;
Strong-tempered steel his stronger strength obeyed,
Yet was he servile to my coy disdain.
    O, be not proud, nor brag not of thy might,
    For mastering her that foiled the god of fight!

'Touch but my lips with those fair lips of thine –
Though mine be not so fair, yet are they red –
The kiss shall be thine own as well as mine.
What see'st thou in the ground? hold up thy head,
    Look in mine eyeballs, there thy beauty lies;
    Then why not lips on lips, since eyes in eyes?

'Art thou ashamed to kiss? then wink again,
And I will wink; so shall the day seem night.
Love keeps his revels where there are but twain;
Be bold to play, our sport is not in sight.
    These blue-veined violets whereon we lean
    Never can blab, nor know not what we mean.

'The tender spring upon thy tempting lip
Shews thee unripe; yet mayst thou well be tasted:
Make use of time, let not advantage slip;
Beauty within itself should not be wasted.
    Fair flowers that are not gathered in their prime
    Rot, and consume themselves in little time.

100

105

110

115

120

125

130

'Were I hard-favoured, foul, or wrinkled-old,
Ill-nurtured, crooked, churlish, harsh in voice,
O'erworn, despisèd, rheumatic and cold,       135
Thick-sighted, barren, lean, and lacking juice,
 Then mightst thou pause, for then I were not for thee;
 But having no defects, why dost abhor me?

'Thou canst not see one wrinkle in my brow;
Mine eyes are grey and bright and quick in turning;       140
My beauty as the spring doth yearly grow,
My flesh is soft and plump, my marrow burning;
 My smooth moist hand, were it with thy hand felt,
 Would in thy palm dissolve, or seem to melt.

'Bid me discourse, I will enchant thine ear,       145
Or, like a fairy, trip upon the green,
Or, like a nymph, with long dishevelled hair,
Dance on the sands, and yet no footing seen.
 Love is a spirit all compact of fire,
 Not gross to sink, but light, and will aspire.       150

'Witness this primrose bank whereon I lie;
These forceless flowers like sturdy trees support me;
Two strengthless doves will draw me through the sky
From morn till night, even where I list to sport me.
 Is love so light, sweet boy, and may it be       155
 That thou should think it heavy unto thee?

'Is thine own heart to thine own face affected?
Can thy right hand seize love upon thy left?
Then woo thyself, be of thyself rejected,
Steal thine own freedom, and complain on theft.       160
 Narcissus so himself himself forsook,
 And died to kiss his shadow in the brook.

'Torches are made to light, jewels to wear,
Dainties to taste, fresh beauty for the use,
Herbs for their smell, and sappy plants to bear;       165
Things growing to themselves are growth's abuse.
 Seeds spring from seeds and beauty breedeth beauty;
 Thou wast begot; to get it is thy duty.

'Upon the earth's increase why shouldst thou feed,
170 Unless the earth with thy increase be fed?
By law of nature thou art bound to breed,
That thine may live when thou thyself art dead;
    And so in spite of death thou dost survive,
    In that thy likeness still is left alive.'

175 By this, the love-sick queen began to sweat,
For where they lay the shadow had forsook them,
And Titan, tirèd in the mid-day heat,
With burning eye did hotly overlook them,
    Wishing Adonis had his team to guide,
180     So he were like him, and by Venus' side.

And now Adonis, with a lazy sprite,
And with a heavy, dark, disliking eye,
His louring brows o'erwhelming his fair sight,
Like misty vapours when they blot the sky,
185     Souring his cheeks, cries 'Fie, no more of love!
    The sun doth burn my face; I must remove.'

'Ay me,' quoth Venus, 'young, and so unkind!
What bare excuses mak'st thou to be gone!
I'll sigh celestial breath, whose gentle wind
190 Shall cool the heat of this descending sun;
    I'll make a shadow for thee of my hairs;
    If they burn too, I'll quench them with my tears.

'The sun that shines from heaven shines but warm,
And lo, I lie between that sun and thee;
195 The heat I have from thence doth little harm,
Thine eye darts forth the fire that burneth me;
    And were I not immortal, life were done
    Between this heavenly and earthly sun.

'Art thou obdurate, flinty, hard as steel?
200 Nay, more than flint, for stone at rain relenteth.
Art thou a woman's son, and canst not feel
What 'tis to love, how want of love tormenteth?
    O, had thy mother borne so hard a mind,
    She had not brought forth thee, but died unkind.

'What am I that thou shouldst contemn me this?               205
Or what great danger dwells upon my suit?
What were thy lips the worse for one poor kiss?
Speak, fair; but speak fair words, or else be mute.
    Give me one kiss, I'll give it thee again,
    And one for interest, if thou wilt have twain.          210

'Fie, lifeless picture, cold and senseless stone,
Well painted idol, image dull and dead,
Statue contenting but the eye alone,
Thing like a man, but of no woman bred!
    Thou art no man, though of a man's complexion,          215
    For men will kiss even by their own direction.'

This said, impatience chokes her pleading tongue,
And swelling passion doth provoke a pause;
Red cheeks and fiery eyes blaze forth her wrong;
Begin judge in love, she cannot right her cause;           220
    And now she weeps, and now she fain would speak,
    And now her sobs do her intendments break.

Sometime she shakes her head, and then his hand;
Now gazeth she on him, now on the ground;
Sometime her arms infold him like a band;                  225
She would, he will not in her arms be bound;
    And when from thence he struggles to be gone,
    She locks her lily fingers one in one.

'Fondling,' she saith, 'since I have hemmed thee here
Within the circuit of this ivory pale,                     230
I'll be a park, and thou shalt be my deer;
Feed where thou wilt, on mountain or in dale;
    Graze on my lips, and if those hills be dry,
    Stray lower, where the pleasant fountains lie.

'Within this limit is relief enough,                       235
Sweet bottom-grass and high delightful plain,
Round rising hillocks, brakes obscure and rough,
To shelter thee from tempest and from rain:
    Then be my deer, since I am such a park;
    No dog shall rouse thee, though a thousand bark.'       240

At this Adonis smiles as in disdain,
That in each cheek appears a pretty dimple;
Love made those hollows, if himself were slain,
He might be buried in a tomb so simple,
245    Foreknowing well, if there he came to lie,
    Why, there Love lived, and there he could not die.

These lovely caves, these round enchanting pits,
Opened their mouths to swallow Venus' liking.
Being mad before, how doth she now for wits?
250  Struck dead at first, what needs a second striking?
    Poor queen of love, in thine own law forlorn,
    To love a cheek that smiles at thee in scorn!

Now which way shall she turn? what shall she say?
Her words are done, her woes the more increasing;
255  The time is spent, her object will away,
And from her twining arms doth urge releasing.
    'Pity,' she cries, 'some favour, some remorse!'
    Away he springs, and hasteth to his horse.

But lo, from forth a copse that neighbours by,
260  A breeding jennet, lusty, young and proud,
Adonis' trampling courser doth espy,
And forth she rushes, snorts and neighs aloud.
    The strong-necked steed, being tied unto a tree,
    Breaketh his rein and to her straight goes he.

265  Imperiously he leaps, he neighs, he bounds,
And now his woven girths he breaks asunder;
The bearing earth with his hard hoof he wounds,
Whose hollow womb resounds like heaven's thunder;
    The iron bit he crusheth 'tween his teeth,
270    Controlling what he was controllèd with.

His ears up-pricked; his braided hanging mane
Upon his compassed crest now stand on end;
His nostrils drink the air, and forth again,
As from a furnace, vapours doth he send;
275    His eye, which scornfully glisters like fire,
    Shows his hot courage and his high desire.

Sometime he trots, as if he told the steps,
With gentle majesty and modest pride;
Anon he rears upright, curvets and leaps,
As who should say 'Lo, thus my strength is tried,      280
   And this I do to captivate the eye
   Of the fair breeder that is standing by.'

What recketh he his rider's angry stir,
His flattering 'Holla' or his 'Stand, I say'?
What cares he now for curb or pricking spur?           285
For rich caparisons or trappings gay?
   He sees his love, and nothing else he sees,
   For nothing else with his proud sight agrees.

Look when a painter would surpass the life
In limning out a well-proportioned steed,              290
His art with nature's workmanship at strife,
As if the dead the living should exceed;
   So did this horse excel a common one
   In shape, in courage, colour, pace and bone.

Round-hoofed, short-jointed, fetlocks shag and long,   295
Broad breast, full eye, small head and nostril wide,
High crest, short ears, straight legs and passing strong,
Thin mane, thick tail, broad buttock, tender hide;
   Look what a horse should have he did not lack,
   Save a proud rider on so proud a back.            300

Sometime he scuds far off, and there he stares;
Anon he starts at stirring of a feather;
To bid the wind a base he now prepares,
And whe'er he run or fly they know not whether;
   For through his mane and tail the high wind sings,  305
   Fanning the hairs, who wave like feathered wings.

He looks upon his love and neighs unto her;
She answers him as if she knew his mind;
Being proud, as females are, to see him woo her,
She puts on outward strangeness, seems unkind,         310
   Spurns at his love and scorns the heat he feels,
   Beating his kind embracements with her heels.

Then, like a melancholy malcontent,
He vails his tail, that, like a falling plume,
Cool shadow to his melting buttock lent;
He stamps, and bites the poor flies in his fume.
 His love, perceiving how he was enraged,
 Grew kinder, and his fury was assuaged.

His testy master goeth about to take him,
When, lo, the unbacked breeder, full of fear,
Jealous of catching, swiftly doth forsake him,
With her the horse, and left Adonis there.
 As they were mad, unto the wood they hie them,
 Out-stripping crows that strive to over-fly them.

All swoln with chafing, down Adonis sits,
Banning his boisterous and unruly beast;
And now the happy season once more fits
That love-sick Love by pleading may be blest;
 For lovers say the heart hath treble wrong
 When it is barred the aidance of the tongue.

An oven that is stopped, or river stayed,
Burneth more hotly, swelleth with more rage;
So of concealèd sorrow may be said,
Free vent of words love's fire doth assuage;
 But when the heart's attorney once is mute,
 The client breaks, as desperate in his suit.

He sees her coming, and begins to glow,
Even as a dying coal revives with wind,
And with his bonnet hides his angry brow,
Looks on the dull earth with disturbed mind,
 Taking no notice that she is so nigh,
 For all askance he holds her in his eye.

O, what a sight it was, wistly to view
How she came stealing to the wayward boy!
To note the fighting conflict of her hue,
How white and red each other did destroy!
 But now her cheek was pale, and by and by
 It flashed forth fire, as lightning from the sky.

Now was she just before him as he sat,
And like a lowly lover down she kneels;                    350
With one fair hand she heaveth up his hat,
Her other tender hand his fair cheek feels;
　　His tend'rer cheek receives her soft hand's print
　　As apt as new-fall'n snow takes any dint.

O, what a war of looks was then between them,             355
Her eyes petitioners to his eyes suing!
His eyes saw her eyes as they had not seen them;
Her eyes wooed still, his eyes disdained the wooing;
　　And all this dumb play had his acts made plain
　　With tears which chorus-like her eyes did rain.        360

Full gently now she takes him by the hand,
A lily prisoned in a gaol of snow,
Or ivory in an alabaster band;
So white a friend engirts so white a foe:
　　This beauteous combat, wilful and unwilling,           365
　　Showed like two silver doves that sit a-billing.

Once more the engine of her thoughts began:
'O fairest mover on this mortal round,
Would thou wert as I am, and I a man,
My heart all whole as thine, thy heart my wound;          370
　　For one sweet look thy help I would assure thee,
　　Though nothing but my body's bane would cure thee.'

'Give me my hand,' saith he; 'why dost thou feel it?'
'Give me my heart,' saith she, 'and thou shalt have it;
O, give it me, lest thy hard heart do steel it,           375
And being steeled, soft sighs can never grave it;
　　Then love's deep groans I never shall regard,
　　Because Adonis' heart hath made mine hard.'

'For shame,' he cries, 'let go, and let me go;
My day's delight is past, my horse is gone,               380
And 'tis your fault I am bereft him so.
I pray you hence, and leave me here alone;
　　For all my mind, my thought, my busy care,
　　Is how to get my palfrey from the mare.'

385 Thus she replies: 'Thy palfrey, as he should,
Welcomes the warm approach of sweet desire.
Affection is a coal that must be cooled;
Else, suffered, it will set the heart on fire.
  The sea hath bounds, but deep desire hath none,
390   Therefore no marvel though thy horse be gone.

'How like a jade he stood tied to the tree,
Servilely mastered with a leathern rein!
But when he saw his love, his youth's fair fee,
He held such petty bondage in disdain,
395   Throwing the base thong from his bending crest,
  Enfranchising his mouth, his back, his breast.

'Who sees his true-love in her naked bed,
Teaching the sheets a whiter hue than white,
But, when his glutton eye so full hath fed,
400 His other agents aim at like delight?
  Who is so faint that dares not be so bold
  To touch the fire, the weather being cold?

'Let me excuse thy courser, gentle boy;
And learn of him, I heartily beseech thee,
405 To take advantage on presented joy;
Though I were dumb, yet his proceedings teach thee.
  O, learn to love; the lesson is but plain,
  And once made perfect, never lost again.'

'I know not love,' quoth he, 'nor will not know it,
410 Unless it be a boar, and then I chase it.
'Tis much to borrow, and I will not owe it.
My love to love is love but to disgrace it;
  For I have heard it is a life in death,
  That laughs, and weeps, and all but with a breath.

415 'Who wears a garment shapeless and unfinished?
Who plucks the bud before one leaf put forth?
If springing things be any jot diminished,
They wither in their prime, prove nothing worth.
  The colt that's backed and burdened being young
420   Loseth his pride, and never waxeth strong.

82

'You hurt my hand with wringing; let us part,
And leave this idle theme, this bootless chat;
Remove your siege from my unyielding heart;
To love's alarms it will not ope the gate.
   Dismiss your vows, your feignèd tears, your flattery;    425
   For where a heart is hard they make no battery.'

'What, canst thou talk?' quoth she, 'hast thou a tongue?
O, would thou hadst not, or I had no hearing!
Thy mermaid's voice hath done me double wrong;
I had my load before, now pressed with bearing:    430
   Melodious discord, heavenly tune harsh sounding,
   Ears' deep-sweet music, and heart's deep-sore wounding.

'Had I no eyes but ears, my ears would love
That inward beauty and invisible;
Or were I deaf, thy outward parts would move    435
Each part in me that were but sensible.
   Though neither eyes nor ears, to hear nor see,
   Yet should I be in love by touching thee.

'Say that the sense of feeling were bereft me,
And that I could not see, nor hear, nor touch,    440
And nothing but the very smell were left me,
Yet would my love to thee be still as much;
   For from the stillitory of thy face excelling
   Comes breath perfumed, that breedeth love by smelling.

'But O, what banquet wert thou to the taste,    445
Being nurse and feeder of the other four!
Would they not wish the feast might ever last,
And bid Suspicion double-lock the door,
   Lest Jealousy, that sour unwelcome guest,
   Should by his stealing in disturb the feast?'    450

Once more the ruby-coloured portal opened,
Which to his speech did honey passage yield;
Like a red morn, that ever yet betokened
Wrack to the seaman, tempest to the field,
   Sorrow to shepherds, woe unto the birds,    455
   Gusts and foul flaws to herdmen and to herds.

This ill presage advisedly she marketh:
Even as the wind is hushed before it raineth,
Or as the wolf doth grin before he barketh,
460　Or as the berry breaks before it staineth,
　　　Or like the deadly bullet of a gun,
　　　His meaning struck her ere his words begun.

And at his look she flatly falleth down,
For looks kill love, and love by looks reviveth;
465　A smile recures the wounding of a frown.
But blessèd bankrupt that by loss so thriveth!
　　　The silly boy, believing she is dead,
　　　Claps her pale cheek, till clapping makes it red;

And all amazed brake off his late intent,
470　For sharply he did think to reprehend her,
Which cunning love did wittily prevent.
Fair fall the wit that can so well defend her!
　　　For on the grass she lies as she were slain,
　　　Till his breath breatheth life in her again.

475　He wrings her nose, he strikes her on the cheeks,
He bends her fingers, holds her pulses hard,
He chafes her lips, a thousand ways he seeks
To mend the hurt that his unkindness marred;
　　　He kisses her; and she, by her good will,
480　　Will never rise, so he will kiss her still.

The night of sorrow now is turned to day:
Her two blue windows faintly she upheaveth,
Like the fair sun, when in his fresh array
He cheers the morn, and all the earth relieveth;
485　　And as the bright sun glorifies the sky,
　　　So is her face illumined with her eye;

Whose beams upon his hairless face are fixèd,
As if from thence they borrowed all their shine.
Were never four such lamps together mixèd,
490　Had not his clouded with his brow's repine;
　　　But hers, which through the crystal tears gave light,
　　　Shone like the moon in water seen by night.

'O, where am I?' quoth she; 'in earth or heaven,
Or in the ocean drenched, or in the fire?
What hour is this? or morn or weary even?      495
Do I delight to die, or life desire?
   But now I lived, and life was death's annoy;
   But now I died, and death was lively joy.

'O, thou didst kill me: kill me once again.
Thy eyes' shrewd tutor, that hard heart of thine,      500
Hath taught them scornful tricks, and such disdain
That they have murdered this poor heart of mine;
   And these mine eyes, true leaders to their queen,
   But for thy piteous lips no more had seen.

'Long may they kiss each other, for this cure!      505
O, never let their crimson liveries wear!
And as they last, their verdure still endure
To drive infection from the dangerous year!
   That the star-gazers, having writ on death,
   May say, the plague is banished by thy breath.      510

'Pure lips, sweet seals in my soft lips imprinted,
What bargains may I make, still to be sealing?
To sell myself I can be well contented,
So thou wilt buy, and pay, and use good dealing;
   Which purchase if thou make, for fear of slips      515
   Set thy seal manual on my wax-red lips.

'A thousand kisses buys my heart from me;
And pay them at thy leisure, one by one.
What is ten hundred touches unto thee?
Are they not quickly told and quickly gone?      520
   Say for non-payment that the debt should double,
   Is twenty hundred kisses such a trouble?'

'Fair queen,' quoth he, 'if any love you owe me,
Measure my strangeness with my unripe years;
Before I know myself, seek not to know me;      525
No fisher but the ungrown fry forbears:
   The mellow plum doth fall, the green sticks fast,
   Or being early plucked is sour to taste.

'Look, the world's comforter, with weary gait,
His day's hot task hath ended in the west;
The owl, night's herald, shrieks 'tis very late;
The sheep are gone to fold, birds to their nest;
 And coal-black clouds that shadow heaven's light
 Do summon us to part, and bid good night.

'Now let me say "Good night", and so say you;
If you will say so, you shall have a kiss.'
'Good night', quoth she; and, ere he says 'Adieu',
The honey fee of parting tendered is:
 Her arms do lend his neck a sweet embrace;
 Incorporate then they seem; face grows to face.

Till breathless he disjoined, and backward drew
The heavenly moisture, that sweet coral mouth,
Whose precious taste her thirsty lips well knew,
Whereon they surfeit, yet complain on drouth.
 He with her plenty pressed, she faint with dearth,
 Their lips together glued, fall to the earth.

Now quick desire hath caught the yielding prey,
And glutton-like she feeds, yet never filleth;
Her lips are conquerors, his lips obey,
Paying what ransom the insulter willeth;
 Whose vulture thought doth pitch the price so high
 That she will draw his lips' rich treasure dry.

And having felt the sweetness of the spoil,
With blindfold fury she begins to forage;
Her face doth reek and smoke, her blood doth boil,
And careless lust stirs up a desperate courage,
 Planting oblivion, beating reason back,
 Forgetting shame's pure blush and honour's wrack.

Hot, faint and weary, with her hard embracing,
Like a wild bird being tamed with too much handling,
Or as the fleet-foot roe that's tired with chasing,
Or like the froward infant stilled with dandling,
 He now obeys and now no more resisteth,
 While she takes all she can, not all she listeth.

What wax so frozen but dissolves with temp'ring,    565
And yields at last to every light impression?
Things out of hope are compassed oft with vent'ring,
Chiefly in love, whose leave exceeds commission:
  Affection faints not like a pale-faced coward,
  But then woos best when most his choice is froward.    570

When he did frown, O, had she then gave over,
Such nectar from his lips she had not sucked.
Foul words and frowns must not repel a lover;
What though the rose have prickles, yet 'tis plucked.
  Were beauty under twenty locks kept fast,    575
  Yet love breaks through, and picks them all at last.

For pity now she can no more detain him;
The poor fool prays her that he may depart.
She is resolved no longer to restrain him;
Bids him farewell, and look well to her heart,    580
  The which by Cupid's bow she doth protest
  He carries thence incagèd in his breast.

'Sweet boy,' she says, 'this night I'll waste in sorrow,
For my sick heart commands mine eyes to watch.
Tell me, love's master, shall we meet to-morrow?    585
Say, shall we? shall we? wilt thou make the match?'
  He tells her, no; to-morrow he intends
  To hunt the boar with certain of his friends.

'The boar!' quoth she; whereat a sudden pale,
Like lawn being spread upon the blushing rose,    590
Usurps her cheek; she trembles at his tale,
And on his neck her yoking arms she throws.
  She sinketh down, still hanging by his neck,
  He on her belly falls, she on her back.

Now is she in the very lists of love,    595
Her champion mounted for the hot encounter.
All is imaginary she doth prove;
He will not manage her, although he mount her;
  That worse than Tantalus' is her annoy,
  To clip Elysium and to lack her joy.    600

Even so poor birds, deceived with painted grapes,
Do surfeit by the eye and pine the maw;
Even so she languisheth in her mishaps
As those poor birds that helpless berries saw.
605   The warm effect which she in him finds missing
    She seeks to kindle with continual kissing.

But all in vain, good queen, it will not be,
She hath assayed as much as may be proved:
Her pleading hath deserved a greater fee;
610   She's Love, she loves, and yet she is not loved.
    'Fie, fie,' he says, 'you crush me; let me go;
    You have no reason to withhold me so.'

'Thou hadst been gone,' quoth she, 'sweet boy, ere this,
But that thou toldst me thou wouldst hunt the boar.
615   O, be advised: thou knowst not what it is
With javelin's point a churlish swine to gore,
    Whose tushes never sheathed he whetteth still,
    Like to a mortal butcher bent to kill.

'On his bow-back he hath a battle set
620   Of bristly pikes that ever threat his foes;
His eyes like glow-worms shine when he doth fret;
His snout digs sepulchres where'er he goes;
    Being moved, he strikes whate'er is in his way,
    And whom he strikes his crookèd tushes slay.

625   'His brawny sides, with hairy bristles armed,
Are better proof than thy spear's point can enter;
His short thick neck cannot be easily harmed;
Being ireful, on the lion he will venter:
    The thorny brambles and embracing bushes,
630       As fearful of him, part, through whom he rushes.

'Alas, he nought esteems that face of thine,
To which Love's eyes pays tributary gazes;
Nor thy soft hands, sweet lips and crystal eyne,
Whose full perfection all the world amazes;
635   But having thee at vantage – wondrous dread! –
    Would root these beauties as he roots the mead.

'O, let him keep his loathsome cabin still;
Beauty hath nought to do with such foul fiends.
Come not within his danger by thy will;
They that thrive well take counsel of their friends.        640
   When thou didst name the boar, not to dissemble,
   I feared thy fortune, and my joints did tremble.

'Didst thou not mark my face? was it not white?
Sawst thou not signs of fear lurk in mine eye?
Grew I not faint? and fell I not downright?                 645
Within my bosom, whereon thou dost lie,
   My boding heart pants, beats, and takes no rest,
   But, like an earthquake, shakes thee on my breast.

'For where Love reigns, disturbing Jealousy
Doth call himself Affection's sentinel;                     650
Gives false alarms, suggesteth mutiny,
And in a peaceful hour doth cry "Kill, kill!"
   Distempering gentle Love in his desire,
   As air and water do abate the fire.

'This sour informer, this bate-breeding spy,               655
This canker that eats up Love's tender spring,
This carry-tale, dissentious Jealousy,
That sometime true news, sometime false doth bring,
   Knocks at my heart, and whispers in mine ear
   That if I love thee I thy death should fear;          660

'And more than so, presenteth to mine eye
The picture of an angry chafing boar
Under whose sharp fangs on his back doth lie
An image like thyself, all stained with gore;
   Whose blood upon the fresh flowers being shed         665
   Doth make them droop with grief and hang the head.

'What should I do, seeing thee so indeed,
That tremble at th'imagination?
The thought of it doth make my faint heart bleed,
And fear doth teach it divination:                         670
   I prophesy thy death, my living sorrow,
   If thou encounter with the boar to-morrow.

'But if thou needs wilt hunt, be ruled by me;
Uncouple at the timorous flying hare,
675  Or at the fox which lives by subtlety,
Or at the roe which no encounter dare.
    Pursue these fearful creatures o'er the downs,
    And on thy well-breathed horse keep with thy hounds.

'And when thou hast on foot the purblind hare,
680  Mark the poor wretch, to overshoot his troubles,
How he outruns the wind, and with what care
He cranks and crosses with a thousand doubles.
    The many musits through the which he goes
    Are like a labyrinth to amaze his foes.

685  'Sometime he runs among a flock of sheep,
To make the cunning hounds mistake their smell,
And sometime where earth-delving conies keep,
To stop the loud pursuers in their yell;
    And sometime sorteth with a herd of deer.
690    Danger deviseth shifts; wit waits on fear.

'For there his smell with others being mingled,
The hot scent-snuffing hounds are driven to doubt,
Ceasing their clamorous cry till they have singled
With much ado the cold fault cleanly out.
695    Then do they spend their mouths; Echo replies,
    As if another chase were in the skies.

'By this, poor Wat, far off upon a hill,
Stands on his hinder legs with listening ear,
To hearken if his foes pursue him still:
700  Anon their loud alarums he doth hear;
    And now his grief may be comparèd well
    To one sore sick that hears the passing-bell.

'Then shalt thou see the dew-bedabbled wretch
Turn, and return, indenting with the way;
705  Each envious brier his weary legs do scratch,
Each shadow makes him stop, each murmur stay;
    For misery is trodden on by many,
    And being low, never relieved by any.

'Lie quietly and hear a little more;
Nay, do not struggle, for thou shalt not rise.          710
To make thee hate the hunting of the boar,
Unlike myself thou hear'st me moralize,
    Applying this to that, and so to so;
    For love can comment upon every woe.

'Where did I leave?' 'No matter where,' quoth he;       715
'Leave me, and then the story aptly ends.
The night is spent.' 'Why, what of that?' quoth she.
'I am', quoth he, 'expected of my friends;
    And now 'tis dark, and going I shall fall.'
    'In night', quoth she, 'desire sees best of all.       720

'But if thou fall, O, then imagine this,
The earth, in love with thee, thy footing trips,
And all is but to rob thee of a kiss.
Rich preys make true men thieves; so do thy lips
    Make modest Dian cloudy and forlorn,               725
    Lest she should steal a kiss, and die forsworn.

'Now of this dark night I perceive the reason:
Cynthia for shame obscures her silver shine,
Till forging Nature be condemned of treason,
For stealing moulds from heaven that were divine,      730
    Wherein she framed thee, in high heaven's despite,
    To shame the sun by day and her by night.

'And therefore hath she bribed the Destinies
To cross the curious workmanship of Nature,
To mingle beauty with infirmities                      735
And pure perfection with impure defeature,
    Making it subject to the tyranny
    Of mad mischances and much misery;

'As burning fevers, agues pale and faint,
Life-poisoning pestilence and frenzies wood,           740
The marrow-eating sickness whose attaint
Disorder breeds by heating of the blood,
    Surfeits, imposthumes, grief and damned despair,
    Swear Nature's death for framing thee so fair.

745 'And not the least of all these maladies
But in one minute's fight brings beauty under:
Both favour, savour, hue and qualities,
Whereat th'impartial gazer late did wonder,
 Are on the sudden wasted, thawed and done,
750  As mountain snow melts with the midday sun.

'Therefore, despite of fruitless chastity,
Love-lacking vestals and self-loving nuns,
That on the earth would breed a scarcity
And barren dearth of daughters and of sons,
755  Be prodigal: the lamp that burns by night
 Dries up his oil to lend the world his light.

'What is thy body but a swallowing grave,
Seeming to bury that posterity
Which by the rights of time thou needs must have,
760 If thou destroy them not in dark obscurity?
 If so, the world will hold thee in disdain,
 Sith in thy pride so fair a hope is slain.

'So in thyself thyself art made away;
A mischief worse than civil home-bred strife,
765 Or theirs whose desperate hands themselves do slay,
Or butcher sire that reaves his son of life.
 Foul cankering rust the hidden treasure frets,
 But gold that's put to use more gold begets.'

'Nay, then,' quoth Adon, 'you will fall again
770 Into your idle over-handled theme;
The kiss I gave you is bestowed in vain,
And all in vain you strive against the stream;
 For, by this black-faced night, desire's foul nurse,
 Your treatise makes me like you worse and worse.

775 'If love have lent you twenty thousand tongues,
And every tongue more moving than your own,
Bewitching like the wanton mermaid's songs,
Yet from mine ear the tempting tune is blown;
 For know, my heart stands armèd in mine ear,
780  And will not let a false sound enter there;

'Lest the deceiving harmony should run
Into the quiet closure of my breast;
And then my little heart were quite undone,
In his bedchamber to be barred of rest.
   No, lady, no; my heart longs not to groan,     785
   But soundly sleeps, while now it sleeps alone.

'What have you urged that I cannot reprove?
The path is smooth that leadeth on to danger;
I hate not love, but your device in love
That lends embracements unto every stranger.    790
   You do it for increase: O strange excuse,
   When reason is the bawd to lust's abuse!

'Call it not love, for Love to heaven is fled
Since sweating Lust on earth usurped his name;
Under whose simple semblance he hath fed    795
Upon fresh beauty, blotting it with blame;
   Which the hot tyrant stains and soon bereaves,
   As caterpillars do the tender leaves.

'Love comforteth like sunshine after rain,
But Lust's effect is tempest after sun;    800
Love's gentle spring doth always fresh remain,
Lust's winter comes ere summer half be done;
   Love surfeits not, Lust like a glutton dies;
   Love is all truth, Lust full of forgèd lies.

'More I could tell, but more I dare not say;    805
The text is old, the orator too green.
Therefore, in sadness, now I will away;
My face is full of shame, my heart of teen:
   Mine ears that to your wanton talk attended
   Do burn themselves for having so offended.'    810

With this, he breaketh from the sweet embrace
Of those fair arms which bound him to her breast,
And homeward through the dark laund runs apace;
Leaves Love upon her back deeply distressed.
   Look how a bright star shooteth from the sky,    815
   So glides he in the night from Venus' eye;

Which after him she darts, as one on shore
Gazing upon a late-embarkèd friend,
Till the wild waves will have him seen no more,
820 Whose ridges with the meeting clouds contend;
    So did the merciless and pitchy night
    Fold in the object that did feed her sight.

Whereat amazed as one that unaware
Hath dropped a precious jewel in the flood,
825 Or 'stonished as night-wanderers often are,
Their light blown out in some mistrustful wood;
    Even so confounded in the dark she lay
    Having lost the fair discovery of her way.

And now she beats her heart, whereat it groans,
830 That all the neighbour caves, as seeming troubled,
Make verbal repetition of her moans;
Passion on passion deeply is redoubled:
    'Ay me!' she cries, and twenty times, 'Woe, woe!'
    And twenty echoes twenty times cry so.

835 She, marking them, begins a wailing note,
And sings extemporally a woeful ditty;
How love makes young men thrall, and old men dote;
How love is wise in folly, foolish witty:
    Her heavy anthem still concludes in woe,
840     And still the choir of echoes answer so.

Her song was tedious, and outwore the night,
For lovers' hours are long, though seeming short:
If pleased themselves, others, they think, delight
In such-like circumstance, with such-like sport.
845     Their copious stories, oftentimes begun,
    End without audience, and are never done.

For who hath she to spend the night withal
But idle sounds resembling parasites,
Like shrill-tongued tapsters answering every call,
850 Soothing the humour of fantastic wits?
    She says ' 'Tis so'; they answer all ' 'Tis so',
    And would say after her, if she said 'No'.

Lo, here the gentle lark, weary of rest,
From his moist cabinet mounts up on high,
And wakes the morning, from whose silver breast    855
The sun ariseth in his majesty;
   Who doth the world so gloriously behold
   That cedar-tops and hills seem burnished gold.

Venus salutes him with this fair good-morrow:
'O thou clear god, and patron of all light,    860
From whom each lamp and shining star doth borrow
The beauteous influence that makes him bright,
   There lives a son that sucked an earthly mother
   May lend thee light, as thou dost lend to other.'

This said, she hasteth to a myrtle grove,    865
Musing the morning is so much o'erworn,
And yet she hears no tidings of her love;
She hearkens for his hounds and for his horn.
   Anon she hears them chant it lustily,
   And all in haste she coasteth to the cry.    870

And as she runs, the bushes in the way
Some catch her by the neck, some kiss her face,
Some twined about her thigh to make her stay;
She wildly breaketh from their strict embrace,
   Like a milch doe, whose swelling dugs do ache,    875
   Hasting to feed her fawn hid in some brake.

By this she hears the hounds are at a bay;
Whereat she starts, like one that spies an adder
Wreathed up in fatal folds just in his way,
The fear whereof doth make him shake and shudder:    880
   Even so the timorous yelping of the hounds
   Appals her senses and her spirit confounds.

For now she knows it is no gentle chase,
But the blunt boar, rough bear, or lion proud,
Because the cry remaineth in one place,    885
Where fearfully the dogs exclaim aloud.
   Finding their enemy to be so curst,
   They all strain court'sy who shall cope him first.

890
This dismal cry rings sadly in her ear,
Through which it enters to surprise her heart;
Who, overcome by doubt and bloodless fear,
With cold-pale weakness numbs each feeling part;
 Like soldiers, when their captain once doth yield,
 They basely fly and dare not stay the field.

895
Thus stands she in a trembling ecstasy;
Till, cheering up her senses all dismayed,
She tells them 'tis a causeless fantasy,
And childish error, that they are afraid;
 Bids them leave quaking, bids them fear no more;
900
 And with that word she spied the hunted boar,

Whose frothy mouth, bepainted all with red,
Like milk and blood being mingled both together,
A second fear through all her sinews spread,
Which madly hurries her she knows not whither:
905
 This way she runs, and now she will no further,
 But back retires to rate the boar for murther.

A thousand spleens bear her a thousand ways;
She treads the path that she untreads again;
Her more than haste is mated with delays,
910
Like the proceedings of a drunken brain,
 Full of respects, yet nought at all respecting,
 In hand with all things, nought at all effecting.

Here kennelled in a brake she finds a hound,
And asks the weary caitiff for his master;
915
And there another licking of his wound,
'Gainst venomed sores the only sovereign plaster;
 And here she meets another sadly scowling,
 To whom she speaks, and he replies with howling.

When he hath ceased his ill-resounding noise,
920
Another flap-mouthed mourner, black and grim,
Against the welkin volleys out his voice;
Another and another answer him,
 Clapping their proud tails to the ground below,
 Shaking their scratched ears, bleeding as they go.

Look how the world's poor people are amazed 925
At apparitions, signs and prodigies,
Whereon with fearful eyes they long have gazed,
Infusing them with dreadful prophecies;
   So she at these sad signs draws up her breath,
   And, sighing it again, exclaims on Death. 930

'Hard-favoured tyrant, ugly, meagre, lean,
Hateful divorce of love' – thus chides she Death –
'Grim-grinning ghost, earth's worm, what dost thou mean
To stifle beauty and to steal his breath
   Who when he lived, his breath and beauty set 935
   Gloss on the rose, smell to the violet?

'If he be dead – O no, it cannot be,
Seeing his beauty, thou shouldst strike at it –
O yes, it may; thou hast no eyes to see,
But hatefully at random dost thou hit. 940
   Thy mark is feeble age; but thy false dart
   Mistakes that aim, and cleaves an infant's heart.

'Hadst thou but bid beware, then he had spoke,
And, hearing him, thy power had lost his power.
The Destinies will curse thee for this stroke; 945
They bid thee crop a weed, thou pluckst a flower.
   Love's golden arrow at him should have fled,
   And not Death's ebon dart, to strike him dead.

'Dost thou drink tears, that thou provok'st such weeping?
What may a heavy groan advantage thee? 950
Why hast thou cast into eternal sleeping
Those eyes that taught all other eyes to see?
   Now Nature cares not for thy mortal vigour,
   Since her best work is ruined with thy rigour.'

Here overcome as one full of despair, 955
She vailed her eyelids, who, like sluices, stopped
The crystal tide that from her two cheeks fair
In the sweet channel of her bosom dropped;
   But through the flood-gates breaks the silver rain,
   And with his strong course opens them again. 960

O, how her eyes and tears did lend and borrow!
Her eye seen in the tears, tears in her eye;
Both crystals, where they viewed each other's sorrow,
Sorrow that friendly sighs sought still to dry;
    But like a stormy day, now wind, now rain,
     Sighs dry her cheeks, tears make them wet again.

Variable passions throng her constant woe,
As striving who should best become her grief;
All entertained, each passion labours so
That every present sorrow seemeth chief,
    But none is best. Then join they all together,
     Like many clouds consulting for foul weather.

By this, far off she hears some huntsman holloa;
A nurse's song ne'er pleased her babe so well.
The dire imagination she did follow
This sound of hope doth labour to expel;
    For now reviving joy bids her rejoice,
     And flatters her it is Adonis' voice.

Whereat her tears began to turn their tide,
Being prisoned in her eye like pearls in glass;
Yet sometimes falls an orient drop beside,
Which her cheek melts, as scorning it should pass
    To wash the foul face of the sluttish ground,
     Who is but drunken when she seemeth drowned.

O hard-believing love, how strange it seems
Not to believe, and yet too credulous!
Thy weal and woe are both of them extremes;
Despair, and hope, makes thee ridiculous:
    The one doth flatter thee in thoughts unlikely,
     In likely thoughts the other kills thee quickly.

Now she unweaves the web that she hath wrought:
Adonis lives, and Death is not to blame;
It was not she that called him all to nought:
Now she adds honours to his hateful name;
    She clepes him king of graves, and grave for kings,
     Imperious supreme of all mortal things.

'No, no,' quoth she, 'sweet Death, I did but jest;
Yet pardon me, I felt a kind of fear
When as I met the boar, that bloody beast,
Which knows no pity, but is still severe:                    1000
    Then, gentle shadow – truth I must confess –
    I railed on thee, fearing my love's decease.

'''Tis not my fault: the boar provoked my tongue;
Be wreaked on him, invisible commander;
'Tis he, foul creature, that hath done thee wrong;          1005
I did but act, he's author of thy slander.
    Grief hath two tongues, and never woman yet
    Could rule them both without ten women's wit.'

Thus, hoping that Adonis is alive,
Her rash suspect she doth extenuate;                        1010
And that his beauty may the better thrive,
With Death she humbly doth insinuate;
    Tells him of trophies, statues, tombs, and stories
    His victories, his triumphs and his glories.

'O Jove,' quoth she, 'how much a fool was I                 1015
To be of such a weak and silly mind
To wail his death who lives, and must not die
Till mutual overthrow of mortal kind!
    For he being dead, with him is Beauty slain,
    And, Beauty dead, black Chaos comes again.              1020

'Fie, fie, fond love, thou art as full of fear
As one with treasure laden, hemmed with thieves;
Trifles unwitnessèd with eye or ear
Thy coward heart with false bethinking grieves.'
    Even at this word she hears a merry horn,                1025
    Whereat she leaps that was but late forlorn.

As falcons to the lure, away she flies;
The grass stoops not, she treads on it so light;
And in her haste unfortunately spies
The foul boar's conquest on her fair delight;              1030
    Which seen, her eyes, as murdered with the view,
    Like stars ashamed of day, themselves withdrew;

Or as the snail, whose tender horns being hit,
Shrinks backward in his shelly cave with pain,
1035 And there all smothered up in shade doth sit,
Long after fearing to creep forth again;
    So at his bloody view her eyes are fled
    Into the deep-dark cabins of her head;

Where they resign their office and their light
1040 To the disposing of her troubled brain;
Who bids them still consort with ugly night,
And never wound the heart with looks again;
    Who, like a king perplexèd in his throne,
    By their suggestion gives a deadly groan:

1045 Whereat each tributary subject quakes,
As when the wind, imprisoned in the ground,
Struggling for passage, earth's foundation shakes,
Which with cold terror doth men's minds confound.
    This mutiny each part doth so surprise,
1050     That from their dark beds once more leap her eyes;

And being opened, threw unwilling light
Upon the wide wound that the boar had trenched
In his soft flank; whose wonted lily-white
With purple tears that his wound wept was drenched:
1055     No flower was nigh, no grass, herb, leaf or weed,
    But stole his blood and seemed with him to bleed.

This solemn sympathy poor Venus noteth:
Over one shoulder doth she hang her head;
Dumbly she passions, franticly she doteth;
1060 She thinks he could not die, he is not dead.
    Her voice is stopped, her joints forget to bow;
    Her eyes are mad that they have wept till now.

Upon his hurt she looks so steadfastly
That her sight dazzling makes the wound seem three;
1065 And then she reprehends her mangling eye
That makes more gashes where no breach should be:
    His face seems twain, each several limb is doubled,
    For oft the eye mistakes, the brain being troubled.

'My tongue cannot express my grief for one,
And yet,' quoth she, 'behold two Adons dead!    1070
My sighs are blown away, my salt tears gone,
Mine eyes are turned to fire, my heart to lead;
    Heavy heart's lead, melt at mine eyes' red fire!
    So shall I die by drops of hot desire.

'Alas, poor world, what treasure hast thou lost!    1075
What face remains alive that's worth the viewing?
Whose tongue is music now? what canst thou boast
Of things long since, or any thing ensuing?
    The flowers are sweet, their colours fresh and trim;
    But true sweet beauty lived and died with him.    1080

'Bonnet nor veil henceforth no creature wear;
Nor sun nor wind will ever strive to kiss you.
Having no fair to lose, you need not fear;
The sun doth scorn you, and the wind doth hiss you.
    But when Adonis lived, sun and sharp air    1085
    Lurked like two thieves to rob him of his fair;

'And therefore would he put his bonnet on,
Under whose brim the gaudy sun would peep;
The wind would blow it off, and, being gone,
Play with his locks. Then would Adonis weep;    1090
    And straight, in pity of his tender years,
    They both would strive who first should dry his tears.

'To see his face the lion walked along
Behind some hedge, because he would not fear him;
To recreate himself when he hath sung,    1095
The tiger would be tame and gently hear him;
    If he had spoke, the wolf would leave his prey,
    And never fright the silly lamb that day.

'When he beheld his shadow in the brook,
The fishes spread on it their golden gills;    1100
When he was by, the birds such pleasure took
That some would sing, some other in their bills
    Would bring him mulberries and ripe-red cherries;
    He fed them with his sight, they him with berries.

1105 'But this foul, grim, and urchin-snouted boar,
Whose downward eye still looketh for a grave,
Ne'er saw the beauteous livery that he wore;
Witness the entertainment that he gave.
    If he did see his face, why then I know
1110     He thought to kiss him, and hath killed him so.

'''Tis true, 'tis true; thus was Adonis slain:
He ran upon the boar with his sharp spear,
Who did not whet his teeth at him again,
But by a kiss thought to persuade him there;
1115     And nuzzling in his flank, the loving swine
    Sheathed unaware the tusk in his soft groin.

'Had I been toothed like him, I must confess,
With kissing him I should have killed him first;
But he is dead, and never did he bless
1120 My youth with his; the more am I accurst.'
    With this, she falleth in the place she stood,
    And stains her face with his congealed blood.

She looks upon his lips, and they are pale;
She takes him by the hand, and that is cold;
1125 She whispers in his ears a heavy tale,
As if they heard the woeful words she told;
    She lifts the coffer-lids that close his eyes,
    Where, lo, two lamps, burnt out, in darkness lies;

Two glasses, where herself herself beheld
1130 A thousand times, and now no more reflect,
Their virtue lost wherein they late excelled,
And every beauty robbed of his effect.
    'Wonder of time,' quoth she, 'this is my spite,
    That, thou being dead, the day should yet be light.

1135 'Since thou art dead, lo, here I prophesy
Sorrow on love hereafter shall attend:
It shall be waited on with jealousy,
Find sweet beginning but unsavoury end;
    Ne'er settled equally, but high or low,
1140     That all love's pleasure shall not match his woe.

'It shall be fickle, false and full of fraud;
Bud, and be blasted, in a breathing while;
The bottom poison, and the top o'erstrawed
With sweets that shall the truest sight beguile;
    The strongest body shall it make most weak,          1145
    Strike the wise dumb, and teach the fool to speak.

'It shall be sparing, and too full of riot,
Teaching decrepit age to tread the measures;
The staring ruffian shall it keep in quiet,
Pluck down the rich, enrich the poor with treasures;    1150
    It shall be raging-mad, and silly-mild,
    Make the young old, the old become a child.

'It shall suspect where is no cause of fear;
It shall not fear where it should most mistrust;
It shall be merciful, and too severe,                1155
And most deceiving when it seems most just;
    Perverse it shall be where it shows most toward,
    Put fear to valour, courage to the coward.

'It shall be cause of war and dire events,
And set dissension 'twixt the son and sire;         1160
Subject and servile to all discontents,
As dry combustious matter is to fire.
    Sith in his prime death doth my love destroy,
    They that love best their loves shall not enjoy.'

By this the boy that by her side lay killed         1165
Was melted like a vapour from her sight,
And in his blood that on the ground lay spilled
A purple flower sprung up, chequered with white,
    Resembling well his pale cheeks, and the blood
    Which in round drops upon their whiteness stood.    1170

She bows her head the new-sprung flower to smell,
Comparing it to her Adonis' breath;
And says within her bosom it shall dwell,
Since he himself is reft from her by death.
    She crops the stalk, and in the breach appears    1175
    Green-dropping sap, which she compares to tears.

'Poor flower,' quoth she, 'this was thy father's guise –
Sweet issue of a more sweet-smelling sire –
For every little grief to wet his eyes.
To grow unto himself was his desire,
    And so 'tis thine; but know, it is as good
    To wither in my breast as in his blood.

'Here was thy father's bed, here in my breast;
Thou art the next of blood, and 'tis thy right.
Lo, in this hollow cradle take thy rest;
My throbbing heart shall rock thee day and night;
    There shall not be one minute in an hour
    Wherein I will not kiss my sweet love's flower.'

Thus weary of the world, away she hies,
And yokes her silver doves, by whose swift aid
Their mistress, mounted, through the empty skies
In her light chariot quickly is conveyed,
    Holding their course to Paphos, where their queen
    Means to immure herself and not be seen.

# THE RAPE OF LUCRECE

## TO THE RIGHT HONOURABLE
## HENRY WRIOTHESLEY,

### EARL OF SOUTHAMPTON AND BARON OF
### TITCHFIELD

The love I dedicate to your lordship is without end;
whereof this pamphlet without beginning is but a
superfluous moiety. The warrant I have of your
honourable disposition, not the worth of my untu-
tored lines, makes it assured of acceptance. What I
have done is yours; what I have to do is yours; being
part in all I have, devoted yours. Were my worth
greater, my duty would show greater; meantime,
as it is, it is bound to your lordship, to whom I wish
long life still lengthened with all happiness.

> Your lordship's in all duty,
> William Shakespeare

# THE ARGUMENT

Lucius Tarquinius, for his excessive pride surnamed Superbus, after he had caused his own father-in-law Servius Tullius to be cruelly murdered, and, contrary to the Roman laws and customs, not requiring or staying for the people's suffrages, had possessed himself of the kingdom, went, accompanied with his sons and other noblemen of Rome, to besiege Ardea. During which siege, the principal men of the army meeting one evening at the tent of Sextus Tarquinius, the King's son, in their discourses after supper everyone commended the virtues of his own wife; among whom Collatinus extolled the incomparable chastity of his wife Lucretia. In that pleasant humour they all posted to Rome; and intending, by their secret and sudden arrival, to make trial of that which everyone had before avouched, only Collatinus finds his wife, though it were late in the night, spinning amongst her maids: the other ladies were all found dancing and revelling, or in several disports. Whereupon the noblemen yielded Collatinus the victory and his wife the fame. At that time Sextus Tarquinius, being inflamed with Lucrece' beauty, yet smothering his passions for the present, departed with the rest back to the camp; from whence he shortly after privily withdrew himself, and was according to his estate royally entertained and lodged by Lucrece at Collatium. The same night he treacherously stealeth into her chamber, violently ravished her, and early in the morning speedeth away. Lucrece, in this lamentable plight, hastily dispatcheth messengers, one to Rome for her father, another to the camp for Collatine. They came, the one accompanied with Junius Brutus, the other with Publius Valerius; and finding

Lucrece attired in mourning habit, demanded the cause of her
30 sorrow. She, first taking an oath of them for her revenge,
revealed the actor and whole manner of his dealing, and withal
suddenly stabbed herself. Which done, with one consent they
all vowed to root out the whole hated family of the Tarquins;
and, bearing the dead body to Rome, Brutus acquainted the
35 people with the doer and manner of the vile deed, with a bitter
invective against the tyranny of the King. Wherewith the
people were so moved that with one consent and a general
acclamation the Tarquins were all exiled, and the state govern-
ment changed from kings to consuls.

From the besiegèd Ardea all in post,
Borne by the trustless wings of false desire,
Lust-breathèd Tarquin leaves the Roman host
And to Collatium bears the lightless fire
Which, in pale embers hid, lurks to aspire 5
   And girdle with embracing flames the waist
   Of Collatine's fair love, Lucrece the chaste.

Haply the name of 'chaste' unhapp'ly set
This bateless edge on his keen appetite,
When Collatine unwisely did not let 10
To praise the clear unmatchèd red and white
Which triumphed in that sky of his delight,
   Where mortal stars as bright as heaven's beauties
   With pure aspects did him peculiar duties.

For he the night before in Tarquin's tent 15
Unlocked the treasure of his happy state;
What priceless wealth the heavens had him lent
In the possession of his beauteous mate;
Reckoning his fortune at such high-proud rate
   That kings might be espousèd to more fame, 20
   But king nor peer to such a peerless dame.

O happiness enjoyed but of a few,
And, if possessed, as soon decayed and done
As is the morning silver melting dew
Against the golden splendour of the sun! 25
An expired date cancelled ere well begun!
   Honour and beauty in the owner's arms
   Are weakly fortressed from a world of harms.

Beauty itself doth of itself persuade
30 The eyes of men without an orator;
What needeth then apology be made
To set forth that which is so singular?
Or why is Collatine the publisher
  Of that rich jewel he should keep unknown
35   From thievish ears, because it is his own?

Perchance his boast of Lucrece' sovereignty
Suggested this proud issue of a king;
For by our ears our hearts oft tainted be:
Perchance that envy of so rich a thing,
40 Braving compare, disdainfully did sting
  His high-pitched thoughts, that meaner men should vaunt
  That golden hap which their superiors want.

But some untimely thought did instigate
His all too timeless speed, if none of those;
45 His honour, his affairs, his friends, his state
Neglected all, with swift intent he goes
To quench the coal which in his liver glows.
  O rash false heat, wrapped in repentant cold,
  Thy hasty spring still blasts and ne'er grows old.

50 When at Collatium this false lord arrived,
Well was he welcomed by the Roman dame,
Within whose face beauty and virtue strived
Which of them both should underprop her fame:
When virtue bragged, beauty would blush for shame;
55   When beauty boasted blushes, in despite
  Virtue would stain that or with silver white.

But beauty, in that white entitulèd
From Venus' doves, doth challenge that fair field;
Then virtue claims from beauty beauty's red,
60 Which virtue gave the golden age to gild
Their silver cheeks, and called it then their shield;
  Teaching them thus to use it in the fight,
  When shame assailed, the red should fence the white.

This heraldry in Lucrece' face was seen,
Argued by beauty's red and virtue's white;           65
Of either's colour was the other queen,
Proving from world's minority their right;
Yet their ambition makes them still to fight,
    The sovereignty of either being so great
    That oft they interchange each other's seat.      70

This silent war of lilies and of roses
Which Tarquin viewed in her fair face's field
In their pure ranks his traitor eye encloses;
Where, lest between them both it should be killed,
The coward captive vanquishèd doth yield             75
    To those two armies that would let him go
    Rather than triumph in so false a foe.

Now thinks he that her husband's shallow tongue,
The niggard prodigal that praised her so,
In that high task hath done her beauty wrong,        80
Which far exceeds his barren skill to show;
Therefore that praise which Collatine doth owe
    Enchanted Tarquin answers with surmise,
    In silent wonder of still-gazing eyes.

This earthly saint adorèd by this devil              85
Little suspecteth the false worshipper;
For unstained thoughts do seldom dream on evil;
Birds never limed no secret bushes fear:
So, guiltless, she securely gives good cheer
    And reverend welcome to her princely guest,      90
    Whose inward ill no outward harm expressed.

For that he coloured with his high estate,
Hiding base sin in pleats of majesty,
That nothing in him seemed inordinate
Save sometime too much wonder of his eye,            95
Which, having all, all could not satisfy;
    But poorly rich so wanteth in his store
    That cloyed with much he pineth still for more.

But she that never coped with stranger eyes
100    Could pick no meaning from their parling looks,
Nor read the subtle shining secrecies
Writ in the glassy margents of such books:
She touched no unknown baits; nor feared no hooks;
    Nor could she moralize his wanton sight
105        More than his eyes were opened to the light.

He stories to her ears her husband's fame,
Won in the fields of fruitful Italy;
And decks with praises Collatine's high name,
Made glorious by his manly chivalry
110    With bruisèd arms and wreaths of victory.
    Her joy with heaved–up hand she doth express,
    And wordless so greets heaven for his success.

Far from the purpose of his coming thither
He makes excuses for his being there.
115    No cloudy show of stormy blustering weather
Doth yet in his fair welkin once appear;
Till sable Night, mother of dread and fear,
    Upon the world dim darkness doth display
    And in her vaulty prison stows the day.

120    For then is Tarquin brought unto his bed,
Intending weariness with heavy sprite;
For after supper long he questionèd
With modest Lucrece, and wore out the night.
Now leaden slumber with life's strength doth fight,
125        And every one to rest himself betakes,
    Save thieves and cares and troubled minds that wakes.

As one of which doth Tarquin lie revolving
The sundry dangers of his will's obtaining;
Yet ever to obtain his will resolving,
130    Though weak-built hopes persuade him to abstaining.
Despair to gain doth traffic oft for gaining,
    And when great treasure is the meed proposed,
    Though death be adjunct, there's no death supposed.

Those that much covet are with gain so fond
That what they have not, that which they possess,      135
They scatter and unloose it from their bond;
And so by hoping more they have but less,
Or, gaining more, the profit of excess
  Is but to surfeit, and such griefs sustain
  That they prove bankrupt in this poor-rich gain.      140

The aim of all is but to nurse the life
With honour, wealth, and ease in waning age;
And in this aim there is such thwarting strife
That one for all or all for one we gage:
As life for honour in fell battle's rage;      145
  Honour for wealth; and oft that wealth doth cost
  The death of all, and all together lost.

So that in venturing ill we leave to be
The things we are for that which we expect;
And this ambitious foul infirmity      150
In having much torments us with defect
Of that we have; so then we do neglect
  The thing we have, and all for want of wit
  Make something nothing by augmenting it.

Such hazard now must doting Tarquin make,      155
Pawning his honour to obtain his lust;
And for himself himself he must forsake.
Then where is truth if there be no self-trust?
When shall he think to find a stranger just
  When he himself himself confounds, betrays      160
  To slanderous tongues and wretched hateful days?

Now stole upon the time the dead of night,
When heavy sleep had closed up mortal eyes;
No comfortable star did lend his light,
No noise but owls' and wolves' death-boding cries;      165
Now serves the season that they may surprise
  The silly lambs; pure thoughts are dead and still,
  While lust and murder wakes to stain and kill.

And now this lustful lord leaped from his bed,
170    Throwing his mantle rudely o'er his arm;
Is madly tossed between desire and dread:
Th'one sweetly flatters, th'other feareth harm;
But honest fear, bewitched with lust's foul charm,
    Doth too too oft betake him to retire,
175    Beaten away by brain-sick rude desire.

His falchion on a flint he softly smiteth,
That from the cold stone sparks of fire do fly;
Whereat a waxen torch forthwith he lighteth,
Which must be lodestar to his lustful eye;
180    And to the flame thus speaks advisedly:
    'As from this cold flint I enforced this fire,
    So Lucrece must I force to my desire.'

Here pale with fear he doth premeditate
The dangers of his loathsome enterprise,
185    And in his inward mind he doth debate
What following sorrow may on this arise;
Then, looking scornfully, he doth despise
    His naked armour of still-slaughtered lust,
    And justly thus controls his thoughts unjust:

190    'Fair torch, burn out thy light, and lend it not
To darken her whose light excelleth thine;
And die, unhallowed thoughts, before you blot
With your uncleanness that which is divine;
Offer pure incense to so pure a shrine;
195    Let fair humanity abhor the deed
    That spots and stains love's modest snow-white weed.

'O shame to knighthood and to shining arms!
O foul dishonour to my household's grave!
O impious act including all foul harms!
200    A martial man to be soft fancy's slave!
True valour still a true respect should have;
    Then my digression is so vile, so base,
    That it will live engraven in my face.

'Yea, though I die the scandal will survive
And be an eye-sore in my golden coat:                            205
Some loathsome dash the herald will contrive,
To cipher me how fondly I did dote,
That my posterity, shamed with the note,
    Shall curse my bones, and hold it for no sin
    To wish that I their father had not been.                   210

'What win I if I gain the thing I seek?
A dream, a breath, a froth of fleeting joy.
Who buys a minute's mirth to wail a week?
Or sells eternity to get a toy?
For one sweet grape who will the vine destroy?                  215
    Or what fond beggar, but to touch the crown,
    Would with the sceptre straight be strucken down?

'If Collatinus dream of my intent,
Will he not wake, and in a desperate rage
Post hither, this vile purpose to prevent?                      220
This siege that hath engirt his marriage,
This blur to youth, this sorrow to the sage,
    This dying virtue, this surviving shame,
    Whose crime will bear an ever-during blame?

'O what excuse can my invention make                            225
When thou shalt charge me with so black a deed?
Will not my tongue be mute, my frail joints shake,
Mine eyes forgo their light, my false heart bleed?
The guilt being great, the fear doth still exceed;
    And extreme fear can neither fight nor fly,                 230
    But coward-like with trembling terror die.

'Had Collatinus killed my son or sire,
Or lain in ambush to betray my life,
Or were he not my dear friend, this desire
Might have excuse to work upon his wife,                        235
As in revenge or quittal of such strife;
    But as he is my kinsman, my dear friend,
    The shame and fault finds no excuse nor end.

'Shameful it is – ay, if the fact be known;
Hateful it is – there is no hate in loving;
I'll beg her love – but she is not her own.
The worst is but denial and reproving.
My will is strong past reason's weak removing:
    Who fears a sentence or an old man's saw
    Shall by a painted cloth be kept in awe.'

Thus graceless holds he disputation
'Tween frozen conscience and hot-burning will,
And with good thoughts makes dispensation,
Urging the worser sense for vantage still;
Which in a moment doth confound and kill
    All pure effects, and doth so far proceed
    That what is vile shows like a virtuous deed.

Quoth he, 'She took me kindly by the hand,
And gazed for tidings in my eager eyes,
Fearing some hard news from the warlike band
Where her belovèd Collatinus lies.
O how her fear did make her colour rise!
    First red as roses that on lawn we lay,
    Then white as lawn, the roses took away.

'And how her hand in my hand being locked
Forced it to tremble with her loyal fear!
Which struck her sad, and then it faster rocked
Until her husband's welfare she did hear;
Whereat she smilèd with so sweet a cheer
    That had Narcissus seen her as she stood
    Self-love had never drowned him in the flood.

'Why hunt I then for colour or excuses?
All orators are dumb when beauty pleadeth;
Poor wretches have remorse in poor abuses;
Love thrives not in the heart that shadows dreadeth;
Affection is my captian, and he leadeth;
    And when his gaudy banner is displayed
    The coward fights and will not be dismayed.

'Then childish fear avaunt, debating die!
Respect and reason wait on wrinkled age!                          275
My heart shall never countermand mine eye;
Sad pause and deep regard beseems the sage:
My part is Youth, and beats these from the stage.
  Desire my pilot is, beauty my prize;
  Then who fears sinking where such treasure lies?'              280

As corn o'ergrown by weeds, so heedful fear
Is almost choked by unresisted lust.
Away he steals with open listening ear,
Full of foul hope and full of fond mistrust;
Both which, as servitors to the unjust,                           285
  So cross him with their opposite persuasion
  That now he vows a league, and now invasion.

Within his thought her heavenly image sits,
And in the selfsame seat sits Collatine.
That eye which looks on her confounds his wits;                   290
That eye which him beholds, as more divine,
Unto a view so false will not incline;
  But with a pure appeal seeks to the heart,
  Which once corrupted takes the worser part;

And therein heartens up his servile powers,                       295
Who, flattered by their leader's jocund show,
Stuff up his lust, as minutes fill up hours;
And as their captain, so their pride doth grow,
Paying more slavish tribute than they owe.
  By reprobate desire thus madly led                              300
  The Roman lord marcheth to Lucrece' bed.

The locks between her chamber and his will,
Each one by him enforced, retires his ward;
But as they open, they all rate his ill,
Which drives the creeping thief to some regard.                   305
The threshold grates the door to have him heard;
  Night-wandering weasels shriek to see him there;
  They fright him, yet he still pursues his fear.

As each unwilling portal yields him way,
310 Through little vents and crannies of the place
The wind wars with his torch to make him stay,
And blows the smoke of it into his face,
Extinguishing his conduct in this case;
　　But his hot heart, which fond desire doth scorch,
315 　　Puffs forth another wind that fires the torch.

And being lighted, by the light he spies
Lucretia's glove, wherein her needle sticks;
He takes it from the rushes where it lies,
And griping it, the needle his finger pricks,
320 As who should say 'This glove to wanton tricks
　　Is not inured; return again in haste;
　　Thou seest our mistress' ornaments are chaste.'

But all these poor forbiddings could not stay him;
He in the worst sense consters their denial:
325 The doors, the wind, the glove, that did delay him
He takes for accidental things of trial;
Or as those bars which stop the hourly dial,
　　Who with a lingering stay his course doth let
　　Till every minute pays the hour his debt.

330 'So, so,' quoth he, 'these lets attend the time,
Like little frosts that sometime threat the spring,
To add a more rejoicing to the prime
And give the sneapèd birds more cause to sing.
Pain pays the income of each precious thing:
335 　　Huge rocks, high winds, strong pirates, shelves, and sands
　　The merchant fears, ere rich at home he lands.'

Now is he come unto the chamber door
That shuts him from the heaven of his thought,
Which with a yielding latch, and with no more,
340 Hath barred him from the blessèd thing he sought.
So from himself impiety hath wrought
　　That for his prey to pray he doth begin,
　　As if the heavens should countenance his sin.

But in the midst of his unfruitful prayer,
Having solicited the eternal power                              345
That his foul thoughts might compass his fair fair,
And they would stand auspicious to the hour,
Even there he starts; quoth he, 'I must deflower:
　　The powers to whom I pray abhor this fact;
　　How can they then assist me in the act?                     350

'Then Love and Fortune be my gods, my guide!
My will is backed with resolution;
Thoughts are but dreams till their effects be tried;
The blackest sin is cleared with absolution;
Against love's fire fear's frost hath dissolution.             355
　　The eye of heaven is out, and misty night
　　Covers the shame that follows sweet delight.'

This said, his guilty hand plucked up the latch,
And with his knee the door he opens wide.
The dove sleeps fast that this night-owl will catch;           360
Thus treason works ere traitors be espied.
Who sees the lurking serpent steps aside;
　　But she, sound sleeping, fearing no such thing,
　　Lies at the mercy of his mortal sting.

Into the chamber wickedly he stalks,                           365
And gazeth on her yet unstainèd bed.
The curtains being close, about he walks,
Rolling his greedy eyeballs in his head;
By their high treason is his heart misled,
　　Which gives the watchword to his hand full soon            370
　　To draw the cloud that hides the silver moon.

Look as the fair and fiery-pointed sun
Rushing from forth a cloud bereaves our sight:
Even so, the curtain drawn, his eyes begun
To wink, being blinded with a greater light.                   375
Whether it is that she reflects so bright
　　That dazzleth them, or else some shame supposed,
　　But blind they are, and keep themselves enclosed.

O, had they in that darksome prison died,
380 Then had they seen the period of their ill!
Then Collatine again by Lucrece' side
In his clear bed might have reposèd still.
But they must ope, this blessèd league to kill;
    And holy-thoughted Lucrece to their sight
385     Must sell her joy, her life, her world's delight.

Her lily hand her rosy cheek lies under,
Cozening the pillow of a lawful kiss;
Who therefore angry seems to part in sunder,
Swelling on either side to want his bliss;
390 Between whose hills her head entombèd is;
    Where like a virtuous monument she lies
    To be admired of lewd unhallowed eyes.

Without the bed her other fair hand was,
On the green coverlet, whose perfect white
395 Showed like an April daisy on the grass,
With pearly sweat resembling dew of night.
Her eyes like marigolds had sheathed their light,
    And canopied in darkness sweetly lay
    Till they might open to adorn the day.

400 Her hair like golden threads played with her breath:
O modest wantons, wanton modesty!
Showing life's triumph in the map of death,
And death's dim look in life's mortality:
Each in her sleep themselves so beautify
405     As if between them twain there were no strife,
    But that life lived in death and death in life.

Her breasts like ivory globes circled with blue,
A pair of maiden worlds unconquerèd,
Save of their lord no bearing yoke they knew,
410 And him by oath they truly honourèd.
These worlds in Tarquin new ambition bred,
    Who like a foul usurper went about
    From this fair throne to heave the owner out.

What could he see but mightily he noted?
What did he note but strongly he desired?                    415
What he beheld, on that he firmly doted,
And in his will his wilful eye he tired.
With more than admiration he admired
  Her azure veins, her alabaster skin,
  Her coral lips, her snow-white dimpled chin.               420

As the grim lion fawneth o'er his prey,
Sharp hunger by the conquest satisfied,
So o'er this sleeping soul doth Tarquin stay,
His rage of lust by gazing qualified –
Slacked not suppressed; for standing by her side,           425
  His eye which late this mutiny restrains
  Upon a greater uproar tempts his veins.

And they like straggling slaves for pillage fighting,
Obdurate vassals fell exploits effecting,
In bloody death and ravishment delighting,                  430
Nor children's tears nor mothers' groans respecting,
Swell in their pride, the onset still expecting.
  Anon his beating heart, alarum striking,
  Gives the hot charge, and bids them do their liking.

His drumming heart cheers up his burning eye,               435
His eye commends the leading to his hand;
His hand, as proud of such a dignity,
Smoking with pride, marched on to make his stand
On her bare breast, the heart of all her land;
  Whose ranks of blue veins as his hand did scale           440
  Left their round turrets destitute and pale.

They, mustering to the quiet cabinet
Where their dear governess and lady lies,
Do tell her she is dreadfully beset,
And fright her with confusion of their cries.               445
She much amazed breaks ope her locked-up eyes,
  Who, peeping forth this tumult to behold,
  Are by his flaming torch dimmed and controlled.

Imagine her as one in dead of night
450 From forth dull sleep by dreadful fancy waking,
That thinks she hath beheld some ghastly sprite
Whose grim aspect sets every joint a-shaking;
What terror 'tis! but she in worser taking,
 From sleep disturbèd, heedfully doth view
455  The sight which makes supposèd terror true.

Wrapped and confounded in a thousand fears,
Like to a new-killed bird she trembling lies;
She dares not look, yet, winking, there appears
Quick-shifting antics, ugly in her eyes.
460 Such shadows are the weak brain's forgeries,
 Who, angry that the eyes fly from their lights,
 In darkness daunts them with more dreadful sights.

His hand that yet remains upon her breast –
Rude ram, to batter such an ivory wall –
465 May feel her heart, poor citizen, distressed,
Wounding itself to death, rise up and fall,
Beating her bulk, that his hand shakes withal.
 This moves in him more rage and lesser pity
 To make the breach and enter this sweet city.

470 First like a trumpet doth his tongue begin
To sound a parley to his heartless foe,
Who o'er the white sheet peers her whiter chin,
The reason of this rash alarm to know,
Which he by dumb demeanour seeks to show;
475  But she with vehement prayers urgeth still
 Under what colour he commits this ill.

Thus he replies: 'The colour in thy face,
That even for anger makes the lily pale
And the red rose blush at her own disgrace,
480 Shall plead for me and tell my loving tale.
Under that colour am I come to scale
 Thy never-conquered fort: the fault is thine,
 For those thine eyes betray thee unto mine.

'Thus I forestall thee, if thou mean to chide:
Thy beauty hath ensnared thee to this night, 485
Where thou with patience must my will abide,
My will that marks thee for my earth's delight,
Which I to conquer sought with all my might;
　　But as reproof and reason beat it dead,
　　By thy bright beauty was it newly bred. 490

'I see what crosses my attempt will bring;
I know what thorns the growing rose defends;
I think the honey guarded with a sting;
All this beforehand counsel comprehends.
But Will is deaf, and hears no heedful friends; 495
　　Only he hath an eye to gaze on Beauty,
　　And dotes on what he looks, 'gainst law or duty.

'I have debated even in my soul
What wrong, what shame, what sorrow I shall breed;
But nothing can affection's course control, 500
Or stop the headlong fury of his speed.
I know repentant tears ensue the deed,
　　Reproach, disdain, and deadly enmity;
　　Yet strive I to embrace mine infamy.'

This said, he shakes aloft his Roman blade, 505
Which like a falcon towering in the skies
Coucheth the fowl below with his wings' shade,
Whose crooked beak threats, if he mount he dies.
So under his insulting falchion lies
　　Harmless Lucretia, marking what he tells 510
　　With trembling fear, as fowl hear falcons' bells.

'Lucrece,' quoth he, 'this night I must enjoy thee.
If thou deny, then force must work my way,
For in thy bed I purpose to destroy thee;
That done, some worthless slave of thine I'll slay, 515
To kill thine honour with thy life's decay;
　　And in thy dead arms do I mean to place him,
　　Swearing I slew him, seeing thee embrace him.

'So thy surviving husband shall remain
520   The scornful mark of every open eye;
Thy kinsmen hang their heads at this disdain,
Thy issue blurred with nameless bastardy;
And thou, the author of their obloquy,
    Shalt have thy trespass cited up in rhymes
525     And sung by children in succeeding times.

'But if thou yield, I rest thy secret friend;
The fault unknown is as a thought unacted;
A little harm done to a great good end
For lawful policy remains enacted;
530   The poisonous simple sometime is compacted
    In a pure compound; being so applied,
    His venom in effect is purified.

'Then for thy husband and thy children's sake,
Tender my suit; bequeath not to their lot
535   The shame that from them no device can take,
The blemish that will never be forgot,
Worse than a slavish wipe or birth-hour's blot;
    For marks descried in men's nativity
    Are nature's faults, not their own infamy.'

540   Here with a cockatrice' dead-killing eye
He rouseth up himself, and makes a pause;
While she, the picture of pure piety,
Like a white hind under the gripe's sharp claws,
Pleads in a wilderness where are no laws
545    To the rough beast that knows no gentle right,
    Nor aught obeys but his foul appetite.

But when a black-faced cloud the world doth threat,
In his dim mist th'aspiring mountains hiding,
From earth's dark womb some gentle gust doth get,
550   Which blow these pitchy vapours from their biding,
Hindering their present fall by this dividing;
    So his unhallowed haste her words delays,
    And moody Pluto winks while Orpheus plays.

Yet, foul night-waking cat, he doth but dally
While in his hold-fast foot the weak mouse panteth;     555
Her sad behaviour feeds his vulture folly,
A swallowing gulf that even in plenty wanteth;
His ear her prayers admits, but his heart granteth
   No penetrable entrance to her plaining:
   Tears harden lust, though marble wear with raining.     560

Her pity-pleading eyes are sadly fixed
In the remorseless wrinkles of his face;
Her modest eloquence with sighs is mixed,
Which to her oratory adds more grace.
She puts the period often from his place,     565
   And 'midst the sentence so her accent breaks
   That twice she doth begin ere once she speaks.

She conjures him by high almighty Jove,
By knighthood, gentry, and sweet friendship's oath,
By her untimely tears, her husband's love,     570
By holy human law and common troth,
By heaven and earth, and all the power of both,
   That to his borrowed bed he make retire,
   And stoop to honour, not to foul desire.

Quoth she, 'Reward not hospitality     575
With such black payment as thou hast pretended;
Mud not the fountain that gave drink to thee;
Mar not the thing that cannot be amended;
End thy ill aim before thy shoot be ended;
   He is no woodman that doth bend his bow     580
   To strike a poor unseasonable doe.

'My husband is thy friend; for his sake spare me:
Thyself art mighty; for thine own sake leave me:
Myself a weakling; do not then ensnare me:
Thou look'st not like deceit; do not deceive me.     585
My sighs like whirlwinds labour hence to heave thee.
   If ever man were moved with woman's moans,
   Be movèd with my tears, my sighs, my groans:

'All which together, like a troubled ocean,
590 Beat at thy rocky and wrack-threatening heart,
To soften it with their continual motion;
For stones dissolved to water do convert.
O, if no harder than a stone thou art,
  Melt at my tears and be compassionate;
595   Soft pity enters at an iron gate.

'In Tarquin's likeness I did entertain thee:
Hast thou put on his shape to do him shame?
To all the host of heaven I complain me
Thou wrong'st his honour, wound'st his princely name:
600 Thou art not what thou seem'st; and if the same,
  Thou seem'st not what thou art, a god, a king;
  For kings like gods should govern every thing.

'How will thy shame be seeded in thine age,
When thus thy vices bud before thy spring?
605 If in thy hope thou dar'st do such outrage,
What dar'st thou not when once thou art a king?
O, be remembered, no outrageous thing
  From vassal actors can be wiped away;
  Then kings' misdeeds cannot be hid in clay.

610 'This deed will make thee only loved for fear,
But happy monarchs still are feared for love;
With foul offenders thou perforce must bear,
When they in thee the like offences prove.
If but for fear of this, thy will remove;
615   For princes are the glass, the school, the book,
  Where subjects' eyes do learn, do read, do look.

'And wilt thou be the school where lust shall learn?
Must he in thee read lectures of such shame?
Wilt thou be glass wherein it shall discern
620 Authority for sin, warrant for blame,
To privilege dishonour in thy name?
  Thou back'st reproach against long-living laud,
  And mak'st fair reputation but a bawd.

'Hast thou command? By him that gave it thee,
From a pure heart command thy rebel will.                          625
Draw not thy sword to guard iniquity,
For it was lent thee all that brood to kill.
Thy princely office how canst thou fulfil,
   When patterned by thy fault foul sin may say
   He learned to sin, and thou didst teach the way?                630

'Think but how vile a spectacle it were
To view thy present trespass in another.
Men's faults do seldom to themselves appear;
Their own transgressions partially they smother.
This guilt would seem death-worthy in thy brother.                 635
   O, how are they wrapped in with infamies
   That from their own misdeeds askance their eyes!

'To thee, to thee, my heaved-up hands appeal,
Not to seducing lust, thy rash relier:
I sue for exiled majesty's repeal;                                 640
Let him return, and flattering thoughts retire:
His true respect will prison false desire,
   And wipe the dim mist from thy doting eyne,
   That thou shalt see thy state, and pity mine.'

'Have done,' quoth he; 'my uncontrollèd tide                       645
Turns not, but swells the higher by this let.
Small lights are soon blown out; huge fires abide,
And with the wind in greater fury fret;
The petty streams that pay a daily debt
   To their salt sovereign, with their fresh falls' haste         650
   Add to his flow, but alter not his taste.'

'Thou art', quoth she, 'a sea, a sovereign king;
And lo, there falls into thy boundless flood
Black lust, dishonour, shame, misgoverning,
Who seek to stain the ocean of thy blood.                          655
If all these petty ills shall change thy good,
   Thy sea within a puddle's womb is hearsed,
   And not the puddle in thy sea dispersed.

'So shall these slaves be king, and thou their slave;
660    Thou nobly base, they basely dignified;
Thou their fair life, and they thy fouler grave;
Thou loathèd in their shame, they in thy pride.
The lesser thing should not the greater hide:
    The cedar stoops not to the base shrub's foot,
665       But low shrubs wither at the cedar's root.

'So let thy thoughts, low vassals to thy state' –
'No more,' quoth he; 'by heaven I will not hear thee.
Yield to my love; if not, enforcèd hate
Instead of love's coy touch shall rudely tear thee.
670    That done, despitefully I mean to bear thee
    Unto the base bed of some rascal groom,
    To be thy partner in this shameful doom.'

This said, he sets his foot upon the light,
For light and lust are deadly enemies:
675    Shame folded up in blind concealing night,
When most unseen, then most doth tyrannize.
The wolf hath seized his prey, the poor lamb cries,
    Till with her own white fleece her voice controlled
    Entombs her outcry in her lips' sweet fold.

680    For with the nightly linen that she wears
He pens her piteous clamours in her head,
Cooling his hot face in the chastest tears
That ever modest eyes with sorrow shed.
O, that prone lust should stain so pure a bed!
685      The spots whereof could weeping purify,
    Her tears should drop on them perpetually.

But she hath lost a dearer thing than life,
And he hath won what he would lose again.
This forcèd league doth force a further strife;
690    This momentary joy breeds months of pain;
This hot desire converts to cold disdain;
    Pure Chastity is rifled of her store,
    And Lust the thief far poorer than before.

Look as the full-fed hound or gorged hawk,
Unapt for tender smell or speedy flight,          695
Make slow pursuit, or altogether balk
The prey wherein by nature they delight,
So surfeit-taking Tarquin fares this night;
    His taste delicious, in digestion souring,
    Devours his will that lived by foul devouring.   700

O deeper sin than bottomless conceit
Can comprehend in still imagination!
Drunken Desire must vomit his receipt
Ere he can see his own abomination.
While Lust is in his pride, no exclamation        705
    Can curb his heat or rein his rash desire,
    Till, like a jade, Self-will himself doth tire.

And then with lank and lean discoloured cheek,
With heavy eye, knit brow, and strengthless pace,
Feeble Desire, all recreant, poor, and meek,      710
Like to a bankrupt beggar wails his case.
The flesh being proud, Desire doth fight with Grace;
    For there it revels, and when that decays,
    The guilty rebel for remission prays.

So fares it with this faultful lord of Rome,      715
Who this accomplishment so hotly chased;
For now against himself he sounds this doom,
That through the length of times he stands disgraced.
Besides, his soul's fair temple is defaced,
    To whose weak ruins muster troops of cares     720
    To ask the spotted princess how she fares.

She says her subjects with foul insurrection
Have battered down her consecrated wall,
And by their mortal fault brought in subjection
Her immortality, and made her thrall              725
To living death and pain perpetual;
    Which in her prescience she controllèd still,
    But her foresight could not forestall their will.

Even in this thought through the dark night he stealeth,
730    A captive victor that hath lost in gain;
Bearing away the wound that nothing healeth,
The scar that will, despite of cure, remain;
Leaving his spoil perplexed in greater pain.
    She bears the load of lust he left behind,
735      And he the burden of a guilty mind.

He like a thievish dog creeps sadly thence;
She like a wearied lamb lies panting there;
He scowls, and hates himself for his offence;
She, desperate, with her nails her flesh doth tear.
740    He faintly flies, sweating with guilty fear;
    She stays, exclaiming on the direful night;
      He runs, and chides his vanished loathed delight.

He thence departs a heavy convertite;
She there remains a hopeless castaway;
745    He in his speed looks for the morning light;
She prays she never may behold the day.
'For day,' quoth she, 'night's scapes doth open lay,
    And my true eyes have never practised how
      To cloak offences with a cunning brow.

750    'They think not but that every eye can see
The same disgrace which they themselves behold;
And therefore would they still in darkness be,
To have their unseen sin remain untold.
For they their guilt with weeping will unfold,
755    And grave, like water that doth eat in steel,
      Upon my cheeks what helpless shame I feel.'

Here she exclaims against repose and rest,
And bids her eyes hereafter still be blind;
She wakes her heart by beating on her breast,
760    And bids it leap from thence, where it may find
Some purer chest, to close so pure a mind.
    Frantic with grief thus breathes she forth her spite
      Against the unseen secrecy of night:

'O comfort-killing Night, image of hell,
Dim register and notary of shame,                           765
Black stage for tragedies and murders fell,
Vast sin-concealing chaos, nurse of blame!
Blind muffled bawd, dark harbour for defame,
    Grim cave of death, whispering conspirator
    With close-tongued treason and the ravisher!          770

'O hateful, vaporous, and foggy Night,
Since thou art guilty of my cureless crime,
Muster thy mists to meet the eastern light,
Make war against proportioned course of time;
Or if thou wilt permit the sun to climb                    775
    His wonted height, yet ere he go to bed
    Knit poisonous clouds about his golden head.

'With rotten damps ravish the morning air;
Let their exhaled unwholesome breaths make sick
The life of purity, the supreme fair,                      780
Ere he arrive his weary noontide prick;
And let thy musty vapours march so thick
    That in their smoky ranks his smothered light
    May set at noon and make perpetual night.

'Were Tarquin Night, as he is but Night's child,          785
The silver-shining queen he would distain;
Her twinkling handmaids too, by him defiled,
Through Night's black bosom should not peep again.
So should I have co-partners in my pain;
    And fellowship in woe doth woe assuage,               790
    As palmers' chat makes short their pilgrimage.

'Where now I have no one to blush with me,
To cross their arms and hang their heads with mine,
To mask their brows and hide their infamy;
But I alone alone must sit and pine,                       795
Seasoning the earth with showers of silver brine,
    Mingling my talk with tears, my grief with groans,
    Poor wasting monuments of lasting moans.

'O Night, thou furnace of foul reeking smoke,
Let not the jealous Day behold that face
Which underneath thy black all-hiding cloak
Immodestly lies martyred with disgrace!
Keep still possession of thy gloomy place,
 That all the faults which in thy reign are made
 May likewise be sepulchred in thy shade.

'Make me not object to the tell-tale Day:
The light will show charactered in my brow
The story of sweet chastity's decay,
The impious breach of holy wedlock vow;
Yea, the illiterate that know not how
 To cipher what is writ in learnèd books
 Will quote my loathsome trespass in my looks.

'The nurse to still her child will tell my story,
And fright her crying babe with Tarquin's name;
The orator to deck his oratory
Will couple my reproach to Tarquin's shame;
Feast-finding minstrels tuning my defame
 Will tie the hearers to attend each line,
 How Tarquin wrongèd me, I Collatine.

'Let my good name, that senseless reputation,
For Collatine's dear love be kept unspotted;
If that be made a theme for disputation,
The branches of another root are rotted,
And undeserved reproach to him allotted
 That is as clear from this attaint of mine
 As I ere this was pure to Collatine.

'O unseen shame, invisible disgrace!
O unfelt sore, crest-wounding private scar!
Reproach is stamped in Collatinus' face,
And Tarquin's eye may read the mot afar,
How he in peace is wounded, not in war.
 Alas, how many bear such shameful blows,
 Which not themselves but he that gives them knows!

'If, Collatine, thine honour lay in me,
From me by strong assault it is bereft:                                    835
My honey lost, and I, a drone-like bee,
Have no perfection of my summer left,
But robbed and ransacked by injurious theft.
   In thy weak hive a wandering wasp hath crept,
   And sucked the honey which thy chaste bee kept.                 840

'Yet am I guilty of thy honour's wrack;
Yet for thy honour did I entertain him;
Coming from thee, I could not put him back,
For it had been dishonour to disdain him;
Besides, of weariness he did complain him,                               845
   And talked of virtue: O unlooked-for evil,
   When virtue is profaned in such a devil!

'Why should the worm intrude the maiden bud,
Or hateful cuckoos hatch in sparrows' nests?
Or toads infect fair founts with venom mud?                             850
Or tyrant folly lurk in gentle breasts?
Or kings be breakers of their own behests?
   But no perfection is so absolute
   That some impurity doth not pollute.

'The agèd man that coffers up his gold                                   855
Is plagued with cramps and gouts and painful fits,
And scarce hath eyes his treasure to behold;
But like still-pining Tantalus he sits,
And useless barns the harvest of his wits,
   Having no other pleasure of his gain                          860
   But torment that it cannot cure his pain.

'So then he hath it when he cannot use it,
And leaves it to be mastered by his young,
Who in their pride do presently abuse it;
Their father was too weak and they too strong                           865
To hold their cursèd-blessèd fortune long.
   The sweets we wish for turn to loathèd sours
   Even in the moment that we call them ours.

'Unruly blasts wait on the tender spring;
870 Unwholesome weeds take root with precious flowers;
The adder hisses where the sweet birds sing;
What virtue breeds iniquity devours.
We have no good that we can say is ours
  But ill-annexèd Opportunity
875   Or kills his life or else his quality.

'O Opportunity, thy guilt is great!
'Tis thou that execut'st the traitor's treason;
Thou sets the wolf where he the lamb may get;
Whoever plots the sin, thou point'st the season.
880 'Tis thou that spurn'st at right, at law, at reason;
  And in thy shady cell where none may spy him
  Sits Sin, to seize the souls that wander by him.

'Thou mak'st the vestal violate her oath;
Thou blow'st the fire when temperance is thawed;
885 Thou smother'st honesty, thou murd'rest troth,
Thou foul abettor, thou notorious bawd;
Thou plantest scandal, and displacest laud.
  Thou ravisher, thou traitor, thou false thief,
  Thy honey turns to gall, thy joy to grief.

890 'Thy secret pleasure turns to open shame,
Thy private feasting to a public fast,
Thy smoothing titles to a ragged name,
Thy sugared tongue to bitter wormwood taste;
Thy violent vanities can never last.
895   How comes it then, vile Opportunity,
  Being so bad, such numbers seek for thee?

'When wilt thou be the humble suppliant's friend,
And bring him where his suit may be obtained?
When wilt thou sort an hour great strifes to end,
900 Or free that soul which wretchedness hath chained,
Give physic to the sick, ease to the pained?
  The poor, lame, blind, halt, creep, cry out for thee;
  But they ne'er meet with Opportunity.

'The patient dies while the physician sleeps;
The orphan pines while the oppressor feeds;          905
Justice is feasting while the widow weeps;
Advice is sporting while infection breeds.
Thou grant'st no time for charitable deeds;
    Wrath, envy, treason, rape, and murder's rages,
    Thy heinous hours wait on them as their pages.    910

'When Truth and Virtue have to do with thee,
A thousand crosses keep them from thy aid;
They buy thy help, but Sin ne'er gives a fee:
He gratis comes, and thou art well appaid
As well to hear as grant what he hath said.          915
    My Collatine would else have come to me
    When Tarquin did, but he was stayed by thee.

'Guilty thou art of murder and of theft,
Guilty of perjury and subornation,
Guilty of treason, forgery, and shift,               920
Guilty of incest, that abomination:
An accessary by thine inclination
    To all sins past and all that are to come
    From the creation to the general doom.

'Misshapen Time, copesmate of ugly Night,            925
Swift subtle post, carrier of grisly care,
Eater of youth, false slave to false delight,
Base watch of woes, sin's pack-horse, virtue's snare;
Thou nursest all, and murderest all that are.
    O hear me then, injurious shifting Time;          930
    Be guilty of my death, since of my crime.

'Why hath thy servant Opportunity
Betrayed the hours thou gav'st me to repose,
Cancelled my fortunes and enchainèd me
To endless date of never-ending woes?                935
Time's office is to fine the hate of foes,
    To eat up errors by opinion bred,
    Not spend the dowry of a lawful bed.

'Time's glory is to calm contending kings,
To unmask falsehood and bring truth to light,
To stamp the seal of time in agèd things,
To wake the morn and sentinel the night,
To wrong the wronger till he render right,
    To ruinate proud buildings with thy hours,
    And smear with dust their glittering golden towers;

'To fill with worm-holes stately monuments,
To feed oblivion with decay of things,
To blot old books and alter their contents,
To pluck the quills from ancient ravens' wings,
To dry the old oak's sap and cherish springs,
    To spoil antiquities of hammered steel,
    And turn the giddy round of Fortune's wheel;

'To show the beldame daughters of her daughter,
To make the child a man, the man a child,
To slay the tiger that doth live by slaughter,
To tame the unicorn and lion wild,
To mock the subtle in themselves beguiled,
    To cheer the ploughman with increaseful crops,
    And waste huge stones with little water-drops.

'Why work'st thou mischief in thy pilgrimage,
Unless thou couldst return to make amends?
One poor retiring minute in an age
Would purchase thee a thousand thousand friends,
Lending him wit that to bad debtors lends.
    O this dread night, wouldst thou one hour come back,
    I could prevent this storm and shun thy wrack!

'Thou ceaseless lackey to Eternity,
With some mischance cross Tarquin in his flight;
Devise extremes beyond extremity,
To make him curse this cursèd crimeful night.
Let ghastly shadows his lewd eyes affright,
    And the dire thought of his committed evil
    Shape every bush a hideous shapeless devil.

'Disturb his hours of rest with restless trances;
Afflict him in his bed with bedrid groans;                    975
Let there bechance him pitiful mischances,
To make him moan, but pity not his moans.
Stone him with hardened hearts harder than stones,
    And let mild women to him lose their mildness,
    Wilder to him than tigers in their wildness.             980

'Let him have time to tear his curlèd hair,
Let him have time against himself to rave,
Let him have time of time's help to despair,
Let him have time to live a loathèd slave,
Let him have time a beggar's orts to crave,                   985
    And time to see one that by alms doth live
    Disdain to him disdainèd scraps to give.

'Let him have time to see his friends his foes,
And merry fools to mock at him resort;
Let him have time to mark how slow time goes                  990
In time of sorrow, and how swift and short
His time of folly and his time of sport;
    And ever let his unrecalling crime
    Have time to wail the abusing of his time.

'O Time, thou tutor both to good and bad,                     995
Teach me to curse him that thou taught'st this ill;
At his own shadow let the thief run mad,
Himself himself seek every hour to kill;
Such wretched hands such wretched blood should spill;
    For who so base would such an office have                1000
    As slanderous deathsman to so base a slave?

'The baser is he, coming from a king,
To shame his hope with deeds degenerate;
The mightier man, the mightier is the thing
That makes him honoured or begets him hate;                  1005
For greatest scandal waits on greatest state.
    The moon being clouded presently is missed,
    But little stars may hide them when they list.

'The crow may bathe his coal-black wings in mire,
1010 And unperceived fly with the filth away;
But if the like the snow-white swan desire,
The stain upon his silver down will stay.
Poor grooms are sightless night, kings glorious day;
    Gnats are unnoted wheresoe'er they fly,
1015     But eagles gazed upon with every eye.

'Out, idle words, servants to shallow fools,
Unprofitable sounds, weak arbitrators!
Busy yourselves in skill-contending schools;
Debate where leisure serves with dull debaters;
1020 To trembling clients be you mediators:
    For me, I force not argument a straw,
    Since that my case is past the help of law.

'In vain I rail at Opportunity,
At Time, at Tarquin, and uncheerful Night;
1025 In vain I cavil with mine infamy,
In vain I spurn at my confirmed despite;
This helpless smoke of words doth me no right:
    The remedy indeed to do me good
    Is to let forth my foul defilèd blood.

1030 'Poor hand, why quiver'st thou at this decree?
Honour thyself to rid me of this shame;
For if I die, my honour lives in thee,
But if I live, thou liv'st in my defame.
Since thou couldst not defend thy loyal dame,
1035     And wast afeard to scratch her wicked foe,
    Kill both thyself and her for yielding so.'

This said, from her betumbled couch she starteth,
To find some desperate instrument of death;
But this no-slaughterhouse no tool imparteth
1040 To make more vent for passage of her breath,
Which thronging through her lips so vanisheth
    As smoke from Etna that in air consumes,
    Or that which from dischargèd cannon fumes.

'In vain', quoth she, 'I live, and seek in vain
Some happy mean to end a hapless life.                    1045
I feared by Tarquin's falchion to be slain,
Yet for the selfsame purpose seek a knife;
But when I feared, I was a loyal wife:
   So am I now – O no, that cannot be;
   Of that true type hath Tarquin rifled me.               1050

'O, that is gone for which I sought to live,
And therefore now I need not fear to die.
To clear this spot by death, at least I give
A badge of fame to slander's livery,
A dying life to living infamy.                           1055
   Poor helpless help, the treasure stolen away,
   To burn the guiltless casket where it lay!

'Well, well, dear Collatine, thou shalt not know
The stainèd taste of violated troth;
I will not wrong thy true affection so                    1060
To flatter thee with an infringèd oath;
This bastard graff shall never come to growth:
   He shall not boast who did thy stock pollute
   That thou art doting father of his fruit.

'Nor shall he smile at thee in secret thought,           1065
Nor laugh with his companions at thy state;
But thou shalt know thy interest was not bought
Basely with gold, but stolen from forth thy gate.
For me, I am the mistress of my fate,
   And with my trespass never will dispense,            1070
   Till life to death acquit my forced offence.

'I will not poison thee with my attaint,
Nor fold my fault in cleanly-coined excuses;
My sable ground of sin I will not paint
To hide the truth of this false night's abuses.          1075
My tongue shall utter all; mine eyes, like sluices,
   As from a mountain spring that feeds a dale,
   Shall gush pure streams to purge my impure tale.'

By this, lamenting Philomel had ended
1080 The well-tuned warble of her nightly sorrow,
And solemn night with slow sad gait descended
To ugly hell; when lo, the blushing morrow
Lends light to all fair eyes that light will borrow;
But cloudy Lucrece shames herself to see,
1085 And therefore still in night would cloistered be.

Revealing day through every cranny spies,
And seems to point her out where she sits weeping;
To whom she sobbing speaks: 'O eye of eyes,
Why pry'st thou through my window? Leave thy peeping;
1090 Mock with thy tickling beams eyes that are sleeping;
Brand not my forehead with thy piercing light,
For day hath naught to do what's done by night.'

Thus cavils she with every thing she sees.
True grief is fond and testy as a child,
1095 Who wayward once, his mood with naught agrees;
Old woes, not infant sorrows, bear them mild.
Continuance tames the one; the other wild,
Like an unpractised swimmer plunging still,
With too much labour drowns for want of skill.

1100 So she deep drenchèd in a sea of care
Holds disputation with each thing she views,
And to herself all sorrow doth compare;
No object but her passion's strength renews,
And as one shifts, another straight ensues.
1105 Sometime her grief is dumb and hath no words,
Sometime 'tis mad and too much talk affords.

The little birds that tune their morning's joy
Make her moans mad with their sweet melody;
For mirth doth search the bottom of annoy;
1110 Sad souls are slain in merry company;
Grief best is pleased with grief's society.
True sorrow then is feelingly sufficed
When with like semblance it is sympathized.

'Tis double death to drown in ken of shore;
He ten times pines that pines beholding food; 1115
To see the salve doth make the wound ache more;
Great grief grieves most at that would do it good;
Deep woes roll forward like a gentle flood,
　　Who, being stopped, the bounding bank o'erflows;
　　Grief dallied with nor law nor limit knows. 1120

'You mocking birds,' quoth she, 'your tunes entomb
Within your hollow-swelling feathered breasts,
And in my hearing be you mute and dumb;
My restless discord loves no stops nor rests;
A woeful hostess brooks not merry guests. 1125
　　Relish your nimble notes to pleasing ears;
　　Distress likes dumps, when time is kept with tears.

'Come, Philomel, that sing'st of ravishment,
Make thy sad grove in my dishevelled hair.
As the dank earth weeps at thy languishment, 1130
So I at each sad strain will strain a tear,
And with deep groans the diapason bear;
　　For burden-wise I'll hum on Tarquin still,
　　While thou on Tereus descants better skill.

'And whiles against a thorn thou bear'st thy part 1135
To keep thy sharp woes waking, wretched I,
To imitate thee well, against my heart
Will fix a sharp knife to affright mine eye,
Who if it wink shall thereon fall and die:
　　These means as frets upon an instrument 1140
　　Shall tune our heart-strings to true languishment.

'And for, poor bird, thou sing'st not in the day,
As shaming any eye should thee behold,
Some dark deep desert seated from the way,
That knows not parching heat nor freezing cold, 1145
Will we find out; and there we will unfold
　　To creatures stern sad tunes to change their kinds:
　　Since men prove beasts, let beasts bear gentle minds.'

As the poor frighted deer that stands at gaze,
1150 Wildly determining which way to fly,
Or one encompassed with a winding maze,
That cannot tread the way out readily,
So with herself is she in mutiny,
    To live or die which of the twain were better
1155    When life is shamed and death reproach's debtor.

'To kill myself,' quoth she, 'alack, what were it,
But with my body my poor soul's pollution?
They that lose half with greater patience bear it
Than they whose whole is swallowed in confusion.
1160 That mother tries a merciless conclusion
    Who, having two sweet babes, when death takes one,
    Will slay the other and be nurse to none.

'My body or my soul, which was the dearer,
When the one pure the other made divine?
1165 Whose love of either to myself was nearer,
When both were kept for heaven and Collatine?
Ay me, the bark pilled from the lofty pine,
    His leaves will wither and his sap decay;
    So must my soul, her bark being pilled away.

1170 'Her house is sacked, her quiet interrupted,
Her mansion battered by the enemy,
Her sacred temple spotted, spoiled, corrupted,
Grossly engirt with daring infamy.
Then let it not be called impiety
1175    If in this blemished fort I make some hole
    Through which I may convey this troubled soul.

'Yet die I will not till my Collatine
Have heard the cause of my untimely death,
That he may vow in that sad hour of mine
1180 Revenge on him that made me stop my breath.
My stainèd blood to Tarquin I'll bequeath,
    Which by him tainted shall for him be spent,
    And as his due writ in my testament.

'My honour I'll bequeath unto the knife
That wounds my body so dishonourèd.            1185
'Tis honour to deprive dishonoured life;
The one will live, the other being dead.
So of shame's ashes shall my fame be bred;
  For in my death I murder shameful scorn:
  My shame so dead, mine honour is new born.     1190

'Dear lord of that dear jewel I have lost,
What legacy shall I bequeath to thee?
My resolution, love, shall be thy boast,
By whose example thou revenged mayst be.
How Tarquin must be used, read it in me:         1195
  Myself thy friend will kill myself thy foe;
  And for my sake serve thou false Tarquin so.

'This brief abridgement of my will I make:
My soul and body to the skies and ground;
My resolution, husband, do thou take;          1200
Mine honour be the knife's that makes my wound;
My shame be his that did my fame confound;
  And all my fame that lives disbursèd be
  To those that live and think no shame of me.

'Thou, Collatine, shalt oversee this will;       1205
How was I overseen that thou shalt see it!
My blood shall wash the slander of mine ill;
My life's foul deed, my life's fair end shall free it.
Faint not, faint heart, but stoutly say "So be it";
  Yield to my hand, my hand shall conquer thee:    1210
  Thou dead, both die, and both shall victors be.'

This plot of death when sadly she had laid,
And wiped the brinish pearl from her bright eyes,
With untuned tongue she hoarsely calls her maid,
Whose swift obedience to her mistress hies;      1215
For fleet-winged duty with thought's feathers flies.
  Poor Lucrece' cheeks unto her maid seem so
  As winter meads when sun doth melt their snow.

Her mistress she doth give demure good-morrow
1220 With soft slow tongue, true mark of modesty,
And sorts a sad look to her lady's sorrow,
For why her face wore sorrow's livery;
But durst not ask of her audaciously
 Why her two suns were cloud-eclipsèd so,
1225  Nor why her fair cheeks over-washed with woe.

But as the earth doth weep, the sun being set,
Each flower moistened like a melting eye,
Even so the maid with swelling drops 'gan wet
Her circled eyne, enforced by sympathy
1230 Of those fair suns set in her mistress' sky,
 Who in a salt-waved ocean quench their light,
 Which makes the maid weep like the dewy night.

A pretty while these pretty creatures stand,
Like ivory conduits coral cisterns filling.
1235 One justly weeps; the other takes in hand
No cause but company of her drops' spilling.
Their gentle sex to weep are often willing,
 Grieving themselves to guess at others' smarts,
 And then they drown their eyes or break their hearts.

1240 For men have marble, women waxen, minds,
And therefore are they formed as marble will;
The weak oppressed, the impression of strange kinds
Is formed in them by force, by fraud, or skill.
Then call them not the authors of their ill,
1245  No more than wax shall be accounted evil
 Wherein is stamped the semblance of a devil.

Their smoothness, like a goodly champaign plain,
Lays open all the little worms that creep;
In men, as in a rough-grown grove, remain
1250 Cave-keeping evils that obscurely sleep;
Through crystal walls each little mote will peep.
 Though men can cover crimes with bold stern looks,
 Poor women's faces are their own faults' books.

No man inveigh against the withered flower,
But chide rough winter that the flower hath killed; 1255
Not that devoured, but that which doth devour,
Is worthy blame. O, let it not be hild
Poor women's faults that they are so fulfilled
   With men's abuses: those proud lords to blame
   Make weak-made women tenants to their shame. 1260

The precedent whereof in Lucrece view,
Assailed by night with circumstances strong
Of present death, and shame that might ensue
By that her death, to do her husband wrong;
Such danger to resistance did belong 1265
   That dying fear through all her body spread;
   And who cannot abuse a body dead?

By this, mild patience bid fair Lucrece speak
To the poor counterfeit of her complaining.
'My girl,' quoth she, 'on what occasion break 1270
Those tears from thee that down thy cheeks are raining?
If thou dost weep for grief of my sustaining,
   Know, gentle wench, it small avails my mood:
   If tears could help, mine own would do me good.

'But tell me, girl, when went' – and there she stayed, 1275
Till after a deep groan – 'Tarquin from hence?'
'Madam, ere I was up,' replied the maid,
'The more to blame my sluggard negligence.
Yet with the fault I thus far can dispense:
   Myself was stirring ere the break of day, 1280
   And ere I rose was Tarquin gone away.

'But lady, if your maid may be so bold,
She would request to know your heaviness.'
'O, peace,' quoth Lucrece. 'If it should be told,
The repetition cannot make it less; 1285
For more it is than I can well express,
   And that deep torture may be called a hell,
   When more is felt than one hath power to tell.

'Go, get me hither paper, ink, and pen;
1290 Yet save that labour, for I have them here.
What should I say? One of my husband's men
Bid thou be ready by and by to bear
A letter to my lord, my love, my dear.
  Bid him with speed prepare to carry it;
1295   The cause craves haste, and it will soon be writ.'

Her maid is gone, and she prepares to write,
First hovering o'er the paper with her quill;
Conceit and grief an eager combat fight;
What wit sets down is blotted straight with will;
1300 This is too curious-good, this blunt and ill.
  Much like a press of people at a door
  Throng her inventions, which shall go before.

At last she thus begins: 'Thou worthy lord
Of that unworthy wife that greeteth thee,
1305 Health to thy person! Next, vouchsafe t'afford –
If ever, love, thy Lucrece thou wilt see –
Some present speed to come and visit me.
  So I commend me, from our house in grief;
  My woes are tedious, though my words are brief.'

1310 Here folds she up the tenor of her woe,
Her certain sorrow writ uncertainly.
By this short schedule Collatine may know
Her grief, but not her grief's true quality;
She dares not thereof make discovery,
1315 Lest he should hold it her own gross abuse,
  Ere she with blood had stained her stained excuse.

Besides, the life and feeling of her passion
She hoards, to spend when he is by to hear her,
When sighs and groans and tears may grace the fashion
1320 Of her disgrace, the better so to clear her
From that suspicion which the world might bear her.
  To shun this blot, she would not blot the letter
  With words, till action might become them better.

To see sad sights moves more than hear them told,
For then the eye interprets to the ear                          1325
The heavy motion that it doth behold,
When every part a part of woe doth bear.
'Tis but a part of sorrow that we hear;
  Deep sounds make lesser noise than shallow fords,
  And sorrow ebbs, being blown with wind of words.            1330

Her letter now is sealed, and on it writ
'At Ardea to my lord with more than haste'.
The post attends, and she delivers it,
Charging the sour-faced groom to hie as fast
As lagging fowls before the northern blast.                    1335
  Speed more than speed but dull and slow she deems:
  Extremity still urgeth such extremes.

The homely villain curtsies to her low,
And blushing on her, with a steadfast eye
Receives the scroll without or yea or no,                      1340
And forth with bashful innocence doth hie.
But they whose guilt within their bosoms lie
  Imagine every eye beholds their blame;
  For Lucrece thought he blushed to see her shame:

When, silly groom, God wot, it was defect                      1345
Of spirit, life, and bold audacity;
Such harmless creatures have a true respect
To talk in deeds, while others saucily
Promise more speed, but do it leisurely.
  Even so this pattern of the worn-out age                     1350
  Pawned honest looks, but laid no words to gage.

His kindled duty kindled her mistrust,
That two red fires in both their faces blazed;
She thought he blushed as knowing Tarquin's lust,
And blushing with him, wistly on him gazed.                    1355
Her earnest eye did make him more amazed;
  The more she saw the blood his cheeks replenish,
  The more she thought he spied in her some blemish.

But long she thinks till he return again,
1360  And yet the duteous vassal scarce is gone.
The weary time she cannot entertain,
For now 'tis stale to sigh, to weep, and groan;
So woe hath wearied woe, moan tired moan,
    That she her plaints a little while doth stay,
1365    Pausing for means to mourn some newer way.

At last she calls to mind where hangs a piece
Of skilful painting made for Priam's Troy,
Before the which is drawn the power of Greece,
For Helen's rape the city to destroy,
1370  Threatening cloud-kissing Ilion with annoy;
    Which the conceited painter drew so proud
    As heaven, it seemed, to kiss the turrets bowed.

A thousand lamentable objects there
In scorn of nature art gave lifeless life;
1375  Many a dry drop seemed a weeping tear,
Shed for the slaughtered husband by the wife;
The red blood reeked to show the painter's strife,
    And dying eyes gleamed forth their ashy lights
    Like dying coals burnt out in tedious nights.

1380  There might you see the labouring pioneer
Begrimed with sweat and smearèd all with dust;
And from the towers of Troy there would appear
The very eyes of men through loop-holes thrust,
Gazing upon the Greeks with little lust.
1385    Such sweet observance in this work was had
    That one might see those far-off eyes look sad.

In great commanders, grace and majesty
You might behold, triumphing in their faces;
In youth, quick bearing and dexterity;
1390  And here and there the painter interlaces
Pale cowards marching on with trembling paces,
    Which heartless peasants did so well resemble
    That one would swear he saw them quake and tremble.

In Ajax and Ulysses, O what art
Of physiognomy might one behold! 1395
The face of either ciphered either's heart;
Their face their manners most expressly told:
In Ajax' eyes blunt rage and rigour rolled,
    But the mild glance that sly Ulysses lent
    Showed deep regard and smiling government. 1400

There pleading might you see grave Nestor stand,
As 'twere encouraging the Greeks to fight,
Making such sober action with his hand
That it beguiled attention, charmed the sight;
In speech it seemed his beard all silver white 1405
    Wagged up and down, and from his lips did fly
    Thin winding breath which purled up to the sky.

About him were a press of gaping faces
Which seemed to swallow up his sound advice;
All jointly listening, but with several graces, 1410
As if some mermaid did their ears entice;
Some high, some low, the painter was so nice.
    The scalps of many almost hid behind
    To jump up higher seemed, to mock the mind.

Here one man's hand leaned on another's head, 1415
His nose being shadowed by his neighbour's ear;
Here one being thronged bears back, all bollen and red;
Another smothered seems to pelt and swear;
And in their rage such signs of rage they bear
    As, but for loss of Nestor's golden words, 1420
    It seemed they would debate with angry swords.

For much imaginary work was there;
Conceit deceitful, so compact, so kind,
That for Achilles' image stood his spear
Gripped in an arméd hand; himself behind 1425
Was left unseen, save to the eye of mind:
    A hand, a foot, a face, a leg, a head,
    Stood for the whole to be imaginéd.

And from the walls of strong-besiegèd Troy,
1430   When their brave hope, bold Hector, marched to field,
Stood many Trojan mothers sharing joy
To see their youthful sons bright weapons wield;
And to their hope they such odd action yield
    That through their light joy seemèd to appear,
1435     Like bright things stained, a kind of heavy fear.

And from the strand of Dardan where they fought
To Simois' reedy banks the red blood ran,
Whose waves to imitate the battle sought
With swelling ridges, and their ranks began
1440 To break upon the gallèd shore, and then
    Retire again, till meeting greater ranks
    They join, and shoot their foam at Simois' banks.

To this well-painted piece is Lucrece come,
To find a face where all distress is stelled.
1445 Many she sees where cares have carvèd some,
But none where all distress and dolour dwelled,
Till she despairing Hecuba beheld,
    Staring on Priam's wounds with her old eyes,
    Which bleeding under Pyrrhus' proud foot lies.

1450 In her the painter had anatomized
Time's ruin, beauty's wrack, and grim care's reign;
Her cheeks with chaps and wrinkles were disguised;
Of what she was no semblance did remain.
Her blue blood changed to black in every vein,
1455     Wanting the spring that those shrunk pipes had fed,
    Showed life imprisoned in a body dead.

On this sad shadow Lucrece spends her eyes,
And shapes her sorrow to the beldame's woes,
Who nothing wants to answer her but cries
1460 And bitter words to ban her cruel foes;
The painter was no god to lend her those;
    And therefore Lucrece swears he did her wrong,
    To give her so much grief, and not a tongue.

'Poor instrument,' quoth she, 'without a sound,
I'll tune thy woes with my lamenting tongue, 1465
And drop sweet balm in Priam's painted wound,
And rail on Pyrrhus that hath done him wrong,
And with my tears quench Troy that burns so long;
   And with my knife scratch out the angry eyes
   Of all the Greeks that are thine enemies. 1470

'Show me the strumpet that began this stir,
That with my nails her beauty I may tear.
Thy heat of lust, fond Paris, did incur
This load of wrath that burning Troy doth bear;
Thy eye kindled the fire that burneth here; 1475
   And here in Troy, for trespass of thine eye,
   The sire, the son, the dame and daughter die.

'Why should the private pleasure of some one
Become the public plague of many moe?
Let sin alone committed light alone 1480
Upon his head that hath transgressèd so;
Let guiltless souls be freed from guilty woe:
   For one's offence why should so many fall,
   To plague a private sin in general?

'Lo, here weeps Hecuba, here Priam dies, 1485
Here manly Hector faints, here Troilus swounds,
Here friend by friend in bloody channel lies,
And friend to friend gives unadvisèd wounds,
And one man's lust these many lives confounds.
   Had doting Priam checked his son's desire, 1490
   Troy had been bright with fame, and not with fire.'

Here feelingly she weeps Troy's painted woes;
For sorrow, like a heavy hanging bell
Once set on ringing, with his own weight goes;
Then little strength rings out the doleful knell. 1495
So Lucrece, set a-work, sad tales doth tell
  To pencilled pensiveness and coloured sorrow:
  She lends them words, and she their looks doth borrow.

She throws her eyes about the painting round,
And who she finds forlorn she doth lament.
At last she sees a wretched image bound,
That piteous looks to Phrygian shepherds lent;
His face, though full of cares, yet showed content;
    Onward to Troy with the blunt swains he goes,
    So mild that patience seemed to scorn his woes.

In him the painter laboured with his skill
To hide deceit and give the harmless show
An humble gait, calm looks, eyes wailing still,
A brow unbent that seemed to welcome woe;
Cheeks neither red nor pale, but mingled so
    That blushing red no guilty instance gave,
    Nor ashy pale the fear that false hearts have.

But like a constant and confirmèd devil,
He entertained a show so seeming just,
And therein so ensconced his secret evil,
That jealousy itself could not mistrust
False creeping craft and perjury should thrust
    Into so bright a day such black-faced storms,
    Or blot with hell-born sin such saint-like forms.

The well-skilled workman this mild image drew
For perjured Sinon, whose enchanting story
The credulous old Priam after slew;
Whose words like wildfire burnt the shining glory
Of rich-built Ilion, that the skies were sorry,
    And little stars shot from their fixèd places,
    When their glass fell, wherein they viewed their faces.

This picture she advisedly perused,
And chid the painter for his wondrous skill,
Saying, some shape in Sinon's was abused:
So fair a form lodged not a mind so ill.
And still on him she gazed, and gazing still,
    Such signs of truth in his plain face she spied
    That she concludes the picture was belied.

'It cannot be', quoth she, 'that so much guile' –
She would have said, 'can lurk in such a look';                    1535
But Tarquin's shape came in her mind the while,
And from her tongue 'can lurk' from 'cannot' took:
'It cannot be' she in that sense forsook,
    And turned it thus: 'It cannot be, I find,
    But such a face should bear a wicked mind:                     1540

'For even as subtle Sinon here is painted,
So sober-sad, so weary, and so mild,
As if with grief or travel he had fainted,
To me came Tarquin armèd to beguild
With outward honesty, but yet defiled                              1545
    With inward vice. As Priam him did cherish,
    So did I Tarquin; so my Troy did perish.

'Look, look, how listening Priam wets his eyes,
To see those borrowed tears that Sinon sheeds.
Priam, why art thou old and yet not wise?                          1550
For every tear he falls a Trojan bleeds.
His eye drops fire, no water thence proceeds;
    Those round clear pearls of his that move thy pity.
    Are balls of quenchless fire to burn thy city.

'Such devils steal effects from lightless hell,                    1555
For Sinon in his fire doth quake with cold,
And in that cold hot-burning fire doth dwell.
These contraries such unity do hold
Only to flatter fools and make them bold;
    So Priam's trust false Sinon's tears doth flatter              1560
    That he finds means to burn his Troy with water.'

Here, all enraged, such passion her assails
That patience is quite beaten from her breast.
She tears the senseless Sinon with her nails,
Comparing him to that unhappy guest                                1565
Whose deed hath made herself herself detest.
    At last she smilingly with this gives o'er:
    'Fool, fool,' quoth she, 'his wounds will not be sore.'

Thus ebbs and flows the current of her sorrow,
1570 And time doth weary time with her complaining;
She looks for night, and then she longs for morrow,
And both she thinks too long with her remaining.
Short time seems long in sorrow's sharp sustaining:
    Though woe be heavy, yet it seldom sleeps,
1575     And they that watch see time how slow it creeps.

Which all this time hath overslipped her thought
That she with painted images hath spent,
Being from the feeling of her own grief brought
By deep surmise of others' detriment,
1580 Losing her woes in shows of discontent.
    It easeth some, though none it ever cured,
    To think their dolour others have endured.

But now the mindful messenger come back
Brings home his lord and other company;
1585 Who finds his Lucrece clad in mourning black,
And round about her tear-distainèd eye
Blue circles streamed, like rainbows in the sky:
    These water-galls in her dim element
    Foretell new storms to those already spent.

1590 Which when her sad beholding husband saw,
Amazedly in her sad face he stares:
Her eyes, though sod in tears, looked red and raw,
Her lively colour killed with deadly cares.
He hath no power to ask her how she fares;
1595     Both stood like old acquaintance in a trance,
    Met far from home, wondering each other's chance.

At last he takes her by the bloodless hand,
And thus begins: 'What uncouth ill event
Hath thee befallen, that thou dost trembling stand?
1600 Sweet love, what spite hath thy fair colour spent?
Why art thou thus attired in discontent?
    Unmask, dear dear, this moody heaviness,
    And tell thy grief, that we may give redress.'

Three times with sighs she gives her sorrow fire
Ere once she can discharge one word of woe;                          1605
At length addressed to answer his desire,
She modestly prepares to let them know
Her honour is ta'en prisoner by the foe;
    While Collatine and his consorted lords
    With sad attention long to hear her words.                    1610

And now this pale swan in her watery nest
Begins the sad dirge of her certain ending.
'Few words,' quoth she, 'shall fit the trespass best,
Where no excuse can give the fault amending:
In me moe woes than words are now depending;                        1615
    And my laments would be drawn out too long
    To tell them all with one poor tired tongue.

'Then be this all the task it hath to say:
Dear husband, in the interest of thy bed
A stranger came, and on that pillow lay                             1620
Where thou wast wont to rest thy weary head;
And what wrong else may be imaginèd
    By foul enforcement might be done to me,
    From that, alas, thy Lucrece is not free.

'For in the dreadful dead of dark midnight                          1625
With shining falchion in my chamber came
A creeping creature with a flaming light,
And softly cried "Awake, thou Roman dame,
And entertain my love; else lasting shame
    On thee and thine this night I will inflict,                  1630
    If thou my love's desire do contradict.

'"For some hard-favoured groom of thine," quoth he,
"Unless thou yoke thy liking to my will,
I'll murder straight, and then I'll slaughter thee,
And swear I found you where you did fulfil                          1635
The loathsome act of lust, and so did kill
    The lechers in their deed: this act will be
    My fame, and thy perpetual infamy."

'With this I did begin to start and cry,
1640 And then against my heart he set his sword,
Swearing, unless I took all patiently,
I should not live to speak another word;
So should my shame still rest upon record,
    And never be forgot in mighty Rome
1645   Th'adulterate death of Lucrece and her groom.

'Mine enemy was strong, my poor self weak,
And far the weaker with so strong a fear.
My bloody judge forbade my tongue to speak;
No rightful plea might plead for justice there.
1650 His scarlet lust came evidence to swear
    That my poor beauty had purloined his eyes;
    And when the judge is robbed, the prisoner dies.

'O teach me how to make mine own excuse;
Or at the least this refuge let me find:
1655 Though my gross blood be stained with this abuse,
Immaculate and spotless is my mind;
That was not forced, that never was inclined
    To accessary yieldings, but still pure
    Doth in her poisoned closet yet endure.'

1660 Lo, here the hopeless merchant of this loss,
With head declined and voice dammed up with woe,
With sad set eyes and wretched arms across,
From lips new waxen pale begins to blow
The grief away that stops his answer so;
1665   But wretched as he is, he strives in vain;
    What he breathes out his breath drinks up again.

As through an arch the violent roaring tide
Outruns the eye that doth behold his haste,
Yet in the eddy boundeth in his pride
1670 Back to the strait that forced him on so fast,
In rage sent out, recalled in rage being past;
    Even so his sighs, his sorrows, make a saw,
    To push grief on and back the same grief draw.

Which speechless woe of his poor she attendeth,
And his untimely frenzy thus awaketh:                                    1675
'Dear lord, thy sorrow to my sorrow lendeth
Another power; no flood by raining slaketh;
My woe too sensible thy passion maketh
    More feeling-painful. Let it then suffice
    To drown on woe one pair of weeping eyes.                     1680

'And for my sake, when I might charm thee so,
For she that was thy Lucrece, now attend me:
Be suddenly revengèd on my foe,
Thine, mine, his own. Suppose thou dost defend me
From what is past. The help that thou shalt lend me         1685
    Comes all too late, yet let the traitor die,
    For sparing justice feeds iniquity.

'But ere I name him, you fair lords', quoth she,
Speaking to those that came with Collatine,
'Shall plight your honourable faiths to me,                         1690
With swift pursuit to venge this wrong of mine;
For 'tis a meritorious fair design
    To chase injustice with revengeful arms:
    Knights by their oaths should right poor ladies' harms.'

At this request, with noble disposition                              1695
Each present lord began to promise aid,
As bound in knighthood to her imposition,
Longing to hear the hateful foe bewrayed;
But she, that yet her sad task hath not said,
    The protestation stops. 'O speak,' quoth she:              1700
    'How may this forcèd stain be wiped from me?

'What is the quality of my offence,
Being constrained with dreadful circumstance?
May my pure mind with the foul act dispense,
My low-declinèd honour to advance?                               1705
May any terms acquit me from this chance?
    The poisoned fountain clears itself again;
    And why not I from this compellèd stain?'

With this they all at once began to say

1710   Her body's stain her mind untainted clears,
While with a joyless smile she turns away
The face, that map which deep impression bears
Of hard misfortune, carved in it with tears.
    'No, no,' quoth she, 'no dame hereafter living
1715       By my excuse shall claim excuse's giving.'

Here with a sigh as if her heart would break
She throws forth Tarquin's name: 'He, he,' she says;
But more than 'he' her poor tongue could not speak;
Till after many accents and delays,
1720   Untimely breathings, sick and short assays,
    She utters this: 'He, he, fair lords, 'tis he,
    That guides this hand to give this wound to me.'

Even here she sheathèd in her harmless breast
A harmful knife, that thence her soul unsheathed:
1725   That blow did bail it from the deep unrest
Of that polluted prison where it breathed.
Her contrite sighs unto the clouds bequeathed
    Her wingèd sprite, and through her wounds doth fly
    Life's lasting date from cancelled destiny.

1730   Stone-still, astonished with this deadly deed,
Stood Collatine and all his lordly crew;
Till Lucrece' father, that beholds her bleed,
Himself on her self-slaughtered body threw;
And from the purple fountain Brutus drew
1735     The murd'rous knife; and, as it left the place,
    Her blood in poor revenge held it in chase.

And bubbling from her breast it doth divide
In two slow rivers, that the crimson blood
Circles her body in on every side,
1740   Who like a late-sacked island vastly stood
Bare and unpeopled in this fearful flood.
    Some of her blood still pure and red remained,
    And some looked black, and that false Tarquin stained.

About the mourning and congealèd face
Of that black blood a watery rigol goes,                           1745
Which seems to weep upon the tainted place;
And ever since, as pitying Lucrece' woes,
Corrupted blood some watery token shows;
    And blood untainted still doth red abide,
      Blushing at that which is so putrified.                 1750

'Daughter, dear daughter,' old Lucretius cries,
'That life was mine which thou hast here deprived;
If in the child the father's image lies,
Where shall I live now Lucrece is unlived?
Thou wast not to this end from me derived:                         1755
    If children predecease progenitors,
      We are their offspring, and they none of ours.

'Poor broken glass, I often did behold
In thy sweet semblance my old age new-born;
But now that fair fresh mirror, dim and old,                       1760
Shows me a bare-boned death by time outworn.
O, from thy cheeks my image thou hast torn,
    And shivered all the beauty of my glass,
      That I no more can see what once I was.

'O time, cease thou thy course and last no longer,                 1765
If they surcease to be that should survive!
Shall rotten death make conquest of the stronger,
And leave the faltering feeble souls alive?
The old bees die, the young possess their hive;
    Then live, sweet Lucrece, live again and see              1770
      Thy father die, and not thy father thee!'

By this starts Collatine as from a dream,
And bids Lucretius give his sorrow place;
And then in key-cold Lucrece' bleeding stream
He falls, and bathes the pale fear in his face,                    1775
And counterfeits to die with her a space;
    Till manly shame bids him possess his breath,
      And live to be revengèd on her death.

The deep vexation of his inward soul
1780 Hath served a dumb arrest upon his tongue;
Who, mad that sorrow should his use control,
Or keep him from heart-easing words so long,
Begins to talk; but through his lips do throng
    Weak words, so thick come in his poor heart's aid
1785     That no man could distinguish what he said.

Yet sometime 'Tarquin' was pronouncèd plain,
But through his teeth, as if the name he tore.
This windy tempest, till it blow up rain,
Held back his sorrow's tide to make it more.
1790 At last it rains, and busy winds give o'er;
    Then son and father weep with equal strife
    Who should weep most, for daughter or for wife.

Then one doth call her his, the other his,
Yet neither may possess the claim they lay.
1795 The father says 'She's mine'; 'O, mine she is,'
Replies her husband; 'do not take away
My sorrow's interest; let no mourner say
    He weeps for her, for she was only mine,
    And only must be wailed by Collatine.'

1800 'O,' quoth Lucretius, 'I did give that life
Which she too early and too late hath spilled.'
'Woe, woe,' quoth Collatine, 'she was my wife;
I owed her, and 'tis mine that she hath killed.'
'My daughter' and 'my wife' with clamours filled
1805     The dispersed air, who, holding Lucrece' life,
    Answered their cries, 'my daughter' and 'my wife'.

Brutus, who plucked the knife from Lucrece' side,
Seeing such emulation in their woe
Began to clothe his wit in state and pride,
1810 Burying in Lucrece' wound his folly's show.
He with the Romans was esteemèd so
    As silly jeering idiots are with kings,
    For sportive words and uttering foolish things.

But now he throws that shallow habit by
Wherein deep policy did him disguise,     1815
And armed his long-hid wits advisedly
To check the tears in Collatinus' eyes.
'Thou wrongèd lord of Rome,' quoth he, 'arise;
    Let my unsounded self, supposed a fool,
    Now set thy long-experienced wit to school.     1820

'Why, Collatine, is woe the cure for woe?
Do wounds help wounds, or grief help grievous deeds?
Is it revenge to give thyself a blow
For his foul act by whom thy fair wife bleeds?
Such childish humour from weak minds proceeds;     1825
    Thy wretched wife mistook the matter so
    To slay herself, that should have slain her foe.

'Courageous Roman, do not steep thy heart
In such relenting dew of lamentations,
But kneel with me and help to bear thy part     1830
To rouse our Roman gods with invocations
That they will suffer these abominations –
    Since Rome herself in them doth stand disgraced –
    By our strong arms from forth her fair streets chased.

'Now by the Capitol that we adore,     1835
And by this chaste blood so unjustly stained,
By heaven's fair sun that breeds the fat earth's store,
By all our country rights in Rome maintained,
And by chaste Lucrece' soul that late complained
    Her wrongs to us, and by this bloody knife,     1840
    We will revenge the death of this true wife.'

This said, he struck his hand upon his breast,
And kissed the fatal knife to end his vow,
And to his protestation urged the rest,
Who, wondering at him, did his words allow.     1845
Then jointly to the ground their knees they bow,
    And that deep vow which Brutus made before
    He doth again repeat, and that they swore.

When they had sworn to this advisèd doom,
1850   They did conclude to bear dead Lucrece thence,
To show her bleeding body thorough Rome,
And so to publish Tarquin's foul offence;
Which being done with speedy diligence,
    The Romans plausibly did give consent
    To Tarquin's everlasting banishment.

# 'THE PHOENIX AND TURTLE'

Let the bird of loudest lay,
On the sole Arabian tree,
Herald sad and trumpet be,
To whose sound chaste wings obey.

5    But thou shrieking harbinger,
Foul precurrer of the fiend,
Augur of the fever's end,
To this troop come thou not near!

From this session interdict
10   Every fowl of tyrant wing,
Save the eagle, feathered king:
Keep the obsequy so strict.

Let the priest in surplice white,
That defunctive music can,
15   Be the death-divining swan,
Lest the requiem lack his right.

And thou treble-dated crow,
That thy sable gender mak'st
With the breath thou giv'st and tak'st,
20   'Mongst our mourners shalt thou go.

Here the anthem doth commence:
Love and constancy is dead;
Phoenix and the turtle fled
In a mutual flame from hence.

25   So they loved, as love in twain
Had the essence but in one;
Two distincts, division none:
Number there in love was slain.

Hearts remote, yet not asunder;
30   Distance, and no space was seen
'Twixt this turtle and his queen:
But in them it were a wonder.

So between them love did shine,
That the turtle saw his right
35   Flaming in the phoenix' sight;
Either was the other's mine.

Property was thus appalled,
That the self was not the same;
Single nature's double name
Neither two nor one was called.                    40

Reason, in itself confounded,
Saw division grow together,
To themselves yet either neither,
Simple were so well compounded;

That it cried, How true a twain                    45
Seemeth this concordant one!
Love hath reason, reason none,
If what parts can so remain.

Whereupon it made this threne
To the phoenix and the dove,                       50
Co-supremes and stars of love,
As chorus to their tragic scene.


### THRENOS

Beauty, truth, and rarity,
Grace in all simplicity,
Here enclosed, in cinders lie.                     55

Death is now the phoenix' nest;
And the turtle's loyal breast
To eternity doth rest.

Leaving no posterity,
'Twas not their infirmity,                         60
It was married chastity.

Truth may seem, but cannot be;
Beauty brag, but 'tis not she;
Truth and beauty buried be.

To this urn let those repair                       65
That are either true or fair;
For these dead birds sigh a prayer.

# THE PASSIONATE PILGRIM

## I

When my love swears that she is made of truth,
I do believe her, though I know she lies,
That she might think me some untutored youth,
Unskilful in the world's false forgeries.
Thus vainly thinking that she thinks me young,                    5
Although I know my years be past the best,
I smiling credit her false-speaking tongue,
Outfacing faults in love with love's ill rest.
But wherefore says my love that she is young?
And wherefore say not I that I am old?                            10
O, love's best habit is a soothing tongue,
And age in love loves not to have years told.
 Therefore I'll lie with love, and love with me,
 Since that our faults in love thus smothered be.

## II

Two loves I have, of comfort and despair,
That like two spirits do suggest me still;
My better angel is a man right fair,
My worser spirit a woman coloured ill.
To win me soon to hell, my female evil                           5
Tempteth my better angel from my side,
And would corrupt my saint to be a devil,
Wooing his purity with her fair pride.
And whether that my angel be turned fiend,
Suspect I may, yet not directly tell;                            10

167

For being both to me, both to each friend,
I guess one angel in another's hell.
  The truth I shall not know, but live in doubt,
  Till my bad angel fire my good one out.


### III

Did not the heavenly rhetoric of thine eye,
'Gainst whom the world could not hold argument,
Persuade my heart to this false perjury?
Vows for thee broke deserve not punishment.
A woman I forswore; but I will prove,
Thou being a goddess, I forswore not thee:
My vow was earthly, thou a heavenly love;
Thy grace being gained cures all disgrace in me.
My vow was breath, and breath a vapour is;
Then, thou fair sun, that on this earth doth shine,
Exhal'st this vapour vow; in thee it is:
If broken, then it is no fault of mine.
  If by me broke, what fool is not so wise
  To break an oath, to win a paradise?


### IV

Sweet Cytherea, sitting by a brook
With young Adonis, lovely, fresh and green,
Did court the lad with many a lovely look,
Such looks as none could look but beauty's queen.
She told him stories to delight his ear;
She showed him favours to allure his eye;
To win his heart, she touched him here and there;
Touches so soft still conquer chastity.
But whether unripe years did want conceit,
Or he refused to take her figured proffer,
The tender nibbler would not touch the bait,
But smile and jest at every gentle offer:
  Then fell she on her back, fair queen, and toward:
  He rose and ran away – ah, fool too froward.

## V

If love make me forsworn, how shall I swear to love?
O never faith could hold, if not to beauty vowed:
Though to myself forsworn, to thee I'll constant prove;
Those thoughts, to me like oaks, to thee like osiers bowed.
Study his bias leaves, and makes his book thine eyes,    5
Where all those pleasures live that art can comprehend.
If knowledge be the mark, to know thee shall suffice;
Well learnèd is that tongue that well can thee commend:
All ignorant that soul that sees thee without wonder;
Which is to me some praise, that I thy parts admire.    10
Thine eye Jove's lightning seems, thy voice his dreadful
thunder,
Which, not to anger bent, is music and sweet fire.
Celestial as thou art, O do not love that wrong,
To sing heaven's praise with such an earthly tongue.

## VI

Scarce had the sun dried up the dewy morn,
And scarce the herd gone to the hedge for shade,
When Cytherea, all in love forlorn,
A longing tarriance for Adonis made
Under an osier growing by a brook,    5
A brook where Adon used to cool his spleen.
Hot was the day; she hotter that did look
For his approach, that often there had been.
Anon he comes, and throws his mantle by,
And stood stark naked on the brook's green brim:    10
The sun looked on the world with glorious eye,
Yet not so wistly as this queen on him.
He, spying her, bounced in whereas he stood.
'O Jove,' quoth she, 'why was not I a flood!'

## VII

Fair is my love, but not so fair as fickle;
Mild as a dove, but neither true nor trusty;

Brighter than glass, and yet, as glass is, brittle;
Softer than wax, and yet as iron rusty;
  A lily pale, with damask dye to grace her;
  None fairer, nor none falser to deface her.

Her lips to mine how often hath she joinèd,
Between each kiss her oaths of true love swearing!
How many tales to please me hath she coinèd,
Dreading my love, the loss thereof still fearing!
  Yet in the midst of all her pure protestings,
  Her faith, her oaths, her tears, and all were jestings.

She burnt with love, as straw with fire flameth;
She burnt out love, as soon as straw out-burneth;
She framed the love, and yet she foiled the framing;
She bade love last, and yet she fell a-turning.
  Was this a lover, or a lecher whether?
  Bad in the best, though excellent in neither.

### VIII

'If Music and Sweet Poetry Agree' by Richard Barnfield. From
*Poems: In Divers Humors*, added to *The Encomion of Lady Pecunia*
(1598)

### IX

Fair was the morn, when the fair queen of love,
                    . . .
Paler for sorrow than her milk-white dove,
For Adon's sake, a youngster proud and wild.
  Her stand she takes upon a steep-up hill;
  Anon Adonis comes with horn and hounds;
She, silly queen, with more than love's good will,
Forbade the boy he should not pass those grounds.
'Once', quoth she, 'did I see a fair sweet youth
Here in these brakes deep-wounded with a boar,
Deep in the thigh, a spectacle of ruth!
See, in my thigh,' quoth she, 'here was the sore.'
  She showèd hers; he saw more wounds than one,
  And blushing fled, and left her all alone.

## X

Sweet rose, fair flower, untimely plucked, soon vaded,
Plucked in the bud and vaded in the spring;
Bright orient pearl, alack, too timely shaded,
Fair creature, killed too soon by death's sharp sting;
    Like a green plum that hangs upon a tree,      5
    And falls through wind before the fall should be.

I weep for thee and yet no cause I have;
For why thou leftst me nothing in thy will.
And yet thou leftst me more than I did crave,
For why I cravèd nothing of thee still:      10
    O yes, dear friend, I pardon crave of thee,
    Thy discontent thou didst bequeath to me.

## XI

'Venus with Young Adonis Sitting by Her' by Bartholomew
Griffin. From *Fidessa* (1596)

## XII

Crabbèd age and youth cannot live together:
Youth is full of pleasance, Age is full of care;
Youth like summer morn, Age like winter weather;
Youth like summer brave, Age like winter bare.
Youth is full of sport, Age's breath is short;      5
    Youth is nimble, Age is lame;
Youth is hot and bold, Age is weak and cold;
    Youth is wild and Age is tame.
Age, I do abhor thee; Youth, I do adore thee;
    O, my love, my love is young!      10
Age, I do defy thee. O, sweet shepherd, hie thee,
    For methinks thou stays too long.

## XIII

Beauty is but a vain and doubtful good,
A shining gloss that vadeth suddenly,
A flower that dies when first it 'gins to bud,
A brittle glass that's broken presently;

5  A doubtful good, a gloss, a glass, a flower,
   Lost, vaded, broken, dead within an hour.

   And as goods lost are seld or never found,
   As vaded gloss no rubbing will refresh,
   As flowers dead lie withered on the ground,
10   As broken glass no cement can redress:
       So beauty blemished once, for ever lost,
       In spite of physic, painting, pain and cost.

### XIV

   Good night, good rest: ah, neither be my share;
   She bade good night that kept my rest away;
   And daffed me to a cabin hanged with care,
   To descant on the doubts of my decay.
5    'Farewell,' quoth she, 'and come again to-morrow';
     Fare well I could not, for I supped with sorrow.

   Yet at my parting sweetly did she smile,
   In scorn or friendship nill I conster whether;
   'T may be, she joyed to jest at my exile,
10   'T may be, again to make me wander thither:
     'Wander', a word for shadows like myself,
     As take the pain, but cannot pluck the pelf.

   Lord, how mine eyes throw gazes to the east!
   My heart doth charge the watch; the morning rise
15  Doth cite each moving sense from idle rest.
   Not daring trust the office of mine eyes,
       While Philomela sings, I sit and mark,
       And wish her lays were tunèd like the lark.

   For she doth welcome daylight with her ditty,
20  And drives away dark dreaming night.
   The night so packed, I post unto my pretty;
   Heart hath his hope and eyes their wishèd sight;
       Sorrow changed to solace and solace mixed with sorrow,
       For why she sighed, and bade me come to-morrow.

25  Were I with her, the night would post too soon,
   But now are minutes added to the hours;

To spite me now, each minute seems a moon;
Yet not for me, shine sun to succour flowers!
   Pack night, peep day; good day, of night now borrow;
   Short night, to-night, and length thyself to-morrow.   30

### XV

It was a lording's daughter, the fairest one of three,
That likèd of her master as well as well might be,
Till looking on an Englishman, the fairest that eye could see,
   Her fancy fell a-turning.
Long was the combat doubtful that love with love did fight,  5
To leave the master loveless, or kill the gallant knight;
To put in practice either, alas, it was a spite
   Unto the silly damsel!
But one must be refusèd; more mickle was the pain
That nothing could be usèd to turn them both to gain,   10
For of the two the trusty knight was wounded with disdain:
   Alas, she could not help it!
Thus art with arms contending was victor of the day,
Which by a gift of learning did bear the maid away:
Then, lullaby, the learned man hath got the lady gay;   15
   For now my song is ended.

### XVI

On a day, alack the day!
Love, whose month was ever May,
Spied a blossom passing fair,
Playing in the wanton air.
Through the velvet leaves the wind   5
All unseen 'gan passage find,
That the lover, sick to death,
Wished himself the heaven's breath.
'Air', quoth he, 'thy cheeks may blow;
Air, would I might triumph so!   10
But, alas! my hand hath sworn
Ne'er to pluck thee from thy thorn;
Vow, alack! for youth unmeet,

Youth, so apt to pluck a sweet.
15   Thou for whom Jove would swear
Juno but an Ethiope were;
And deny himself for Jove,
Turning mortal for thy love.'


## XVII

My flocks feed not, my ewes breed not,
My rams speed not, all is amiss;
Love is dying, faith's defying,
Heart's denying, causer of this.
5   All my merry jigs are quite forgot,
All my lady's love is lost, God wot;
Where her faith was firmly fixed in love,
There a nay is placed without remove.
    One silly cross wrought all my loss;
10     O frowning Fortune, cursèd fickle dame!
    For now I see inconstancy
    More in women than in men remain.

In black mourn I, all fears scorn I,
Love hath forlorn me, living in thrall:
15   Heart is bleeding, all help needing,
O cruel speeding, fraughted with gall.
My shepherd's pipe can sound no deal;
My wether's bell rings doleful knell;
My curtal dog that wont to have played,
20   Plays not at all, but seems afraid;
    My sighs so deep procures to weep,
    In howling wise, to see my doleful plight.
    How sighs resound through heartless ground,
    Like a thousand vanquished men in bloody fight!

25   Clear wells spring not, sweet birds sing not,
Green plants bring not forth their dye;
Herds stand weeping, flocks all sleeping,
Nymphs back peeping fearfully.
All our pleasure known to us poor swains,

All our merry meetings on the plains,                    30
All our evening sport from us is fled,
All our love is lost, for Love is dead.
   Farewell, sweet lass, thy like ne'er was
   For a sweet content, the cause of all my moan:
   Poor Corydon must live alone;                    35
   Other help for him I see that there is none.


## XVIII

When as thine eye hath chose the dame,
And stalled the deer that thou shouldst strike,
Let reason rule things worthy blame,
As well as fancy's partial might;
   Take counsel of some wiser head,                    5
   Neither too young nor yet unwed.

And when thou com'st thy tale to tell,
Smooth not thy tongue with filèd talk,
Lest she some subtle practice smell –
A cripple soon can find a halt –                    10
   But plainly say thou lov'st her well,
   And set thy person forth to sell.

And to her will frame all thy ways;
Spare not to spend, and chiefly there
Where thy desert may merit praise,                    15
By ringing in thy lady's ear:
   The strongest castle, tower and town,
   The golden bullet beats it down.

Serve always with assurèd trust,
And in thy suit be humble true;                    20
Unless thy lady prove unjust,
Press never thou to choose a new:
   When time shall serve, be thou not slack
   To proffer, though she put thee back.

What though her frowning brows be bent,                    25
Her cloudy looks will calm ere night,
And then too late she will repent

That thus dissembled her delight;
   And twice desire, ere it be day,
     That which with scorn she put away.

What though she strive to try her strength,
And ban and brawl, and say thee nay,
Her feeble force will yield at length,
When craft hath taught her thus to say:
   'Had women been so strong as men,
     In faith, you had not had it then.'

The wiles and guiles that women work,
Dissembled with an outward show,
The tricks and toys that in them lurk,
The cock that treads them shall not know.
   Have you not heard it said full oft,
     A woman's nay doth stand for nought?

Think women still to strive with men,
To sin and never for to saint:
There is no heaven; be holy then,
When time with age shall them attaint.
   Were kisses all the joys in bed,
     One woman would another wed.

But, soft, enough, too much I fear,
Lest that my mistress hear my song;
She will not stick to round me on th'ear,
To teach my tongue to be so long,
   Yet will she blush, here be it said,
     To hear her secrets so bewrayed.

### XIX

'Live with Me and be My Love' and 'Love's Answer' by
Christopher Marlowe and Walter Ralegh respectively

### XX

'As it Fell upon a Day' by Richard Barnfield. From *Poems: In
Divers Humors*, added to *The Encomiom of Lady Pecunia* (1598)

# 'SHALL I DIE?'

Shall I die? Shall I fly
Lovers' baits and deceits,
                sorrow breeding?
Shall I tend? Shall I send?
    Shall I sue, and not rue
                my proceeding?
    In all duty her beauty
Binds me her servant for ever.
    If she scorn, I mourn,
I retire to despair, joying never.


II

    Yet I must vent my lust
    And explain inward pain
            by my love conceiving.
    If she smiles, she exiles
    All my moan; if she frown,
            all my hopes deceiving.
Suspicious doubt, O keep out,
    For thou art my tormentor.
        Fie, away, pack away;
I will love, for hope bids me venture.

### III

'Twere abuse to accuse
My fair love, ere I prove
      her affection.
Therefore try! Her reply
Gives thee joy – or annoy          25
      or affliction.
    Yet howe'er, I will bear
Her pleasure with patience, for beauty
    Sure will not seem to blot
Her deserts, wronging him doth her duty.    30

### IV

In a dream it did seem –
But alas, dreams do pass
      as do shadows –
I did walk, I did talk
With my love, with my dove          35
      through fair meadows.
Still we passed till at last
We sat to repose us for pleasure.
    Being set, lips met,
Arms twined, and did bind by heart's treasure.    40

### V

Gentle wind sport did find
    Wantonly to make fly
      her gold tresses.
As they shook I did look,
    But her fair did impair          45
      all my senses.
    As amazed, I gazed
On more than a mortal complexion.
    You that love can prove
Such force in beauty's inflection.    50

## VI

Next her hair, forehead fair,
Smooth and high; next doth lie,
          without wrinkle,
Her fair brows; under those,
55   Star-like eyes win love's prize
          when they twinkle.
In her cheeks who seeks
Shall find there displayed beauty's banner:
     O admiring desiring
60   Breeds, as I look still upon her.

## VII

Then lips red; fancy's fed
With all sweets when he meets
          and is granted
There to trade, and is made
65   Happy, sure, to endure
          still undaunted.
Pretty chin doth win
Of all that's called commendation;
     Fairest neck, no speck;
70   All her parts merit high admiration.

## VIII

Pretty bare, past compare,
Parts those plots which besots
          still asunder.
It is meet naught but sweet
75   Should come near that so rare
          'tis a wonder.
No mishap, no scape
Inferior to nature's perfection;
     No blot, no spot:
80   She's beauty's queen in election.

## IX

Whilst I dreamt, I, exempt
From all care, seemed to share
    pleasures plenty:
But awake, care take,
For I find to my mind           85
    pleasures scanty.
Therefore I will try
To compass my heart's chief contenting.
    To delay, some say,
In such a case causeth repenting.         90

# THE EPITAPHS

I    *Upon John Combe* 'An old Gentleman noted thereabouts for his Wealth and Usury'

> Ten in the hundred lies here ingraved,
>   'Tis a Hundred to Ten his soul is not saved:
> If any Man ask 'Who lies in this Tomb?'
>   'Oh! Oh!' quoth the Devil, ''tis my John-a-Combe.'

*Another Epitaph upon John Combe*

'but being dead, and making the poor his heirs, he after writes this for his epitaph':

> How e'er he lived, judge not;
> John Combe shall never be forgot
> While poor hath memory; for he did gather
> To make the poor his issue, he their father,
> As record of his tilth and seed
> Did crown him in his latter deed.

II    *On Elias James*

> When God was pleased, the world unwilling yet,
> Elias James to nature paid his debt,
> And here reposeth; as he lived he died,
> The saying in him strongly verified,
> 'Such life, such death.' Then, the known truth to tell,
> He lived a godly life and died as well.

III  *On Ben Jonson*

'Mr Ben Johnson and Mr Wm Shake-speare being merry at a tavern, Mr Jonson having begun this for his epitaph':

Here lies Ben Jonson that was once one

he gives it to Mr Shakespeare to make up, who presently writes

Who while he lived was a slow thing,
And now being dead is nothing.

*A Later Variant*

Here lies Ben Jonson, who was once one

This he made of himself. Shakespear took the pen from him and made this:

Here lies Benjamin, with short hair upon his chin,
Who while he lived was a slow thing: and now he's buried is no thing.

IV  *Epitaphs on the Stanleys in Tong Church, Shropshire*

*Written upon the East End of the Tomb*

Ask who lies here, but do not weep;
He is not dead, he doth but sleep.
This stony register is for his bones,
His fame is more perpetual than these stones;
And his own goodness, with himself, being gone,
Shall live when earthly monument is none.

*Written upon the West End Thereof*

Not monumental stone preserves our fame,
Nor sky-aspiring pyramids our name;
The memory of him for whom this stands
Shall outlive marble and defacers' hands.
When all to Time's consumption shall be given,
Stanley, for whom this stands, shall stand in heaven.

V  *On Himself*

Made by himself a little before his death

Good friend, for Jesus' sake forbear
To dig the dust enclosèd here!
Bles't be the man that spares these stones
And Curs't be he that moves my bones!

VI  *Upon the King*

Crowns have their compass; length of days, their date;
Triumphs, their tombs; felicity, her fate.
Of more than earth can earth make none partaker,
But knowledge makes the king most like his maker.

# COMMENTARY

## *VENUS AND ADONIS*

*Venus and Adonis* was entered in the Register at Stationers' Hall on 18 April 1593. It was published in quarto in the same year by Richard Field, a fellow-townsman of Shakespeare, with the inscription on the title-page, 'Imprinted by Richard Field, and are to be sold at the signe of the white Greyhound in Paules Church-yard'. Only the First Quarto has any authority. This is an excellent text, carefully supervised, possibly by Shakespeare himself, although there is no direct evidence for this. F. T. Prince has collated the First Quarto with the subsequent editions, and his analysis shows the steady corruption of the text by printers' errors and the ill-judged attempts of compositors and editors to improve it and correct its grammar through the later quartos. Hyder Edward Rollins gives a full account of the history of the text in *The Poems: A New Variorum Edition of Shakespeare*. I have used the First Quarto (Q) for this edition and its very occasional errors are noted in the commentary. The spelling and the punctuation have been modernized.

### THE EPIGRAPH

Ovid, *Amores* (I, xv, 35–6). 'Let what is cheap excite the marvel of the crowd; for me may golden Apollo minister full cups from the Castalian fount' (Loeb). For the significance of this, see Introduction, p. 2.

### THE DEDICATION

Southampton was a great nobleman of the time and a friend and patron of many poets. He was nineteen when *Venus* was dedicated to him. He was a friend of Essex and was later imprisoned at the time of the Essex Rebellion in 1601.

*ear* plough, cultivate

## THE POEM

1–2    *Even as the sun.* For the history and development of this topos, see Baldwin (pp. 4–9).

       *purple-coloured.* Crimson or bright red, often associated with blood. Cf. lines 1054 and 1168.

3    *Rose-cheeked.* Used by Marlowe to describe Adonis in *Hero and Leander* (I, 93).

       *hied him* hastened

5    *Sick-thoughted* love-sick

       *makes amain* hurries with full speed

9    *Stain to* surpassing in beauty and therefore disgracing

11–    *Nature . . . life.* (Nature struggled to surpass herself in making

12    Adonis and, having created a masterpiece, says that she will create no more if he dies.) Cf. line 954.

13    *alight* alight from

14    *saddle-bow* curved front of the saddle. (Rein in the horse tightly so that he will not wander.) Cf. 'bow-back', line 619.

15    *meed* reward

18    *set* seated

24    *wasted* spent

25    *sweating palm.* A sign of amorousness and fertility. See lines 143–4 and *Antony and Cleopatra*: 'Nay, if an oily palm be not a fruitful prognostication / I cannot scratch mine ear' (I, ii, 55–6).

26    *precedent* sign, token

       *pith and livelihood* vigour and energy

29    *enraged* aroused

30    *Courageously* lustfully. Cf. lines 276 and 556.

34    *unapt to toy* unwilling to make love

39    *stalled up* fastened as in a stall

40    *prove* try

42    *lust* desire

46    *chide* scold

47    *broken* interrupted by kisses

53    *miss* misdeed

55    *sharp by fast* famished through fasting

56    *Tires* tears, feeds ravenously on

61    *content* acquiesce

66    *so* so long as

69    *awed resistance* resistance overcome by fear

70    *bred more beauty* made them even more attractive

71    *rank* full

79    *Look how he can* no matter how he looks (whether red or pale)

82    *take truce with* make peace with
      *contending* making war on him

84    *countless* infinite. 'comptless' in Q, the commonest sixteenth-century form.

86    *dive-dapper* dab-chick

90    *winks* shuts his eyes, as at line 121. Presumably he shuts his eyes to give the kiss but, at the last moment, flinches and turns away.

91    *passenger* traveller

92    *good turn.* See *Antony and Cleopatra* (II, v, 58–9): 'For the best turn i' the bed'.

94    *She bathes in water* . . . Prince suggests a reference to Tantalus, up to his chin in water but never able to drink it.

98    *the stern and direful god of war.* Mars, whose love affair with, and subjugation by, Venus was a very common theme of Renaissance iconography, e.g. Botticelli's painting of Mars and Venus in the National Gallery, London.

100    *jar* discord, fight

104    *his uncontrolled crest* 'his helmet which was never bowed in submission' (Prince)

108    *field* of battle, in this case, in Love's war

110    *a red-rose chain.* For the genealogy of this common Renaissance image from Anacreon via Ronsard, see Rollins's note on this line.

119    *Look in mine eyeballs.* (Look in my eyes and see your image reflected there.) For the use of the same conceit, see Donne, 'The Good-Morrow' (line 15): 'My face in thine eye, thine, in mine appears'. See also lines 1129–30.

121    *wink.* Cf. line 90 and Donne, 'The Sunne Rising': (line 13): 'I could eclipse and cloud them with a winke'.

124    *not in sight* not in public view, but also not merely in looking

126    *blab* tell tales. Pooler suggests a reference to Midas, who confided to the reeds that he had asses' ears, and they betrayed his secret.

127    *The tender spring* the down not yet matured into a beard

131–   *Fair flowers* . . . *little time.* Cf. lines 166–74. The theme is that of
2     the first sixteen sonnets.

133    *hard-favoured* ugly, hard-featured. Cf. line 931.

135    *O'erworn* worn out with age
      *despised* despicable

136   *Thick-sighted* dim-sighted

140   *grey*. From the Middle Ages: the equivalent of 'blue' eyes and considered especially attractive.

145–
56   Cf. line 1028.

148   *footing* footprint

149   *compact* composed of

150   *Not gross . . . but light*. Fire was the lightest of the traditional four elements, and its nature was to rise above the heavier ones. Fire formed, therefore, the highest of the sublunar spheres in the Ptolemaic cosmology.

152   *forceless* without strength

153   *doves*. Venus' chariot was traditionally drawn by doves. See line 1190.

154   *list* please

157   *affected* in love with. The reference is to Narcissus, who fell in love with his own reflection in the stream. See lines 161–2.

158   *Can thy right hand . . .* (Can your right hand take hold of love by seizing your own left hand, i.e. can you be in love with yourself?)

161   *on* of

161–   *Narcissus so himself . . . in the brook*. In Marlowe's version, where
2     Narcissus leaps into the water to seize his reflection and is drowned (*Hero and Leander*, I, 73–6), though not in Ovid's, where he merely dies of grief and is turned into a flower (*Metamorphoses*, III, 485ff).

166   *Things growing to themselves*. Cf. line 1180.

177   *Titan* the sun god
      *tired* perhaps attired, clothed. Pooler suggests that the sun is weary from its long climb up the heavens. Cf. lines 529–30.

179   *his team* the fiery horses that drew the chariot of the sun across the sky

180   *So he . . . him* So Titan . . . Adonis

181   *sprite* mood

183   *sight* eyes

187   *unkind* unnatural, as well as the normal modern sense of the word. Cf. lines 204 and 312.

196   *Thine eye darts forth the fire*. A reference to the common theory of the animal spirits which were thought to flow out through the eyes and enter those of the other person, penetrating to the heart and inflaming it with love. This physiological explanation of

falling in love is the source of all the conceits in the period about murdering eyes, Cupid's darts, etc.

201    *relenteth* softens

204    *thy mother . . . died unkind*. There could be irony in this passage. Adonis' mother was Myrrha, who bore him by her own father, Cinyras, and was changed into a myrtle for her sin. She was commonly taken as an example of one who lived 'unkind'. See line 188. The episode in Ovid's *Metamorphoses* (X, 306ff) immediately precedes that of Venus and Adonis.

205    *contemn* refuse scornfully

       *this* an archaic form of 'thus'

215    *complexion*. This is not only natural appearance but also temperament and constitution governed by the individual mixture of the four humours.

216    *even by their own direction* by natural instinct, without the need for prompting.

219    *blaze forth* in the heraldic sense, proclaim

220    *Being judge*. As the goddess of love, she is the arbitrator in all matters of love, yet she cannot arbitrate in her own case.

222    *intendments* intentions to speak

229    *Fondling* a term of endearment, 'darling'

       *hemmed* enclosed

230    *pale* fence, often around a deer park – in this case the enclosure formed by her white arms and locked fingers around him. For the hart/heart and dear/deer conceits, see the Introduction (p. 8) and Orsino's speech at the beginning of *Twelfth Night* (I, i, 16–20).

235    *relief* food, pasture

236    *bottom-grass* grass growing in the valleys

237    *brakes* thickets

240    *rouse*. A hunting term: to drive an animal from its cover or lair.

243    *if himself* so that if he himself were slain

251    *in thine own law forlorn*. (Unhappy under the laws which you yourself have established.) A reference to the traditional plight of lovers as described in Venus' prophecy about lovers at the end of the poem (lines 1135ff).

260    *A breeding jennet* a small Spanish mare

272    *compassed* arched

275    *glisters* glitters

276    *courage* Cf. lines 30 and 556.

277  *told* counted

279  *curvets*. A technical term from the art of horsemanship: when the horse is trained to leap with its front and hind legs fully extended and all off the ground at the same time.

280  *tried* proved

283  *What recketh he* what does he care for
*stir* agitation

288  *agrees* is agreeable to

290  *limning out* painting or drawing

291  *As if the dead the living* . . . See *Lucrece* (lines 1374ff).

295–  This is a stock description of a horse which originated in Virgil's
9     *Georgics* (III, 74ff) and was elaborated in many accounts of the horse and horsemanship in Shakespeare's period. For an account of these, see the notes of Rollins and of Prince on these lines, and the article on hunting in *Shakespeare's England* (vol. II, pp. 334ff).

295  *shag* shaggy, rough

297  *passing* exceedingly

300  *Save a proud rider*. The image of the good rider mastering his horse is a common Renaissance symbol of the rational control of the lower nature. See Thomas Elyot, *Boke Named the Governor* (I, xvii) and Spenser, *The Fairie Queene* (I, i and *passim*). There is an implied moral criticism in the image of the horseless man and the uncontrolled horse.

301  *scuds . . . stares* darts away . . . stands still

303  *To bid the wind a base* challenge the wind to a race. The image is taken from the Elizabethan game of Prisoners' Base, in which two teams occupy contiguous bases and try to intercept any one leaving the other base (*OED*, 'Base sb 2').

304  *whe'er* whether

310  *strangeness* coldness. Cf. line 524.

314  *vails* lowers

316  *fume* anger

320  *unbacked* not yet broken in. Cf. line 419.

321  *Jealous of catching* fearing to be caught

325  *chafing* raging. Cf. line 662.

326  *Banning* cursing

330  *barred the aidance* denied the help

331  *An oven* . . . For the source and history of this image, see Baldwin (pp. 26–9).
*stopped* stopped up

334   *vent.* Used in both literal and metaphorical senses: the vent-hole of the furnace and the outpouring of words.

335   *the heart's attorney* the tongue, which pleads on behalf of the heart

336   *The client* the heart
      *breaks* goes bankrupt

339   *bonnet* hat

342   *all askance.* He watches her without showing it, out of the corner of his eye.

343   *wistly* attentively

351   *heaveth* lifts. Cf. line 482.

354   *apt* readily
      *dint* impression

357   *as* as if

359   *his* its

360   *chorus-like.* This mute exchange of looks is described in terms of a dumb-show; and Venus' tears, in making the meaning clear, are compared to an actor who plays the part of chorus and explains the action.

363   *band* bonds, fetters

364   *engirts* encloses

365   *wilful and unwilling.* This carries the normal sexual associations of 'will': Venus, full of desire, Adonis, lacking in it. The phrase continues the pattern of contrast between 'friend' and 'foe' in line 364.

367   *the engine of her thoughts* her tongue

368   *this mortal round* the earth

370   *thy heart my wound.* (One great wound as mine is.)

372   *bane* ruin, destruction

373   *Give me* give me back

375   *steel* turn to steel

376   *grave* engrave, make an impression on

377   *regard* have any care for

381   *bereft* robbed of

387   *Affection* passion

388   *suffered* allowed to burn

391   *jade* a poor, ill-conditioned horse

393   *fee* the due reward owed to his youth

396   *Enfranchising* liberating

400   *His other agents* his other senses and organs of the body

405   *on* of

408   *made perfect* properly learned

411   *'Tis much to borrow.* (It entails too great a responsibility and I won't accept it.)

412   *My love to love* (My only desire concerning love is a desire to disgrace it.)

414   *all but with a breath* all in the same breath

419   *backed* ridden. Cf. line 320.

426   *battery* breach, entry

429   *mermaid's* associated with the seductive song of the Sirens

430   *now pressed with bearing* weighed down with carrying it. Cf. line 545.

431–  *Melodious discord . . . wounding.* This sequence is in the conven-
2     tion of sonnet rhetoric, the clichés of ice/fire, hot/cold, etc.

433–  *eyes . . . ears . . . banquet.* Shakespeare is drawing on the ima-
45    gery of the traditional 'banquet of the senses'. See the Introduc-
     tion (p. 16) and also George Chapman's *Ovid's Banquet of the Senses* (1595), where the poet feasts on Corinna's beauty with each sense in turn, but, unlike Venus, he seeks in the physical the divine form of the spiritual beauty.

436   *sensible* capable of feeling

443   *stillitory* still for the distillation of perfumes

446   *the other four* the other four senses besides taste

451   *the ruby-coloured portal* Adonis' mouth

454   *Wrack* wreck

456   *flaws* squalls

457   *presage* omen
     *advisedly* carefully

459   *grin* bares his fangs

464   *For looks . . .* (A frown kills love, a smile revives it.)

465   *recures* heals

466   *loss.* 'love' in Q, which Prince retains. Emended by Kinnear to 'looks' and by Walker to 'loss'. (See Rollins, p. 51n.) 'Love' destroys the point of 'bankrupt'; 'looks' is merely repetitive, and both could have been carried over by the compositor from line 464. The force of the paradox depends on 'loss' – in this case, it is the frown that heals the wound.

467   *silly* simple

468   *Claps* slaps

469   *his late intent* his previous intention to reprehend her

470   *sharply* harshly

471   *wittily* cleverly

472   *Fair fall* fair befall, good luck to

475  *wrings* tweaks, plucks

477  *chafes* warms by rubbing with his hand

478  *To mend . . . marred.* Pooler suggests that this is a mixture of two phrases: to mend the hurt that his unkindness caused, and to mend what was marred by his unkindness.

479  *by her good will* willingly

480  *so* so long as

482  *Her two blue windows* either her blue-veined eyelids, or the eyes themselves.
     *upheaveth* lifts. Cf. line 351.

489  *four such lamps* their four eyes

490  *repine* discontent

494  *drenched* immersed

495  *or . . . or* either . . . or

497  *death's annoy* as full of pains as death itself

498  *lively joy* as joyful as life

500  *shrewd* malicious, spiteful

503  *true leaders to their queen.* 'Presumably their queen' is Venus' heart, to which her eyes, truthful bearers of messages, have carried the knowledge of Adonis' disdain, and would have died with it out of loyalty but for the message from his lips.

505  *they* his piteous lips
     *for* as a result of

506  *never . . . wear.* (May their crimson colours never wear out.)

507  *verdure* fragrance, freshness. 'verdour' in Q.

508  *To drive infection.* Malone suggests an allusion to the practice of strewing the house with rue and strong-smelling herbs to keep away the plague. The reference would be particularly relevant in 1592–3 when the plague was especially severe.

509  *the star-gazers.* 'Compilers of almanacs who have prophesied an epidemic' (Prince).

511  *sweet seals.* For the association of kisses with seals, see *Measure for Measure* (IV, i, 6–7): 'But my kisses bring again / Seals of love but sealed in vain'. The reference is to the seals upon a legal document or one involving a financial transaction.

515  *slips* counterfeit coins

516  *seal manual.* On the analogy of 'sign-manual': your personal seal that authenticates your love.

519  *touches.* Touches of the lips, but also, perhaps, a reference to 'touch', an official mark or stamp upon gold or silver, indicating

that it has been tested and its purity guaranteed (*OED*). This links up with 'slips', which lack the official stamp.

520    *told* counted (like coins)

521    *non-payment . . . double.* Where the bond was forfeited for non-payment, the legal penalty was double the original sum involved (Malone).

524    *strangeness.* (Recognize that my bashfulness is a result of my youth.) Cf. line 310.

525    *know* in the sexual, Old Testament sense of the word

526    *No fisher . . .* (There is no fisherman who does not throw back the little fish.)

529–   Baldwin (pp. 30–31) suggests that Shakespeare was drawing on
34     Ovid's *Metamorphoses* (X, 446–52), possibly in Golding's translation (X, 511–17) for this description of nightfall. Ovid is describing Myrrha, the mother-to-be of Adonis, as she sets out on her ill-fated assignment with her own father. See the commentary to lines 203–4.

529    *the world's comforter* the sun. Cf. line 177.

538    *tendered* offered

540    *Incorporate* united in one body

544    *drouth* thirst

545    *pressed* over-pressed. Cf. line 430.

547    *the yielding prey* Adonis. For Shakespeare's use of the bird-of-prey image to describe Venus, see lines 55–8, 63 and 551.

550    *the insulter* the triumphant aggressor

551    *vulture* greedy
      *pitch* set

553    *spoil* plunder. In hunting, the body of the captured prey divided among the hounds.

556    *careless* not caring, reckless
      *courage.* Cf. lines 30 and 276.

557    *Planting oblivion.* (Driving out the thought of everything else.)

558    *wrack.* See line 454.

562    *froward* petulant, fretful
      *stilled* made quiet, soothed

564    *listeth* desires

565    *temp'ring* softening and shaping between the fingers

567    *out of hope* seeming beyond all hope
      *compassed* achieved

568    *whose leave exceeds commission.* A difficult phrase: 'Traditionally

allowed to do more than is laid down in the warrant', i.e. to take more liberties than the mistress is willing to permit.

569 *Affection* passion

570 *when most his choice is froward.* Either 'when the mistress he has chosen is froward – i.e. unwilling' or, alternatively, 'froward' could refer to 'his choice': 'when he has made a perverse choice' (in choosing a mistress who is unwilling). The general meaning is the same in either interpretation: 'the lover woos best when facing resistance'.

575– *under twenty locks* Cf. the common proverb 'Love laughs at
6 locksmiths.'

580 *look well to* take good care of

583 *waste* spend

584 *watch* lie awake

586 *match* bargain

589 *pale* paleness

590 *lawn* very fine, almost transparent linen

595 *lists.* The area where jousts, tiltings and knightly tournaments were held. In this case the battles would be in Love's war.

597 *imaginary* only in the imagination

598 *manage.* A technical term from horse-riding: to put her through her paces.

599 *Tantalus'.* See the commentary to line 94.

600 *clip* embrace
*Elysium* the Elysian fields, the classical equivalent of heaven

601 *Even so* even as
*painted grapes.* The reference is to the picture of grapes which Zeuxis painted so realistically that birds pecked at them. See Pliny's *Natural History* (XXXV, 36).

602 *pine the maw* starve the stomach (though overfeeding through the eyes)

604 *helpless* affording no help

605 *The warm effects.* The normal physical effects that ought to result from his position on top of her.

608 *assayed . . . proved.* (She has tried everything she can.)

609 *fee* reward

612 *reason* right
*withhold* hold me back

616 *churlish* rough, brutal

617 *tushes* tusks
*whetteth* sharpens

618    *mortal* deadly

619–   The sources of this description of the boar are Ovid's account of
30     the Calydonian boar in the *Metamorphoses* (VIII, 284) and
     Golding's translation (VIII, 374). See Rollins (p. 393) and
     Baldwin (pp. 33–7).

619    *bow-back* arched back. Cf. 'saddle-bow', line 14.
     *battle* an army drawn up

621    *fret* become angry

626    *proof* more impenetrable. A term applied to the strength of
     armour.

628    *ireful* angry
     *venter* venture

631–
6     Cf. Ovid's *Metamorphoses* (X, 547ff).

633    *eyne* eyes

635    *at vantage* in a position favourable to himself

636    *root* uproot

637    *cabin* den

639    *danger* within range of his power to harm you

645    *downright* straightway or straight down. Both meanings may be
     intended.

649    *Jealousy*. In addition to its modern meaning, the word still
     carries here some of its older, more general significance:
     apprehension of evil, anxiety.

652    *Kill, kill!* According to Malone, the order given to an army to
     attack.

653    *Distempering* causing disturbance to

655    *bate-breeding* breeding strife

657    *carry-tale* tale-bearer
     *dissentious* causing dissent

662    *chafing* raging. Cf. line 325.

667    *indeed* in reality

670    *divination* the power of prophecy

674    *Uncouple*. (Let your hounds loose.)

678    *well-breathed* sound in wind

679–   For contemporary accounts of hunting the hare of the kind with
700    which Shakespeare was familiar, see Pooler's notes to the
     passage, and his reference to Turbervile's *Booke of Hunting*,
     Topsel's *Four-footed Beasts*, etc. From the verbal parallels
     between *Venus* and such handbooks, it would seem that
     Shakespeare knew them well.

679   *on foot* on the move
     *purblind* weak-sighted. Pooler quotes Topsel for the belief that hares had poor sight.

680   *overshoot* out-run, escape from

682   *cranks* twists and turns
     *doubles* sharp turns

683   *musits* gaps in hedges or fences through which hares habitually run when being hunted

685   *a flock of sheep*. Pooler quotes Turbervile's *Booke of Hunting* for this detail.

687   *earth-delving conies* rabbits that burrow in the ground
     *keep* live, have their burrows

688   *loud pursuers . . . yell* the hounds in full cry

689   *sorteth* consorts, goes in company with

690   *shifts* tricks, stratagems
     *wit* intelligence, cunning

693   *singled* distinguished the scent of the beast being chased from that of other animals (Pooler, quoting Turbervile).

694   *the cold fault* lack of scent, because the scent is cold or confused with that of another animal

695   *spend their mouths* give cry again, having been silent while they had lost the scent

697   *Wat* common name for a hare. Cf. John Skelton's *Phyllyp Sparowe*.

704   *indenting* following a wavy line. From the practice of tearing a legal document in half and giving half to each party so that the fitting together of the two halves is a proof of authenticity. Topsel uses the image to describe the zigzag course of the hounds.

725   *modest Dian* virgin goddess of the moon and of hunting. The thought of Adonis' lips would make her melancholy for the fear that she should steal a kiss and die, having broken her vow of virginity.

728   *Cynthia* another name for Diana, goddess of the moon

729   *forging Nature* all-creating Nature

731   *she* Nature, who has created Adonis according to patterns of beauty stolen from heaven which make him excel both the sun and the moon

732   *her* the moon

733   *she* Cynthia

> *Destinies* the three goddesses of Fate who spin, measure and cut the thread of human life

734 *cross* thwart

*curious* skilfully wrought

736 *defeature* disfigurement

739–
43 Prince cites *Troilus and Cressida*, (V, i, 20–6) as a parallel.

739 *As* such as

*agues* shaking fits

740 *wood* mad

741 *The marrow-eating sickness* probably syphilis, which was very much in the public mind at the period.

*attaint* infecting influence

743 *Surfeits* illnesses resulting from gluttony or drunkenness

*imposthumes* abscesses

744 *Swear Nature's death* swear they will destroy Nature

745–
6 *not the least.* (Even the slightest of these illnesses can overcome beauty in a minute.)

747 *favour* appearance

748 *impartial* unbiased

751 *despite of* in scorn of

752 *vestals* the vestal virgins who were sworn to chastity

*self-loving* Cf. Sonnet 4: 'Unthrifty loveliness, why dost thou spend / Upon thyself thy beauty's legacy?'

757 *a swallowing grave* Cf. Sonnet 3: 'Or who is he so fond will be the tomb / Of his self love to stop posterity'.

762 *Sith* since

766 *reaves* robs

767 *frets* corrodes

770 *over-handled* hackneyed

774 *treatise* discourse, argument

782 *closure* enclosure

787 *reprove* disprove, refute

789 *device* contrivance

792 *When reason is the bawd* when reason is used to justify the evils of lust

795 *Under whose simple semblance* in the disguise of innocent love

797 *the hot tyrant* lust

*bereaves* destroys, takes away

803 *surfeits not* never sickens with over-feeding

806 *green* young and inexperienced

807   *in sadness* in all seriousness

808   *teen* grief

813   *laund* glade

822   *Fold in* enfold

825   *'stonished* dismayed

826   *mistrustful* causing mistrust or anxiety

828   *the fair discovery*. This refers back to and develops the image of
the bright star (line 815), the light blown out (line 826); the way
shown to her by the brightness of Adonis.

830–   Cf. Ovid's *Metamorphoses* (III, 495ff), the lament of Narcissus
4   before he dies, repeated by the nymph Echo – although
Shakespeare exaggerates the number of echoes to the point of
parody.

832   *Passion* passionate speech, lamentation. The individual poems
of Thomas Watson's *Passionate Centurie of Love* are by him called
'Passions', and Shakespeare presents Venus' lament as a love
poem that the echo repeats after her.

836   *a woeful ditty*. As well as Ovid's *Metamorphoses*, Sidney's *Old
Arcadia* (III, pp. 169–71) may have contributed to this scene.
Pyrocles, in the disguise of Cleophila, sings a doleful song of
love 'shee had lately made', and immediately hears a compar-
able song sung with 'Monefull Melody' from within a neigh-
bouring cave. ' "O Venus," sayde Cleophila, "who ys this, so
well acquaynted with mee, that can make so lyvely a Purtraiture
of my myseryes?" ' The singer is Gynecia, who in her unbridled
desire has much in common with Shakespeare's Venus.

837   *thrall* enslaved

839–   *heavy anthem . . . choir* Shakespeare's whole treatment of Venus'
40   'Passion' and its echos is comic, with a touch of parody
throughout.

841   *outwore* outlasted

844   *circumstance* details

845   *oftentimes begun* which they are never tired of telling

848   *parasites* who echo everything she says

849   *tapsters* pot-boys. For their habits referred to here, see *Henry
IV, Part I* (II, iv, 20).

854   *moist cabinet* dewy lodging, nest

859   *him* the sun

863   *that sucked an earthly mother*. This is not, in fact, true, as
Shakespeare must have known, since Adonis was born from a
split in the trunk of the tree into which his mother Myrrha had

been metamorphosed. See Ovid's *Metamorphoses* (X, 500ff). The distortion of the well-known story, and the unusually crude feminine endings in which this commonplace of love poetry is expressed, all contribute to the element of parody in the sequence. They form a startling contrast to the description of the sun rising in the previous verse.

866   *Musing* wondering that the morning is so advanced and yet she has heard nothing of Adonis

869   *Anon* immediately

      *chant it* give cry

870   *coasteth* makes her way in the direction of

873   *twined.* 'twin'd' in Q, emended to 'twine' in Q7. In Maxwell, 'twind' (an alternative form of 'twine'). There seems no necessity to emend Q, as the meaning here is 'some twisted round'.

877   *at a bay* halted because the boar is standing his ground

879   *fatal* promising danger

887   *curst* savage

888   *They all strain courtesy.* They all 'hold back to let another go first' (Prince).

      *cope* tackle

891   *bloodless* pale-faced

892   *each feeling part* all her senses

895   *ecstasy* frenzy, state of violent emotion

907   *spleens* conflicting impulses

909   *mated* either matched with or check-mated by. Both senses are probably intended.

911   *Full of respects.* 'Full of consideration and yet really considering nothing' (Pooler).

912   *In hand . . . effecting.* (Busy with everything, achieving nothing.)

914   *caitiff* wretch

916   *plaster* remedy

920   *flap-mouthed* having broad, hanging lips. These are among the points of a running hound (Pooler).

921   *welkin* sky

928   *Infusing them . . . prophecies.* This refers to the 'signs and prodigies' that the ignorant people interpret as omens of terrible things to come. In the same way, Venus, seeing the unusual behaviour of the hounds, assumes at once that they denote tragedy.

930   *exclaims on* rails against

931 *Hard-favoured*. Cf. line 133.

933 *Grim-grinning*. The image suggests a skull, which leads on to 'earth's worm', the corpse-worm.

936 *Gloss* sheen

941 *Thy mark* proper target

943 *bid beware* give a warning

946 *crop* lop off

947– *golden . . . ebon*. Both are traditional images associated with love
8 and death. 'ebon' is black, like ebony.

953– *Nature . . . rigour*. (Nature does not care what you destroy now
4 since you have already destroyed her best work.) Cf. lines 11–12.

956 *vailed* let fall
*sluices* flood-gates

959 *the silver rain* tears

961 *lend and borrow* give and take images to and from each other

963 *crystals*. Maxwell and Prince interpret them as magic crystals, 'in which one in sympathy with another could see the scene of his distress'; but a simpler interpretation of crystals as looking-glasses seems adequate: the tears and the eyes are reflected in each other, as described in line 962. Donne uses almost the same conceit in 'A Valediction of Weeping'.

968 *become* be the most fitting expression of

969 *All entertained*. All are admitted, none refused entry.

970 *present* while it is in possession

972 *consulting*. The variable passions stop competing with each other and plot together to produce a total grief.

975 *The dire imagination* the death of Adonis, which she had imagined

979 *turn their tide* ebb

980 *pearls in glass*. The image develops out of the 'crystals' of line 963.

981 *orient* where the finest pearls, 'orient', came from

985– *O hard-believing . . . credulous!* love that is sceptical yet credulous
6 at the same time

988 *makes* the fluctuation between despair and hope; hence the singular verb

989 *The one* hope

990 *the other* despair

991 *Now she unweaves* (Now she rejects as false all that she has imagined about Adonis' death.)

992   *to blame* to be blamed
993   *called him all to nought* abused him
995   *clepes* calls
996   *Imperious supreme* supreme emperor
1000  *still severe* ever pitiless
1001  *shadow* spirit, spectre
1004  *Be wreaked* be revenged
1006  *author* (The original cause of my slandering you.)
1010  *suspect* suspicion
1012  *insinuate* insinuate herself into his favour by paying him compliments
1013  *trophies* monuments to his greatness, on tombs
      *stories* Q has a comma after 'stories', but the sense suggests that it is a verb, not a noun: 'and tells stories of'.
1018  *mutual* common
      *mortal kind* the human race.
1019  *Beauty . . . Chaos.* See the Introduction (p. 13) and Marsilio
−20   Ficino's commentary on Plato's *Symposium*. Beauty was the divine form that God out of his overflowing love imposed on formless first matter (Chaos), and the conjunction of these two brought into being all the diverse phenomena of the creation. When Beauty dies, therefore, things fall apart and everything tumbles back into Chaos. See *Othello* (III, iii, 91−2): '. . . and when I love thee not / Chaos is come again'. The relationship between form and chaos is the subject of the allegory in Spenser's *Fairie Queene* (III, vi), in the Garden of Adonis, where Adonis is 'the father of all forms' and Venus is the love that uses him for the purpose of creation.
1022  *hemmed.* See line 229.
1024  *grieves.* The subject of the sentence is 'Trifles' (line 1023), a further example of a plural noun used to govern a singular verb. Cf. line 1128.
1027  *lure.* Here, probably the falconer's call or whistle, but normally a 'bundle of feathers with flesh attached, representing a bird, used to train falcons' (Pooler).
1028  *so light.* Cf. lines 145−56. Love is at its lightest, since Venus thinks Adonis is alive.
1029  *unfortunately* by ill fortune, carrying a stronger sense than modern usage
1030  *The foul boar's conquest* the dead body of Adonis
1031  *as* 'are' in Q

1032 *of* at the approach of

1033 *whose tender horns . . . again.* Cf. *Love's Labour's Lost* (IV, iii,
−6   337–8): 'Love's feeling is more soft and sensible / Than are the
tender horns of cockled snails'.

1041 *still consort with ugly night* for ever keep company with darkness

1043 *Who* the heart

1044 *their suggestion* what the eyes have shown him

1045 *each tributary subject* the faculties governed by the heart

1046 *the wind, imprisoned in the ground.* This was the traditional
Aristotelian explanation of earthquakes. See *Meteorologica* (II,
8).

1052 *trenched* cut. Cf. *Macbeth* (III, iv, 27): 'With twenty trenched
gashes on his head'.

1054 *was drenched* 'had drencht' in Q, an error caused by the carry-
over from line 1052. Corrected in Q7.
*purple tears* crimson blood. Cf. lines 1 and 1168.

1059 *passions* sorrows
*doteth* acts foolishly without control

1062 *that they have wept till now* that they have wept earlier, before
they had adequate cause

1064 *dazzling* blurring with tears

1065 *reprehends . . . eye.* She upbraids her eyes for seeing more
wounds than are actually there; hence 'mangling', creating
wounds.

1078 *ensuing* to come in the future

1081 *no creature wear* let no creature wear

1083 *fair* beauty. Verbal play on fair/fear

1084 *hiss* hiss at

1088 *gaudy* glaringly brilliant. Cf. *Hamlet* (I, iii, 71) 'rich, not gaudy'

1094 *fear* frighten

1095 *recreate* entertain, refresh

1105 *urchin-snouted* with a snout like a hedgehog

1107 *livery* outward appearance

1108 *entertainment* treatment

1114 *persuade him* persuade him to stay there

1115 *nuzzling . . . groin.* The idea of the boar's kiss derives from
−6   Theocritus' idyll *The Dead Adonis*; it was widely known in the
sixteenth century and had been translated into English in 1588.
See Rollins's note on lines 1110–16.

1126 *As if they heard* as if they could hear

1127 *coffer-lids* eye-lids. 'Lids to treasure-chests' (Prince).

1129 *glasses* mirrors

1133 *spite* vexation

1139 *Ne'er settled equally . . . low.* (Never steady but always at one extreme or the other)

1142 *in a breathing while* in a short space of time

1143 *o'erstrawed* strewn over

1147 *sparing . . . riot* miserly yet over-generous, prodigal

1148 *tread the measures* go dancing, like a young man

1149 *staring* aggressive, truculent
   *quiet* peaceful behaviour

1151 *silly-mild* simple

1157 *toward* well disposed, compliant

1158 *Put* impose, add

1168 *a purple flower.* See Ovid's *Metamorphoses* (X, 731–9), though in Ovid's version it is Venus herself who changes Adonis into a flower.
   *purple* blood-red. Cf. lines 1 and 1054.

1174 *reft* stolen

1175 *crops* breaks off

1177 *guise* habit, practice

1180 *To grow unto himself.* Cf. line 166 and Sonnet 16, (line 13): 'To give away yourself keep yourself still'.

1189 *hies* hastens

1190 *silver doves.* Cf. line 153.

1193 *Paphos* the home of Venus and the site of her main temple in Cyprus

# THE RAPE OF LUCRECE

The Rape of Lucrece was entered at Stationers' Hall on 9 May 1594 and printed under the title of Lucrece in the same year. It did not acquire the title of The Rape of Lucrece until the 'Newly revised' Sixth Quarto of 1616. Again the printer was Richard Field and the text is an excellent one, which shows the same progressive corruption through the subsequent quartos as in the case of Venus. Of the eleven known copies of the First Quarto, two have uncorrected sheets and a comparison of these with the corrected versions shows that the proofreader's corrections are of minor significance and in most cases unnecessary. They are discussed by J. C. Maxwell and analysed in full detail by J. W. Lever. The First Quarto prints inverted commas at the beginning of some of the gnomic sayings in the poem, as at lines 87, 88, 460, 530, 560, for example; but the practice is not consistent and I have not included them in this edition. For the fullest account of the text and the subsequent quartos, see Hyder Edward Rollins's *The Poems: A New Variorum Edition of Shakespeare*.

## THE DEDICATION

This is more personal and less formal than that to *Venus*, suggesting that by the time of the second poem, Shakespeare was on terms of friendship with his patron.

2     *pamphlet* a short, written work
      *without beginning* perhaps because the story begins *in medias res*
3     *moiety* part
      *warrant* surety

## THE ARGUMENT

The extent to which this account, based on Ovid and Livy (see the Introduction, p. 26), differs from the poem itself has led to the suggestion by Lever and others that it was not written by Shakespeare but commissioned by the printer as a 'publisher's blurb'.

1     *all in post* in great haste. Cf. line 220.

2     *trustless* not to be trusted

3     *Lust-breathèd* animated by lust

4     *lightless firę* the concealed fire of his lust. Cf. line 1555.

5     *aspire* mount to

8     *Haply* perchance, with a verbal play on 'unhapp'ly'

9     *bateless* not to be blunted

10    *let* forbear

12    *that sky of his delight* Lucrece's face

13    *mortal stars . . . heaven's beauties* her eyes as bright as the stars

14    *pure aspects*. This is an astrological term concerning the position of the stars in relation to the earth, and their influence on it – in this case, wholly benign.
      *peculiar duties* for him alone

16    *Unlocked the treasure* revealed and bragged about

23    *done* consumed

24    *morning* (Uncorrected Q) 'morning' was commonly used as an adjective, and the version 'morning's', which Prince takes from the Corrected Q, is unnecessary. See note on the text, p. 207.

26    *date* a bond with a time-limit

27    *in the owner's arms* part of the military metaphor, 'fortressed', but also used in the literal sense

29–   *persuade . . . orator*. Rhetoric, in which the orator was trained,
30    was by definition the art of persuasion.

31    *apology*. An *apologia*, a full verbal account and description, although not necessary in this case, since such unique beauty as Lucrece's speaks for itself. 'apologies' in the Corrected Q.

37    *Suggested* tempted
      *issue* offspring. Tarquin was the son of Lucius Tarquinius, who had 'possessed himself of the kingdom' (see 'The Argument').

40    *Braving compare* defying comparison

41    *vaunt* brag of

42    *hap* fortune
      *want* lack

44    *all too timeless* too hasty

47    *liver*. In Elizabethan anatomy, the liver was supposed to be the seat of sexual desire.

49   *still blasts* ever is blasted, like a too-early spring

52–   Shakespeare develops an elaborate conceit out of the fact that
63   Lucrece's blushes come and fade. Beauty is initially associated
     with red, virtue with white, as each struggles to become the
     chief source of Lucrece's fame, but they subsequently change
     colours, and ultimately unite in the battle against shame.

53   *underprop* be the chief support of

55   *in despite* in defiance

56   *or* 'ore' in Q, which Prince and Maxwell interpret as 'o'er': over.
     (Virtue would stain over the red of beauty with its own pale-
     ness.) Malone conjectures 'or', the term for gold, as opposed to
     'argent', in heraldic insignia. The same opposition is found in
     *Macbeth* (II, iv, 118): 'His silver skin laced with his golden
     blood'. I follow Lever in preferring 'or', since it stands in natural
     opposition to 'silver' and leads on to the sequence of heraldic
     images that follows: 'challenge that fair field', 'shield', 'This
     heraldry'.

57–   Beauty claims that virtue's white is her colour, since it is the
63   colour of Venus' doves; and virtue claims in turn that beauty's
     colour of red belongs to herself, as it signifies the blushes of
     innocence that defend virtue against shame.

57   *entitulèd* having a claim to

58   *that fair field*. A double metaphor of Lucrece's face: the battle-
     field in which beauty and virtue strive for mastery, and the
     heraldic 'field', the surface of a shield upon which the heraldic
     colours of or and argent are deployed.

59   *from* derived from the white doves which drew the chariot of
     Venus. In *Venus* they are called 'silver' (line 1190).

63   *fence* defend, shield

65   *Argued* demonstrated

67   *world's minority* from time immemorial, the early days of the
     world, the golden age (line 60)

73   *encloses*. This silent war . . . which takes captive Tarquin's eye.

79   *The niggard prodigal* too lavish and yet inadequate in its praise

82   *owe* failed to pay

83   *answers with surmise* pays in his thoughts, which he does not
     speak aloud

84   *still-gazing* which gaze at her continually

88   *limed* caught by bird-lime

89   *securely* without care or apprehension

92   *that* i.e. his 'inward ill'

*coloured* disguised

93 *pleats* folds

97– *poorly rich*. The familiar topos from Ovid, 'Plenty has made me
8 poor' is repeated in various forms through the poem; see, for
example, lines 140, 154, 730 and 858–60.

98 *pineth* starves

99 *coped with* encountered
*stranger* strangers'

100 *parling* speaking

102 *glassy margents*. These are the commentaries printed in the
margins of Renaissance books. Here books are used as a
metaphor for Tarquin's eyes, and their margins, the looks he
casts, reveal the inner truth.

104 *moralize* interpret, draw a lesson from

105 *More than* other than that

106 *stories* gives an account of

111 *heaved-up* uplifted

116 *welkin* sky

121 *Intending* pretending
*sprite* spirit

122 *questionèd* conversed.

126 *wakes*. The use of a singular verb with a plural noun for the sake
of rhyme is common. The Corrected Q has 'wake'.

127 *revolving* turning over in his mind

128 *will's* desire's. This word usually carries strong sexual over-
tones. See lines 243, 417, 487 and 495; also Sonnet 135.

130 *weak-built hopes* built on such weak foundations that they would
deter him from the attempt

131 *Despair to gain* despair of gaining
*Traffic* trade. (Even though despairing of success one goes on
contriving to gain it.)

132 *meed* reward

133 *adjunct . . . supposed*. (Though death is joined to it one doesn't
believe that death will follow.)

134 *fond*. This can mean both 'foolish' and 'eager for'. Both
meanings are present here.

135 *That what they have not, that which they possess* (Q). 'That oft . . .'
in Q6. 'That what they have, not that . . .' (Lever). Malone
notes that the passage is based loosely upon a sententia of
Publilius Syrus with which Elizabethan schoolboys would be
familiar: '*Tam avaro deest quod habet, quam quod non habet*' ("The

miser lacks what he has as much as what he has not'). In modifying this, the syntax seems to have gone astray. The emendation of Q6, 'oft', does not solve the problem. Malone interprets it by making a distinction between 'having' and 'possessing': 'Poetically speaking, they may be said to scatter *what they have not*, i.e. what they cannot be *truly* said to have; what they do not *enjoy*, though possessed of it.' Throwing away what they possess but don't really enjoy, however, would scarcely be called foolish, and cannot be Shakespeare's meaning. Lever places the comma after 'have' and interprets 'possess' in the sense of 'take', hence, they squander what they already have, not what they have seized, and so presumably lose as much as they gain. Maxwell suggests that the sequence is an anacoluthon: 'Shakespeare begins as if about to say "what they have not, they are so eager to obtain that they scatter what they possess", but hastens on to the final clause without expressing what comes between.' This seems much the most plausible explanation of the passage.

136  *bond* ownership

138–9  *the profit of excess* (The only profit they get from gaining more than they need is to fall into a surfeit.)

144  *gage* wager

145  *As* as, for example
     *fell* fierce

148  *in venturing ill* in making a bad gamble
     *leave* cease

149  *expect* hope for

150  *ambitious foul infirmity* foul infirmity of ambition

151  *defect* deficiency

153  *want of wit* lack of good sense

156  *Pawning* risking

160  *confounds* ruins

162–8  *Now stole . . . and kill.* Cf. *Macbeth* (II, i, 49ff): 'Now o'er the one half-world'.

164  *comfortable* affording comfort and help

165  *death-boding* auguring death

167  *silly* helpless, deserving of pity

173  *charm* enchantment

174  *him* himself, i.e. honest fear

175  *brain-sick rude* barbarous and violent

176  *falchion* curved sword

*softly* quietly

179 *lodestar* guiding star

180 *advisedly* with deliberation, having made up his mind

188 *His naked armour of still-slaughtered lust.* Lust which is always destroyed by being fulfilled and hence provides a weak and uncertain motive for action.

189 *justly* in a rational manner

196 *weed* clothing, i.e. chastity

198 *my household's grave* the family tomb with the family escutcheons on it

201 *a true respect* a proper regard for virtue

202 *digression* transgression

205 *an eye-sore* an ugly blot

*my golden coat* coat of arms. The idea develops out of the shields on the family tomb in line 198.

206 *Some loathsome dash* a sign on the coat-of-arms indicating some disgrace, e.g. a baton sinister

207 *cipher me.* (To show forth how foolishly I was infatuated.)

208 *That* so that

*note* sign

214 *toy* a trifle

216 *but* only

220 *Post* hasten. Cf. line 1.

221 *engirt* encompassed

224 *ever-during* everlasting

226 *thou.* Tarquin is addressing posterity or the reader.

229 *doth still exceed* is always greater

235 *to work upon his wife* fulfil itself against

236 *quittal* requital

237 *as he is my kinsman.* Cf. Macbeth's similar debate with himself concerning the killing of Duncan (I, vii, 13): 'First, as I am his kinsman'.

239– This succession of statements and counter-statements is a stan-
42   dard figure of rhetoric that George Puttenham called 'Anti-pophora or the figure of Response'. It was familiar from its use in Senecan tragedy and from Kyd's *Spanish Tragedy* (II, i, 19–28). Cf. *Richard III* (V, iii, 183–93).

243 *will.* See the commentary to line 128.

*past reason's weak removing* beyond the power of weak reason to control. Cf. line 614.

244 *sentence* a moral maxim, the Latin *sententia*

*saw* saying, proverb. See *As You Like It* (II, vii, 156): 'Full of wise saws and modern instances'.

245 *a painted cloth* a wall hanging, either tapestry or painted. Cf. *Macbeth* (II, ii, 53–4): ' 'Tis the eye of childhood / That fears a painted devil', and the picture of the fall of Troy, lines 1366ff. Such pictures often involved moral themes.

246 *graceless* unworthily, with the suggestion of lacking the grace of God.

247 *frozen* numb, inactive

248 *dispensation*. 'A licence granted by ecclesiastical authority to do what is normally forbidden' (*OED*). By means of the form of rational argument, Tarquin justifies his desire to do evil.

249 *Urging . . . vantage* presenting the worst intention in the most favourable light

251 *effects* purposes and results

258 *lawn* fine linen

259 *took* being taken

262 *rocked*. Presumably the theme has changed from the trembling of her hand to the beating of her heart.

265 *Narcissus*. See the commentary to lines 161–2 of *Venus*.

267 *colour* pretext

269 *Poor wretches*. (Weak spirited people feel compunction in committing little wrongs.)

270 *shadows* things in the imagination only, which have no real existence

271 *Affection* passion, desire

273 *The coward fights* even the coward fights

274 *avaunt* be gone
*debating die* let this inner debate stop

275 *Respect* cautious prudence
*wait* let them wait.

276 *countermand* oppose the commands given by. The same debate between the eye and the heart, the eye of reason and of sense, continues in lines 288–95.

277 *Sad pause . . . the sage*. (Sober delay and deep consideration suit the wisdom of age.)

278 *My part is Youth*. Shakespeare is here drawing on the tradition of the Morality Play and Interlude for his metaphor, although no specific source has been found. See the Introduction, p. 34.

279 *Desire my pilot*. This is a common sonnet image, taken from

Petrarch. Compare Wyatt's sonnet 'My Galy Charged with Forgetfulnes' and Spenser's *Amoretti* (34).

281   *heedful* taking heed of the consequences

283   *he* Tarquin

284   *fond mistrust* foolish misgivings. 'Foolish' either because they seem foolish to Tarquin, or because he has been foolish to get himself into such a position where they occur.

285   *servitors* attendants

286   *cross* frustrate, pull in different directions

287   *league* truce, peace, an image which leads on to the long military metaphor of invasion and siege that is used to describe the rape.

288–  The image of Collatine restrains the mad desire aroused by the
94    image of Lucrece, until he looks into his heart which, being already corrupted, encourages him on in his lustful desires. Cf. lines 368–9.

290   *That eye*. Cf. line 369.

295   *his servile powers* his senses

296   *their leader's jocund show* the heart's high-spirited encouragement

297   *Stuff up* fill out

299   *Paying more slavish tribute than they owe*. (Flattered by the heart's approval, the senses play up to it and become even more uncontrollable than they normally would be.)

300   *reprobate* morally depraved

303   *ward*. The indentations in a lock designed to prevent any but the right key from opening it (*OED*). Also conveying the sense of 'guard'.

304   *rate* scold, by their creaking

305   *regard* heed

306   *The threshold grates the door*. The threshold scrapes against the door with a jarring sound to draw attention to him.

307   *Night-wandering weasels*. Traditionally beasts of ill omen and, like Tarquin, robbers of nests. They were kept in Roman houses to kill vermin (Prince).

308   *his fear* the course of action that frightens him, even though he still pursues it

313   *his conduct* his guide, the torch

315   *Puffs forth*. He relights the torch by blowing on it.

318   *rushes* normally used to strew the floors of Elizabethan chambers

319   *griping* grasping

320   *wanton tricks* 'such as dropping a glove for a man to pick up' (Lever)

321  *inured* accustomed

324  *consters* construes, interprets

326  *accidental things of trial*  merely chance occurrences that test his resolution

327  *those bars* the marks for the minutes on a clock face

328  *Who with . . . let.* The bars seem to hinder (let) his course and cause the clock hand to linger over them.

330  *lets* hindrances
     *attend the time* inevitably accompany the occasion

332  *prime* spring

333  *sneapèd* pinched with cold

334  *income* achievement, harvesting. (Pain is the price we pay for every success.)

335  *shelves* sand-banks

341–  *So from himself . . . begin.* His impiety has carried him so far from
2    his better self that he begins to pray for the success of his crime.

342  *prey to pray.* Cf. line 346.

343  *countenance* favour, support

346  *compass* encompass
     *fair fair.* Cf. 'prey . . . pray' in line 342. Within five lines Shakespeare introduces two unusually crude verbal jingles, perhaps to suggest the loss of standards and sensitivity in Tarquin when he is 'so from himself'.

347  *they* the heavens

348  *starts* flinches, recoils suddenly

349  *fact* deed

355  *hath dissolution* is melted

356  *The eye of heaven is out.* Cf. *Macbeth* (II, i, 4–5): 'There's husbandry in heaven; / Their candles are all out'. There is the same association of darkness and sin.

364  *mortal sting* a continuation of the serpent image of line 362, but there is also a sexual connotation. See *Othello* (I, iii, 336): 'our carnal stings'.
     *mortal* deadly

365  *stalks* like a fowler creeping up on a bird. The word was commonly associated with clandestine sexual encounters. See 'Lucrece' in Chaucer's, *The Legend of Good Women*: 'And in the nyght ful thefly gan he stalke'. See also Wyatt: 'They fle from me that sometyme did me seke / With naked fote stalking in my chambre.'

367  *curtains* the curtains drawn around an Elizabethan four-posted bed

369  *By their high treason* the treason of the greedy eyes that undermine the proper moral government of the heart. Cf. line 290.

370  *watchword* signal to attack

371  *To draw the cloud* pull back the curtains

372  *Look as* just as. Cf. line 694.

373  *bereaves* takes away

375  *wink* blink, shut

376  *reflects* shines

377  *supposed* imagined

380  *period* end

383  *this blessèd league* between Collatine and Lucrece

384  *to their sight* because of what they see

387  *Cozening* cheating, robbing

388  *Who* the pillow

389  *Swelling* as in anger
     *to want* at the lack of

391  *monument* like an effigy on a tomb that often showed the head resting on a pillow

392  *unhallowed* profane

393  *Without* outside

397  *marigolds*. These shut at night. See *The Winter's Tale* (IV, iv, 105): 'The marigold, that goes to bed wi' th' sun'.

402  *the map of death* the picture, image, of death, i.e., sleep. Her breathing, revealed by the movement of her hair, shows that she is asleep, not dead.

403  *life's mortality* mortal life

404  *each* i.e. life and death

407–  *ivory globes circled with blue . . . unconquerèd*. Prince suggests that
8     Shakespeare was influenced here by Marlowe's *Hero and Leander* (II, 273–6): 'For though the rising ivory mount he scaled, / Which is with azure circling lines empaled, / Much like a globe (a globe may I term this), / By which love sails to regions full of bliss.' However, Shakespeare has eliminated Marlowe's witty conceit and made the image more simply sensuous.

408  *maiden* chaste

409  *Save of* except for that of her husband

411  *These worlds* the globes of her breasts

413  *the owner* Collatine

417   *will his wilful*. See the commentary to line 128.
      *tired* glutted

419   *alabaster*. 'alablaster' in Q.

424   *qualified* moderated, diminished

425   *Slacked*. 'Slakt' in Q; 'Slaked' (Lever). 'Slake' is an earlier and
      alternative form of 'slack' (Maxwell).

426–  The very extended metaphor of military invasion and conquest
45    that begins here is an application and perversion of the common
      sonnet image of the siege of the fort of love which carries further
      religious associations with it. See the morality play *The Castle
      of Perseverance* or Donne's *Holy Sonnet* XIV, 'Batter My
      Heart'.

426–  *His eye . . . his veins*. The sight of Lucrece, which at first
7     tempered his unruly desires, now kindles an even greater uproar
      in them.

428   *straggling slaves* undisciplined camp-followers

429   *effecting* performing, carrying out. The line is slightly ambigu-
      ous, because the order to carry out the 'fell exploits' and to 'do
      their liking' is not given until line 434. If 'effecting' is retained,
      therefore, it must refer to the normal nature of camp-followers
      who perform evil deeds, delight in ravishing, etc. Steevens's
      emendation, 'affecting', is an attractive one, if it is used in the
      sense of 'liking', being inclined towards. Cf. *King Lear* (I, i,
      1–2): 'I thought the King had more affected the Duke of /
      Albany than Cornwall.'

433   *alarum* the call to arms sounded by the drum

436   *commends the leading* entrusts the initiation of the action

442   *They* the ranks of the blue veins, i.e. the blood
      *mustering* assembling
      *the quiet cabinet* Lucrece's heart, where the understanding has its
      seat.

446   *She* Lucrece

448   *his* Tarquin's

453   *in worser taking* in a worse state of alarm

454   *heedfully* with full awareness

455   *supposèd* imagined

456   *Wrapped* enveloped, with play on 'rapt', carrying some of its
      Latin sense of *raptus*, seized, raped. 'wrapt' in Q.

458   *winking* even with her eyes shut

459   *antics* grotesque figures

462   *daunts* frightens

464    *ram* battering-ram. This is a further extension of the siege image, as is 'poor citizen' in the next line, helpless in a besieged town.

467    *Beating her bulk* shaking her breasts by its beating

470    *trumpet* trumpeter, herald

471    *To sound a parley* sound the trumpet that summons the defenders to the walls

       *heartless* dispirited, terrified

472    *peers* shows a little

474    *dumb demeanour* expression and gesture

476    *colour* pretext. Tarquin takes up the term in its literal sense in line 477, the 'colour in thy face'. In line 481 'colour' is used in a martial metaphor and becomes the flag under which his forces attack.

478    *for anger* out of envy

485    *ensnared thee* caused this night to be the trap in which you are caught

491    *crosses* hostile consequences

492    *defends* See the commentary to line 126.

493    *think* am aware

494    *counsel* consideration, thought

495    *Will* desire, as used throughout. See the Commentary to line 128.

       *heedful* cautious, circumspect

497    *looks* looks at

500    *affection's* passion's, love's

502    *ensue* follow

506    *falcon*. There is a pun here on 'falchion' in line 509, his 'Roman blade'.

507    *Coucheth* causes to cower.

508    *Whose* the falcon's

       *he* the cowering bird below

509    *insulting* triumphing scornfully

511    *bells*. These are bells attached to the feet of falcons to indicate their position when they bring down their prey.

516    *To kill . . . decay* to destroy your honour and your life at the same time

522    *blurred* blotted

       *nameless bastardy*. 'Nameless, because an illegitimate child has no name by inheritance, being considered by the law as *nullius filius*' (Malone).

524    *cited up* called to mind

529    *policy*. This is a term strongly associated with Machiavellianism. The end justifies the means and a small evil is sanctioned if committed with a good end in view.

530    *simple* a single herb used for medical purposes
      *compacted* compounded with others to form a wholesome medicine

534    *Tender* regard favourably

535    *device* contrivance

537    *slavish wipe* the brand with which slaves were marked
      *birth-hour's blot* birth-mark

538    *For marks described in men's nativity* blemishes that are there at birth. Tarquin assails Lucrece with an assortment of arguments that contradict each other, suggesting at line 528 that the act would be virtuous, while at lines 535–7, exploiting the fact that it is shameful and irredeemable.

540    *cockatrice'* a basilisk, a mythological beast credited with the power to kill with the beams from its eyes

542    *the picture* image

543    *gripe's* vulture or eagle.

544    *Pleads . . . laws*. Lever points out that the words imply a crime on both personal and social/legal levels. Similarly 'gentle' in line 546 suggests 'kind' and also 'civilized'.

548    *aspiring* mounting high

549–  *gust . . . blow*. A singular noun is used with a plural verb. The
50     reverse is true with 'her words delays' in line 552.

550    *biding* abode, position

551    *present fall* immediate downpour

553    *moody Pluto*. In Greek myth, Orpheus descended into the underworld and played his lyre so sweetly that the god Pluto, its overlord, slept, and Eurydice was able to escape. The image of the underworld develops out of that of 'earth's dark womb' in line 549.

554    *dally* play as a cat with a mouse

556    *sad* sober, serious, opposed to 'folly'
      *vulture* devouring, preying on flesh

557    *wanteth* still wants more

558    *admits* allows to enter

559    *penetrable* that can be penetrated
      *plaining* lamenting

562    *remorseless* pitiless

565    *period* full stop. In her emotion she breaks off her sentences in the wrong place.

569    *gentry* courtesy

570    *untimely* unfitting, which should never have been caused

571    *troth* good faith and honesty

573    *borrowed bed* the bed which, as a guest, he has been given
      *make retire* make a retreat

574    *stoop to* bow, submit to

576    *pretended* purposed

577    *Mud not* don't muddy. Cf. Sonnet 35 (line 2): 'Roses have thorns, and silver fountains mud'.

579    *shoot* act of shooting. (Change your aim before you actually shoot.)

580    *woodman* sportsman, hunter

581    *unseasonable* out of season for hunting

590    *wrack-threatening* threatening wreck

592    *convert* change

595    *Soft pity* 'Pity can make its way into the hardest heart' (Lever).

597    *put on his shape*. Lucrece suggests that she is addressing an evil spirit who has assumed Tarquin's shape. Hence 'To all the host of heaven' in line 598.

598    Q has a full stop after 'complain me', but most editors omit this and link 'Thou art not what thou seem'st' with the earlier accusation that an evil spirit has taken on Tarquin's appearance.

600    *if the same*. (If you are what you appear to be, you don't behave in a manner appropriate to what you actually are, a king.)

602    *govern every thing* including their own passions

603    *be seeded* bear fruit

605    *If thy hope*. (When you are still only the heir without the full powers of kingship.)

608    *vassal actors* subjects of inferior rank

609    *hid in clay* even after death

610    *for* out of

611    *still* always

613    *like offences prove*. Cf. Angelo's self-accusation in *Measure for Measure* (II, ii, 176–7): 'Thieves for their robbery have authority / When judges steal themselves'.

614    *remove* control. Cf. line 243.

615    *glass* mirror, reflecting an image of how one ought to appear. Cf. *Hamlet* (III, i, 154): 'the glass of fashion'.

618    *read lectures* learn lessons, gain instruction

621    *To privilege* give special privilege to

622    *back'st reproach* give backing to disgrace
      *laud* praise

624    *By him that gave it thee* God

629    *patterned by thy fault* with your fault as a pattern

634    *partially* out of partiality to themselves

637    *askance* turn away

639    *thy rash relier* on which you rashly rely. However, it could mean
      'lust which is rash to rely on you since you may control it'.

640    *repeal* recall from exile

641    *flattering thoughts*. 'Flatterers are traditionally the worst enemies
      of kings' (Maxwell).

642    *respect* consideration for virtue

643    *eyne* eyes

646    *let* hindrance, delay

648    *fret* rage

650    *salt sovereign* the sea

657    *hearsed* enclosed as in a tomb

659    *these slaves* i.e. lust, dishonour, etc.

668    *enforcèd* using force

669    *coy* gentle and delicate

670    *despitefully* cruelly and with malice

671    *rascal* a rascal was an inferior deer in the herd, hence base, mean
      *groom* inferior servant

680    *nightly linen*. Nightdresses were not generally worn in
      Shakespeare's day, and this may refer to a linen stole or shawl
      worn round the head and shoulders, with which Tarquin stifles
      her cries

681    *pens* shuts in, stifles. This is a continuation of the pastoral
      metaphor in lines 677–9: 'lamb', 'fleece', 'fold'.

684    *prone* eager, but also carrying the physical sense of lying face
      downwards

685    *could weeping purify* if weeping could purify them

689    *This forcèd league* union by force between Tarquin and Lucrece

694    *Look as*. See line 372.
      *gorgèd* over-full

695    *unapt* unfit, disinclined
      *tender smell* delicate scent difficult to follow

696    *balk* let slip

700    *Devours his will* his lust is destroyed by being satisfied

701    *bottomless conceit* infinite thought

702 *still* continual

703 *vomit his receipt* spew up what it has received, i.e. be surfeited with pleasure until sick of it

705 *exclamation* denunciation

707 *jade* poor horse
*Self-will* lust, driven on by its own energies without external prompting

710 *recreant* like a coward

711 *wails* bewails

713 *there* in the pride of the flesh

714 *The guilty rebel* desire
*remission* pardon, remission of sins

715 *faultful* full of sin

716 *this accomplishment* i.e. the rape

717 *doom* judgement

719 *his soul's fair temple* his body. See I Corinthians (3:16): 'Know ye not that ye are the temple of God, and that the Spirit of God dwelleth in you?'

721 *the spotted princess* his soul, defiled by sin

722 *She* his soul
*her subjects* the senses and passions

724 *mortal* deadly, death-giving

725 *Thrall* slave

727 *Which* her subjects, the senses
*prescience*. The word normally means foresight, but here it implies the knowledge and purity that the soul formerly possessed, which was sufficient at that time to control the senses but not to anticipate their later rebellion.

732 *despite of cure* in spite of all remedies

733 *spoil* prey, victim
*perplexed* bewildered, distraught. The word carried a stronger meaning than it does now.

740 *faintly* like a coward

741 *exclaiming on* crying out against. Cf. line 757.

743 *convertite* penitent

744 *castaway* lost soul

747 *scapes* transgressions

750 *They*. (My true eyes.)
*not but that* no other than that

755 *grave* engrave, as aqua fortis eats into steel

757 *exclaims against*. See line 741.

761   *chest.* A double meaning: her breast, and a coffer fit to enclose a mind as pure as hers still remains

762   *spite* anger, vexation

765   *notary* recorder

766   *Black stage.* Malone comments that the Elizabethan stage was hung with black for tragedies

767   *blame* evil

768   *harbour for defame* shelter for disgrace

770   *close-tongued* speaking in secret

772   *cureless* beyond cure

774   *proportioned* regular

776   *wonted* customary, usual

780   *The life of purity* the source of all purity, i.e. the sun

781   *noontide prick* the mark on a sundial where the shadow of the gnomon falls at noon

786   *The silver-shining queen* Diana, the moon goddess of virginity and chastity
     *distain* stain, defile

787   *twinkling handmaids* the stars

791   *palmer's chat* the conversation among pilgrims as they make their way to the Holy Land

793   *cross their arms* a traditional and recognized sign of melancholy and grief

794   *To mask their brows* pull their hats down over their eyes

796   *seasoning . . . brine* adding salt in the form of salt tears

798   *wasting monuments* short-lived tokens of griefs which themselves are long-lasting

800   *jealous* suspicious
     *that face* i.e. Lucrece's

803   *still* ever

805   *sepulchred* buried

811   *cipher* decipher

812   *quote* observe. 'cote' in Q, an obsolete form of 'quote'.

816   *Will couple my reproach.* (Will think of my disgrace whenever they think of Tarquin's shame.)

817   *Feast-finding minstrels* travelling minstrels who seek out feasts where they will be employed as entertainers
     *tuning my defame* turning my dishonour into song

818   *tie* hold the attention of

820   *that senseless reputation* a reputation 'unspotted' by sensual sin

822   *a theme for disputation.* A 'theme' was the technical name given to

a proposition or a 'sentence' that would be the subject for debate by students at school or university as a part of their normal training in rhetoric.

823  *another root* that of Collatine, in addition to Lucrece's

825  *attaint* stain

828  *unfelt* not felt by the senses
*crest-wounding* a private scar that yet damages the family honour, the heraldic crest

830  *mot* motto or device beneath the crest in a coat of arms

831  *How he* i.e. Collatine

832  *such shameful blows* a very traditional comment on cuckoldry. Cf. *Othello* (IV, i, 68–70).

835  *bereft* robbed

841  *wrack* wreck

843  *put him back* send him away

848  *intrude* break into

852  *behests* commands

855  *coffers up* shuts up in a coffer

858  *still-pining Tantalus.* This is a common Renaissance emblem of the miser who cannot enjoy the riches he has collected. For a description, see the account of Tantalus in the Mammon's Cave episode in the *Fairie Queene* (II, vii, 57–60). Also see Baldwin (pp. 133–6). The image of 'still-pining' (ever-hungry) Tantalus reiterates the constant theme throughout of the desire for possession that destroys its own pleasure in achieving it. Cf. lines 905 and 1115.

859  *barns* shuts up in a barn. Lever suggests a reference to Luke 12:16–21, the parable of the covetous man.

864  *presently* immediately

867–  *The sweets we wish for . . .* Cf. Sonnet 129 (line 5): 'Enjoyed no
8     sooner but despisèd straight'.

874  *ill-annexèd* evilly attached; accidental circumstances that will pervert what is intrinsically good to evil

877  *execut'st* brings about by providing the occasion

879  *point'st* (Maxwell) appointest. 'poinst' in Q. 'points' (Lever and later quartos).

882  *seize.* 'ceaze' in Q. A possible pun on 'cease'.

885  *troth* faith

887  *displacest laud* bestow praise in the wrong place

892  *smoothing* flattering
*ragged* damaged

899    *sort* choose out

902    *halt* crippled, but here probably used as a verb: to limp or creep

905    *pines* starves. Cf. lines 858 and 1115.

907    *Advice* Medical advice, but as this repeats line 904, it may have a more general application. Malone suggests: 'While infection is spreading, the grave rulers of the state, that ought to guard against its further progress, are careless and inattentive.'

912    *crosses* obstacles
       *from thy aid* from being helped by you

913    *They buy thy help.* Truth and virtue have to pay for a favourable opportunity, but sin can always find an opportunity without having to offer a bribe.

914    *gratis* without a fee
       *appaid* satisfied

916    *else* otherwise

917    *stayed* held back

919    *subornation* procuring a person to commit an evil action

920    *shift* trickery. Cf. line 930.

922    *by thine inclination* by your very nature and disposition

924    *the general doom* the Day of Judgement

925    *copesmate* companion, accessory

926    *post* courier
       *carrier.* An extension of the image of 'post': someone who delivers goods, parcels, etc. Cf. Milton's 'On the University Carrier'. The image is picked up again at line 928: 'sin's pack-horse'.

927    *Eater of youth.* Cf. Sonnet 19, 'Devouring Time' and Sonnet 60: 'Time doth transfix the flourish set on youth, / And delves the parallels in beauty's brow, / Feeds on the rarities of nature's truth'. These are all derived ultimately from Ovid's '*tempus edax rerum*' ('time, consumer of all things').

928    *watch* either a clockface or the cry of the watchman that marks the passing of the hours. Cf. *Macbeth* (II, i, 53–4): '. . . the wolf, / Whose howl's his watch'.

929    *Thou nursest all.* (Time brings everything to birth and to death.)

930    *shifting* moving, with the suggestion of trickery and deceit. Cf. line 920.

934    *fortunes* good fortune. Cf. line 729.

935    *endless date* a bond with sorrow with no 'date of expiry'

936    *office* function
       *fine.* The word carries several contradictory meanings, all

descriptive of the varied activities of time: to bring to an end, to refine and temper, to punish. All meanings are probably present in this context.

937    *opinion*. Used in the Platonic sense here: belief based on inadequate knowledge.

938    *spend the dowry* dissipate the riches of marriage, as it has done in the case of Lucrece

942    *sentinel* guard and control, i.e. see that night does not exceed its proper hours

944    *To ruinate proud buildings with thy hours*. See Sonnet 64: 'When I have seen by Time's fell hand defaced / The rich proud cost of outworn buried age'.

947    *To feed oblivion* to consign things to oblivion by destroying them

948    *To blot old books and alter their contents*. Not only the loss that comes from the physical decay of old books, but the loss of their original meanings through changes in the language and in semantics. This is a common lament from Chaucer onwards. See Chaucer's *Troilus and Criseyde* (II, 22ff).

949    *ancient ravens' wings* for the longevity of ravens, see the 'trebledated crow' of 'The Phoenix and Turtle', line 17.

950    *cherish springs* raise up new growth

952    *Fortune's wheel* the most traditional of all emblems of mutability and perpetual change from success to decay or vice versa

953    *beldame* old woman, grandmother. Cf. line 1458.

954    *To make the child a man, the man a child* the progress from first to second childhood

955– . 
6    *To slay the tiger . . . lion wild*. Cf. Sonnet 19, lines 1–3.

957    *To mock the subtle* mock those who are taken in by their own oversubtle interpretations.

959    *waste* wear away

962    *retiring* returning, allowing one to put the clock back and avoid one's previous mistakes; as in line 964, allowing a second chance to a man who has lent money unwisely

967    *lackey* footman employed to lead the way when travelling at night through city streets. Time conducts the traveller on his journey to eternity. Cf. *Macbeth* (V, v, 22–3): 'And all our yesterdays have lighted fools / The way to dusty death' (Lever).

968    *cross* hinder

973    *Shape every bush* make every bush appear to him . . . Cf. *A*

*Midsummer Night's Dream* (V, i, 22): 'How easy is a bush supposed a bear!'

975 *bedrid* bedridden. 'bedred' in Q.

976 *bechance* happen by chance

981 *curlèd hair* the fashionable Italianate Elizabethan style. Cf. *Othello* (I, ii, 68): 'The wealthy curled darlings of our Nation'.

985 *orts* scraps of food left on the plate. Cf. *Troilus and Cressida* (V, ii, 154): 'The fractions of her faith, orts of her love'.

989 *resort* visit him for the purpose of mocking him

993 *unrecalling* that which cannot be undone, recalled

1001 *deathsman* executioner

1003 *his hope* position as heir

1007 *presently* immediately.

1008 *list* please

1010 *unperceived* without the black mud being noticed

1013 *grooms* servants, subjects
     *sightless* where nothing can be seen

1017 *arbitrators* umpires unable to arbitrate and direct the outcome

1018 *skill-contending* academic debates more concerned to show off skill than to reach the truth

1020 *trembling clients* suitors who depend upon the words of the law (and the skill of the advocate)

1021 *force not argument a straw* care not a straw for argument

1025 *cavil* raise frivolous objections to

1026 *spurn.* (Kick against my irrevocable disgrace.)

1027 *helpless* unhelpful, but also suggesting feeble, weak

1028 *The remedy . . . defilèd blood.* Blood-letting to remove the cor-
-9    rupted blood was standard treatment for illness. Lucrece sees suicide as a healthful cure.

1033 *in my defame* sharing my shame or, perhaps, causing it by failing to perform your duty of killing me

1034 *loyal* virtuous and chaste

1035 *afeard* afraid. A reference to the fact that she did not resist for fear of Tarquin's blackmail.

1037 *betumbled* disordered, possibly with sexual suggestions. Cf. *Antony and Cleopatra* (I, iv, 17): 'to tumble in the bed of Ptolomy'.

1039 *no-slaughterhouse.* Q has no hyphen.
     *imparteth* affords

1042 *consumes* is swallowed up

1043 *fumes* smokes

1045 *mean* means

1050 *true type* true title

1053 *To clear this spot* to remove this moral stain

1054 *A badge of fame* the insignia of their master worn by servants on their livery. In this case the dishonoured livery of ill-repute will be ennobled by the badge of honour.

1057 *To burn the guiltless casket* to kill the innocent body when its chastity has been destroyed. Cf. the same image in line 761. At this point even Lucrece seems to be in some doubt about the value of committing suicide: 'Poor helpless help' in the previous line is a remedy that doesn't really help.

1061 *infringèd* violated

1062 *This bastard graff* a graft inserted into another stock, i.e. a possible child from the rape

1067 *interest* property, ownership

1070 *dispense* condone, pardon

1071 *acquit* atone for

1973 *fold* wrap up
*cleanly-coined* cleverly forged so as to appear like the truth

1074 *sable ground* the background of a shield on which the heraldic signs are painted

1079 *lamenting Philomel.* In Ovid's *Metamorphoses* (V I) Philomela was raped by Tereus and transformed into a nightingale, in which fc ꞈ she sings her grief through the night. A myth very relevant to Lucrece.

1084 *cloudy* sorrowful. Cf. *Venus*, line 725: 'Make modest Dian cloudy and forlorn'.
*shames herself* is ashamed to see herself

1091 *Brand not my forehead* reference to the branding of harlots. Cf. *Hamlet* (III, iv, 40–45): 'Such an act / . . . takes off the rose / From the fair forehead of an innocent love / And sets a blister there'.

1092 *to do* to do with

1096 *bear them mild* make less display since they have become familiar through 'continuance'

1097 *the other* infant sorrows

1103 *No object . . .* (Every object serves to renew her passion since she applies it to herself.)

1109 *search the bottom* probe to the depths of. 'search' is commonly used to describe the probing of a wound.
*annoy* grief

1112 *feelingly sufficed* satisfied in its feelings

1113 *with like semblance* when it is answered by something in sympathy with itself

1114 *ken* sight

1115 *pines* See lines 858 and 905.

1116 *salve* healing ointment

1117 *at that* at that which

1119 *Who* the gentle flood that o'erflows
  *the bounding bank* the bank that confines it

1120 *dallied with* played, trifled with

1121 *entomb* keep shut up

1124 The song of the little birds reminds Lucrece of the song of the
−41 nightingale and of Philomel, whose fate resembles her own. She embarks on a long series of musical metaphors, many of them involving puns, to emphasize the parallel: the 'stops' and 'rests' of their song would interrupt the 'restless' (unresting) flow of her 'discord' (line 1124); 'Relish' (line 1126) is to warble; 'dumps' (line 1127) is a technical term for doleful tunes that has become a metaphor for melancholy ('down in the dumps'); 'strain' (line 1131) is a phrase of a musical composition (cf. *Twelfth Night*, I, i, 4: 'That strain again'); 'diapason' (line 1132) is a tune in the base in concord with the line of the air in the treble; 'burden-wise' (line 1133), as in a burden or base undersong (cf. *The Tempest*, I, ii, 382: 'And, sweet sprites, the burden bear'). Lucrece will bear the burden − sing the base line − while Philomel 'descants' − sings the higher part with better skill. The two lines of song will harmonize because they are inspired by the common grief of rape.

1135 *against a thorn*. A reference to the traditional myth that the nightingale keeps herself awake so that she can sing all night by leaning her breast upon a thorn.
  *bears't thy part* sing your part in the duet

1140 *means* as well as its usual general meaning, the name for the middle register in music between treble and base
  *frets* ridges of wood on the finger-board of a string instrument by which the fingering is regulated. Cf. *Hamlet* (III, ii, 356−7) for the same pun: 'though you can fret me, you cannot play upon me'.

1141 *heart-strings* the final double meaning of the sequence

1142 *And for* and because

1143 *As shaming* being ashamed

1144 *seated from the way* situated out of the way

1147 *kinds* natures. Music was supposed to soften the natures of animals and men alike. See the myth of Orpheus, whose music tamed wild beasts.

1149 *stands at gaze*. A term from hunting: in the attitude of gazing.

1155 *death reproach's debtor* death would incur reproach

1160 *conclusion* experiment

1167 *pilled* peeled

1169 *her bark* her body

1170 *Her house* the soul's

1172 *Her sacred temple*. See line 719.

1175 *this blemished fort*. Following on from 'house . . . mansion . . . temple' (lines 1170–73), the image of the siege used so extensively in relation to Tarquin is now used for Lucrece at the receiving end.

1181 The testament, or will, is a literary convention that goes back to the Middle Ages. Cf. Troilus's will in Chaucer's *Troilus and Criseyde* (V, 305ff) and Donne's 'The Will', written at about the time of *Lucrece*.

1186 *deprive* take away

1188 *So of shame's ashes*. An allusion to the myth of the phoenix and the birth of the new out of the ashes of the old.

1191 *that dear jewel* chastity

1198 *abridgement* précis, shortened version

1203 *disbursèd* paid out, 'unpursed'

1205 *oversee* check the execution of the will

1206 *overseen* deceived

1208 *free* atone for

1214 *untuned* having lost its melody

1215 *hies* hastens

1216 *with thought's feathers* as swift as thought

1218 *meads* meadows

1219 *demure* modest

1221 *sorts* suits

1222 *For why* because

1224 *her two suns* her eyes

1226 *as the earth does weep* i.e. the dews of night

1229 *Her circled eyne* rounded, or perhaps circled with red

1231 *salt-waved ocean* her salt tears

1234 *conduits* pipes for the distribution of water, often culminating in a human figure through the mouth of which the water poured.

Cf. Donne's metaphor for preachers in *Satyre* I (5): 'God's conduits'.

1235 *justly* with proper cause, i.e. Lucrece
*takes in hand* acknowledges no reason except to keep her mistress company in weeping

1241 *as marble will* as the harder marble of men chooses to stamp a shape upon them

1242 *strange kinds* natures different from their own

1247 *champaign* flat and open

1248 *Lays open* exposes

1250 *Cave-keeping* that live hidden in caves

1251 *mote* minute spot

1253 *books* in which their faults can be read

1254 *No man inveigh* let no man inveigh

1257 *hild* (Q). Used instead of 'held' for the sake of the rhyme.

1258 *fulfilled* filled full

1259 *lords to blame . . . to their shame* as if shame were the estate of
-60 which men were the overlords and women were the helpless tenants

1261 *The precedent.* (See the example of this in Lucrece.)

1262 *with circumstances strong* faced with the strong threat of immediate death

1263 *and shame that might ensue* from Tarquin's threat to kill a slave in the bed with her

1266 *dying fear* paralysing fear. In Chaucer's *The Legend of Good Women*, Lucrece actually faints, 'in a swogh she lay, and wex so ded'.

1269 *the poor counterfeit* her maid, who imitates her in weeping

1272 *of my sustaining* which I sustain

1273 *it small avails* it does little to help my grief

1275 *stayed* paused

1279 *dispense* excuse

1298 *Conceit* the thought of how best to write

1299 *wit* reason
*will* in this case, feeling emotion

1300 *curious-good* done with too much art

1302 *which shall go before* which idea shall be expressed first

1307 *present* immediate

1309 *tedious.* For a different use of the same antithesis, see *A Midsummer Night's Dream* (V, i, 56): 'A tedious brief scene'.

1310 *tenor* summary, statement. 'tenure' in Q, an alternative spelling

1311 *uncertainly* without precise definition

1312 *schedule* account, summary

1314 *make discovery* uncover the whole story

1315 *her own gross abuse* lest he should think it her own fault

1316 *stained her stained excuse* before she had given colour to – i.e. vindicated – her explanation of her 'stain' by shedding her own blood

1319 *grace the fashion* set in a good light the appearance of her disgrace

1323 *become* adorn, make more acceptable

1326 *The heavy motion.* Malone suggests that 'motion' carried the meaning of dumb-show or puppet show, with the metaphor extended into 'every part'. The person who spoke for the puppets was called an 'interpreter'. Here the metaphor is reversed: it is the eye that interprets to the ear, not the ear to the eye.

1329 *sounds* straits, channels, with a pun on the normal use of the word

1333 *post* messenger

1334 *sour-faced* solemn, sober-faced

1338 *villain* servant, villein
*curtsies.* 'cursies' in Q.

1339 *on her* as he looks at her
*with a steadfast eye* with his eyes fixed firmly on her

1345 *silly* simple
*God wot* God knows

1348 *To talk in deeds* show true respect by deeds rather than words
*saucily* impertinently

1350 *pattern* example
*worn-out age* age gone by. Cf. the description of Adam in *As You Like It* (II, iii, 56ff).

1351 *Pawned . . . gage.* (Pledged his loyalty by honest looks, not words.)

1355 *wistly* earnestly

1359 *But long.* She thinks the time goes slowly.

1361 *entertain* occupy, fill in

1363 *So* so much

1364 *stay* stop

1366 *a piece / Of skilful painting.* Probably a painted cloth rather than a
–7 tapestry. There is no need to assume that Shakespeare had an actual picture in mind, and it is difficult to conceive of even a Renaissance picture containing so much of the Troy story. The

idea could have been suggested by the *Aeneid* (I, 455–93), where Aeneas admires the picture of the Trojan war in Dido's temple to Juno. Virgil's picture has the same extended narrative content as Shakespeare's, both like that of a strip cartoon, but the account shows none of the interest in the techniques of painting that is found in the *Lucrece* sequence.

1367 *for* of

1368 *drawn* drawn up

1370 *Ilion* Troy. Cf. Marlowe's *Dr Faustus* (V, i, 100): 'the topless towers of Ilium'.

1371 *conceited* clever, ingenious

1374 *In scorn of nature art gave lifeless life.* (Art seemed to outshine nature by making things without life look more living than reality.)

1375 *a dry drop* a painted tear

1377 *reeked* seemed to smell like the real thing
*the painter's strife* the struggle of art to rival nature

1380 *pioneer* sappers who dig trenches and mines, etc. Cf. *Hamlet* (I, v, 163): 'A worthy pioner!'.

1384 *lust* pleasure

1385 *observance* observation of detail

1389 *quick bearing* lively behaviour

1390 *interlaces* interweaves

1392 *heartless* without courage

1394 *Ajax and Ulysses.* The traditional qualities associated with the Greek warriors are treated more fully in *Troilus and Cressida*.

1395 *physiognomy* the art (or science) of recognizing character from the details of the face

1396 *ciphered* expressed, revealed

1400 *regard* thoughtfulness
*smiling government.* This implies both his own assured self-control and his ability to govern others without force.

1401 *Nestor.* See the commentary to line 1394.

1407 *purled* curled

1411 *mermaid.* For the siren song of the mermaids, see the commentary to line 429 of *Venus*.

1412 *high . . . low* tall . . . short
*nice* accurate, precise

1414 *to mock the mind* the suggestion that art feigns and deceives by making stationary things appear to move

1417 *thronged* crushed by the crowd

*bollen* swollen

1418 *pelt* call out angrily

1420 *but for loss of* if it hadn't meant missing Nestor's speech

1422 *imaginary* work of imagination and making appeal to it

1423 *Conceit deceitful* conceptions of art that deceived by looking real.
*compact* well composed
*kind* natural

1424 *That for Achilles' image . . . imaginèd.* Lever notes that the
−8 passage may have been suggested by the account of the Greek
scholar, Philostratus the Elder, born about A D 190, in his work
*Imagines* (Loeb), where he mentions a painting of soldiers, 'some
with the legs hidden, others from the waist up . . . heads only
. . . finally just spear points . . . This, my boy is perspective,
since the problem is to deceive the eye' (I, 4). This work was
well known to the Elizabethans, and was 'required reading' at St
John's College, Oxford, where Thomas Jenkins, the principal
master at Stratford grammar school, had studied. Shakespeare
may have come across the description in his school-days.

1429 *strong-besiegèd* strongly besieged

1433 *such odd action* such ambiguous gestures and attitudes

1434 *through their light* because of these gestures, fear was revealed
behind their appearance of joy

1436 *strand* 'strond' in Q.

1436
−7 *Dardan . . . Simois'* Dardania, another name for Troas, the
region of which Troy was the chief city. Troy itself was inland
on the river Simois.

1440 *gallèd* broken

1444 *stelled* 'steld' in Q. This has been interpreted as 'stalled', penned
up, shut in; as 'stiled', traced as with a stylus; or as 'steeled',
engraved − which ties in with 'carved' in the next line. See
Sonnet 24: 'Mine eye hath played the painter and hath stelled /
Thy beauty's form'. For 'stell' the *O E D* gives to fix (perhaps
associated with the Latin *stella* and fixed stars) and to portray
(identifying it with 'steeled'). All these senses may contribute to
the meaning.

1445 *carvèd* engraved

1447 *Hecuba* grieving for the death of her husband, Priam, killed by
−9 the Greek Pyrrhus when Troy fell. See the Player's speech in
*Hamlet* (I I, ii, 500–20).

1450 *anatomized* dissected, laid open

1452 *chaps* cracks in the skin. 'chops' in Q.

1453 *Of what she was* of what she once was

1454 *Her blue blood . . . black.* This anticipates the changing colour of Lucrece's own blood at lines 1742–3, although the contrast here is between living and dead rather than pure and impure.

1457 *shadow* both the picture as opposed to the reality, and Hecuba, who is only a shadow of her former self

1458 *beldame* old woman. Cf. line 953.
    *shapes her sorrow* models her own sorrow on, and matches it to, that of Hecuba

1459 *Who* Hecuba, who lacks nothing but a voice

1460 *ban* curse

1465 *tune* give voice to

1471 *strumpet* Helen, wife of Menelaus, the Greek leader, who was carried off by Paris, son of Priam; this caused the Trojan war. Cf. *Troilus and Cressida* (IV, i, 68ff).

1473 *fond* infatuated
    *lust.* Lucrece draws attention to the analogy of Troy to herself, both destroyed by lust.

1476 *trespass* crime committed by

1479 *moe* more

1484 *To plague* to punish everyone for the sin committed by a single person

1486 *manly Hector* Priam's eldest son and the greatest of the Trojan warriors
    *Troilus* another of Priam's sons
    *swounds* swoons

1487 *channel* gutter

1488 *unadvised* unintended (in the darkness and chaos when Troy was surprised and captured)

1490 *doting* foolishly overindulgent

1492 *feelingly* with feeling and fellow feeling

1494 *set on ringing* set a-ringing

1496 *set a-work* once started she goes on making her plaint

1497 *pencilled pensiveness* painted sadness
    *coloured sorrow* the sorrows shown in the picture

1498 *words . . . looks.* Identifying with the characters in the painting, she makes up laments suitable to their grief and models her own appearance on theirs.

1499 *She throws her eyes.* She looks at all parts of the painting. The description has a slightly theatrical flavour appropriate to Lucrece's behaviour.

1501 *a wretched image bound*. The image of the man in shackles is that of Sinon, the Greek who pretended to be a deserter from the Greek army. When bound and led in by the Trojans, he told a false story calculated to make the Trojans take the wooden horse into Troy. See the *Aeneid* (II, 25–267).

1502 *that piteous looks*. Sinon's appearance drew pity even from the Trojan shepherds, 'the blunt swains'.
*Phrygian* Trojan. Phrygia was a country in Asia Minor, of which Troas was a part. See line 1436.

1510 *Cheeks neither red nor pale*. Contrast this with the red and white of Lucrece. See the Introduction (p. 36) for its significance.

1511 *no guilty instance* no sign of guilt

1514 *entertained a show* kept up an appearance

1515 *ensconced* concealed

1516 *jealousy* suspicion
*mistrust* suspect that

1519 *saint-like forms* the appearance of patience and humility that Sinon assumes

1521 *whose enchanting story* the story that Sinon told, which bewitched Priam and led to his destruction

1523 *wildfire* a mixture of naphtha, sulphur and pitch that burned fiercely, used in siege warfare

1525 *little stars*. Shakespeare may have taken the idea from Virgil's account of the shooting star when Troy fell. See the *Aeneid* (II, 693–6).

1526 *When their glass fell* the burnished roofs and towers of Troy that reflected the stars. The disorder on earth in the fall of a great kingdom is echoed by disruption of the divine order in the heavens.

1527 *advisedly* very carefully

1529 *some shape . . . abused*. The figure of some other and better person had been abused by presenting it as Sinon.

1530 *lodged not* could not house

1532 *plain* honest

1533 *belied* filled with lies

1534 Shakespeare is playing an amusing game with grammar.
–40 Lucrece's first thought on seeing the innocent-seeming image of Sinon is that 'It cannot be that so much guile can lurk in such a look'; but the memory of Tarquin makes her change her mind

236

before the sentence is finished and omit 'can lurk', leaving the original beginning, 'It cannot be'. If she kept to the same sentence structure, she would have to carry on with a double negative: 'It cannot be that so much guile cannot lurk'. So she changes the structure in mid flight: 'It cannot be but', i.e. 'It can only be that'.

1543 *travel.* 'travail' in Q, carrying also the suggestion of a laborious journey

1544 *armed to beguild* (Q). Malone emends to 'armed: so beguil'd / with outward honesty', meaning 'so beguiling, with the same armour of hypocrisy that Sinon wore'. Most probably 'beguild' is a variant of 'beguile', carrying associations perhaps with 'gilded' and 'guilt'.

1549 *borrowed* feigned
*sheeds* an obsolete form of 'sheds', used for the sake of the rhyme. Cf. Sonnet 34, line 13.

1551 *he* Sinon
*falls* lets fall

1552 *His eye drops fire.* By weeping, he deceives Priam, and in consequence Troy burns.

1554 *balls of quenchless fire.* See the commentary to line 1523.

1555 *lightless hell.* Cf. line 4, where Tarquin bears the fire that cannot be seen but will consume Lucrece.

1558 *such unity.* Sinon's ability to combine hot and cold in his 'cold hot-burning fire' compares with his ability to combine the red and the white in his complexion. See line 1510 and its commentary.

1559 *flatter* please and make overconfident

1561 *he* Sinon
*his* Priam's

1564 *the senseless Sinon* the painted image of Sinon

1565 *unhappy guest* bringing unhappiness, i.e. Tarquin

1567 *with this* with these words

1573 *in sorrow's sharp sustaining* when the sharp pains of sorrow have to be endured

1574 *heavy* the word means both grievous and sleepy

1575 *watch* lie awake

1576 *overslipped* passed away unnoticed

1579 *By deep surmise* by the contemplation of other people's misfortune

1580 *shows* appearances, pictures

1582 *dolour* grief

1583 *mindful* dutiful

1586 *tear-distainèd* stained

1587 *Blue circles* shadows caused by grief

1588 *water-galls* secondary rainbows in the dark sky of her face, foretelling new storms, further tears

1592 *sod . . . raw* boiled, scalded with tears yet looking red and raw, as if uncooked. A typical piece of verbal play that undercuts the tragedy of the situation.

1595 *acquaintance* acquaintances

1596 *wondering each other's chance* conjecturing what has happened to each other

1598 *uncouth* unknown, strange

1600 *spite* outrage, injury
*spent* consumed

1602 *Unmask* uncover

1604 *Three times*. In Ovid's *Fasti* (II, 823), one of Shakespeare's sources, Lucrece makes three attempts to tell her story before succeeding: '*Ter conata loqui: ter destitit*' ('Thrice she essayed to speak, and thrice gave o'er').
*gives her sorrow fire*. A metaphor based on the difficulty of firing an ancient fire-arm by means of a match.

1606 *addressed* ready

1609 *consorted* assembled

1611 *this pale swan* a reference to the common myth of the swan that sings as it dies. Cf. 'The Phoenix and Turtle', line 15.

1612 *her certain ending* the funeral dirge that precedes the death she is resolved on

1614 *give the fault amending* cure the fault

1615 *moe* more
*depending* impending, imminent

1619 *in the interest of*. A legal term: 'the bed which is yours by right'. Cf. line 1797.

1621 *wont* accustomed

1632 *hard-favoured* hard-featured

1633 *yoke thy liking to my will* submit your inclination to my desire

1644 *Rome*. 'Roome' in Q.

1645 *adulterate* adulterous

1648 *forbade*. 'forbod' in Q.

1650 *His scarlet lust* like a judge in his scarlet robes. His lust, which is both judge and witness, prosecutes on the grounds that her beauty has stolen his eyes.

1652   *robbed.* 'rob'd' in Q. Both meanings are implied.

1658   *accessary yieldings* yielding as an accessory to the deed

1659   *her poisoned closet* the polluted body

1660   *the hopeless merchant of this loss.* Collatine, who resembles a merchant who has ventured all his wealth in a ship that has been lost

1662   *wretched arms across* folded arms, a conventional sign of grief

1663   *lips new waxen pale* newly become pale, but also pale as wax

1667   Both the Thames at London Bridge and the Avon at Clopton
–71   Bridge, Stratford, have been suggested as the source of this comparison between the flow and ebb of Collatine's feelings and the water that rushes through a bridge and then turns back in an eddy. The phenomenon is common enough, however, and no specific origin is necessary.

1672   *a saw* which functions by being pushed forward and then pulled back just as grief makes him attempt to speak and then stops him. Shakespeare makes considerable play with this idea of speech starting and stopping.

1675   *untimely* unfitting
      *awaketh* interrupts

1677   *slaketh* abates

1678   *sensible* already too deeply felt. The subject to 'maketh' would seem to be 'thy passion'.

1680   *on woe* in, with woe. Later quartos emend to 'one woe'.

1681   *charm* calm, subdue

1682   *For she that was* for the sake of her who was once

1683   *suddenly* immediately

1684   *Suppose thou dost defend me.* (Imagine, pretend you are still defending me against something, even though it has already happened.)

1694   *Knights by their oaths.* Shakespeare here, as elsewhere, breaks the Roman framework of the poem and draws on the conventions of medieval chivalry.

1695   *disposition* nature, inclination

1697   *imposition* the duty she had imposed

1698   *bewrayed* revealed

1699   *her sad task hath not said.* She has not yet told them on whom to take revenge.

1700   *protestation* their protestation of willingness

1701 *forcèd* by enforcement

1702 *quality* nature

1703 *dreadful* full of fear

1704 *with . . . dispence* give pardon, dispensation for

1706 *terms* words, pleas

*acquit me from this chance.* (Prove me not guilty of what has happened.)

1708 *compellèd* enforced

1713 *carved in it.* 'carv'd it in' in Q.

1715 *By my excuse . . . giving.* (Shall use the fact that I was excused as an excuse for herself.)

1719 *accents* sounds

1720 *assays* attempts

1723 *harmless* innocent

1724 *unsheathed* drew out of her body

1725 *bail* liberate

1729 *Life's lasting date.* 'Eternal life, a lease of endless life, escapes from the life on earth ('destiny') which has been cancelled' (Prince). Lever notes that the line is a precise reversal of Lucrece's complaint against Opportunity (lines 934–5): 'Cancelled my fortunes and enchainèd me / To endless date of never-ending woes?'

1730 *astonished* stunned

1743 *false Tarquin stained.* Lever emends this to 'false Tarquin-stained', turning it into an adjectival phrase.

1745 *rigol* a ring, in this case the clear serum that separates from the clot when blood coagulates.

1754 *unlived* deprived of life

1758 *glass* mirror

1761 *a bare-boned death* a scull, death's head. Her dead face now reflects what he actually is in age instead of what it offered when alive, an image of his youth.

1766 *surcease* cease

1773 *give his sorrow place* give place to his (Collatine's) sorrow

1774 *key-cold* cold in death

1780 *served a dumb arrest* stopped him from speaking

1781 *his use* the use of the tongue

1784 *so thick come* coming so confusedly

1794 *possess the claim they lay* establish the claim they are making, with the suggestion too that neither may ever again possess the object of their claim, Lucrece

1797 *My sorrow's interest.* (My sole right to sorrow for her.) Cf. line 1619.

1801 *too late* presumably, to save her from Tarquin

1803 *I owed her* owned. (She was my possession.)

1805 *dispersed* blown about by their cries

*holding Lucrece life* since her spirit had left the body and soared upwards

1811 *He with the Romans* . . . This description of Brutus throwing off the disguise of fool and buffoon under which he had previously hidden was suggested by Livy. It was a commonplace of Shakespeare's period. Cf. *Henry V* (II, iv, 37–8), the comparison of Henry to 'the Roman Brutus, / Covering discretion with a coat of folly'.

1814 *habit* both the cloak of folly and his general behaviour

1815 *policy* political calculation, contrivance

1816 *advisedly* with deliberate calculation

1819 *unsounded* untested

*supposed* believed to be

1829 *relenting* softening, melting

1834 *chased* to be chased

1835 Lever notes that the Capitol, the Temple of Jupiter, was the place where the second Brutus overthrew another tyrant, Julius Caesar.

1849 *this advisèd doom* this considered, thought-out judgement

1854 *plausibly* with applause, acclamation

# 'THE PHOENIX AND TURTLE'

The only text of authority is that included among the additional poems to Robert Chester's *Loves Martyr*, which is without a title. Since the nineteenth century it has been known indifferently as 'The Phoenix and Turtle' (F. T. Prince, *Oxford Complete Works of Shakespeare* or 'The Phoenix and the Turtle' (Maxwell).

1 *the bird of loudest lay*. For possible candidates, see the Introduction (pp. 53–4).

2 *On the sole Arabian tree*. Cf. *The Tempest* (III, iii, 21–4): '. . . Now I will believe / That there are unicorns; that in Arabia / There is one tree, the phoenix' throne; one phoenix / At this hour reigning there.'

3 *trumpet* trumpeter

5 *shrieking harbinger* the screech-owl. Cf. *A Midsummer Night's Dream* (V, i, 364–6): 'Whilst the screech-owl, screeching loud, / Puts the wretch that lies in woe / In remembrance of a shroud.'

6 *precurrer* precursor, forerunner

7 *Augur* prophet
  *the fever's end* death

9 *interdict* forbid

12 *strict* strictly controlled

14 *defunctive music* music for the funeral
  *can* understands, is skilful in

15 *death-divining swan* a reference to the common myth of the swan that sings before its death. Cf. *Lucrece*, lines 1611–2.

16 *lack his right* be lacking in the music that is due to it

17 *treble-dated crow* living thrice the normal span of life. For the extensive mythology concerning the longevity of crows and ravens from Pliney onwards, see Rollins.

18– *sable gender . . . breath.* This is a reference to the myth that ravens
19   bred by 'billing at the mouth'. The young became black on the
    seventh day, hence 'sable gender', engendering black offspring.
    See Rollins.

25   For a full analysis of the Anthem, see Alvarez.

27   *distincts, division* separate yet undivided. 'In the language of the
    schools, "distinction" implies only verbal, "division", a real
    difference' (Rollins).

28   *Number . . . slain.* (Since two become one, and one is no
    number.)

32   *But in them it were a wonder* except in their case it would be a
    miracle

36   *mine* probably a double meaning: both an external source of
    treasure and a possessive pronoun. See the Introduction (pp.
    55–6).'

37   *Property* carrying the force of the Latin *proprietas*, peculiar or
    essential quality. Property is 'appalled' because the unique and
    individual self is no longer single but double.

39–  What was single is now also double and so cannot be called by
40   either name.

44   *Simple . . . compounded.* A simple is a single element, a com-
    pound, a mixture of elements changed and broken down in the
    process. Here the mixture is both simple and compound at the
    same time, and is thus either both or neither.

45   *it* reason

48   *parts . . . remain* both departs and stays, and divides yet remains
    single

49   *threne* threnos, funeral dirge

55   *in cinders* the ashes of the fire in which the phoenix and the turtle
    burned
    *Here enclosed* in the funeral urn referred to in line 65

60   *'Twas not their infirmity* the fact that they left no posterity was
    not due to impotence

62–3 *Truth may seem . . . Beauty brag.* (Both as they appear in the
    world may pretend to be the real thing, but they are not so in
    fact.)

67   *sigh* let them sigh

# THE PASSIONATE PILGRIM

I

A version of Shakespeare's Sonnet 138 (1609). The extensive differences between the two texts has led to a debate about whether that in *The Passionate Pilgrim* is an inaccurate recall of Sonnet 138 or an earlier version that Shakespeare subsequently worked over. I quote the 1609 version for comparison:

> When my love swears that she is made of truth
> I do believe her, though I know she lies,
> That she might think me some untutored youth,
> Unlearnèd in the world's false subtleties.
> Thus vainly thinking that she thinks me young,
> Although she knows my days are past the best,
> Simply I credit her false-speaking tongue;
> On both sides thus is simple truth suppressed.
> But wherefore says she not she is unjust?
> And wherefore say not I that I am old?
> O, love's best habit is in seeming trust,
> And age in love loves not to have years told.
> > Therefore I lie with her, and she with me,
> > And in our faults by lies we flattered be.

The changes in Sonnet 138 seem too systematic to be explained in terms of bad memory. The control is much tighter, and the sonnet is constructed firmly round the opening couplet as an amplification of the paradox, 'I do believe her, though I know she lies'. 'Subtleties' is more relevant than 'forgeries' (line 4) to this, and the substitution of 'she knows' for 'I know' (line 6) makes the point more strongly. The irrelevant 'love's ill rest' (line 8) and 'young' (line 9) are replaced by 'simple truth' and 'unjust' (untruthful), keeping the emphasis upon truth and lies. The replacement of 'love' by 'her' (line 13) and by 'lies' (line 14) changes the sonnet from a general statement to a personal one about the poet's relationship with his mistress, as in the opening couplet: at the same time it strengthens the force of 'lie' and exploits the common sexual innuendo that the word carried. The 1609 text undoubtedly represents a deliberate revision of the text to which Jaggard had access in *The Passionate Pilgrim*.

7     *credit* believe
8     *Outfacing* defying, pretending they don't exist.
     *with love's ill rest.* A difficult phrase: 'with the help of the ill-grounded sense of security characteristic of love' (Maxwell).
11    *habit is* (Octavo 2). 'habit's in' (Octavo 1).

## II

A version of Sonnet 144. There is no substantive difference between Octavos 1 and 2: and the variations from the text of 1609 are sufficiently minor to be the result of transmission.

2     *That.* 'Which' (1609).
6     *side.* 'sight' (1609), obviously incorrect.
8     *fair pride.* 'foul pride' (1609).
11    *both to me.* 'both from me' (1609). A change of meaning here. In *PP*: 'both are friends to me and to each other'. In 1609: 'both away from me and with each other'.
13    *The truth I shall not know.* 'Yet this shall I ne'er know' (1609).

## III

A version of Longaville's sonnet in *Love's Labour's Lost* (IV, iii, 56–69). Octavos 1 and 2 are virtually identical, with only minor differences from *Loves Labour's Lost*.

9     *My vow was breath* 'Vows are but breath' (*LLL*).
10    *that on this earth doth shine.* 'which on my earth dost shine' (*LLL*).
11    *Exhal'st* (*LLL*). 'Exhalt' (Octavo 1). 'Exhale' (Octavo 2).
14    *To break on oath.* 'To lose an oath' (*LLL*).

IV

This is one of four sonnets in *The Passionate Pilgrim* on the theme of
Venus and Adonis, all showing the influence of Shakespeare's poem,
especially I V. They are I V, V I, I X and X I, the last of which is
identical to Sonnet 3 of Bartholomew Griffin's *Fidessa* (1596). It is
possible, therefore, that the other three are also by Griffin. This poem
is also in Folger M S S 2071.7 and 1.8.

1    *Cytherea* Venus
5    *ear*. 'eares' (Octavo 1 and Folger 1.8).
9    *unripe years did want* whether his youth lacked understanding
10   *figured* as it appeared to him
13   *toward* oncoming, forward
14   *froward* timid, backward

V

A version of Berowne's sonnet in *Love's Labour's Lost* (I V, ii, 101–14).
No significant differences between the Octavos and *Love's Labour's
Lost*.

2    O. 'Ah' (*L L L*).
3    *constant*. 'faithful' (*L L L*).
4    *like oaks*. 'were oaks' (*L L L*).
6    *can*. 'would' (*L L L*).
11   *seems*. 'bears' (*L L L*).
13   *O do not love that wrong*. 'O pardon love this wrong' (*L L L*).
14   *To sing*. 'That sings' (*L L L*).

VI

The debt of this sonnet to Ovid's *Metamorphoses* (I V), the account of
Salmacis and Hermaphroditus, has often been noted. It owes more to
Ovid than to Shakespeare, whose Adonis has no passions to cool.

4    *tarriance* waiting, expectation
6    *spleen* the seat of the emotions
12   *wistly* attentively
13   *bounced in whereas he stood* jumped in from where he was
     standing

### VII

3     *brittle*. 'Brickle' was a common Elizabethan form of the word and may be implied in the poem for the rhyme's sake.

5     *damask* blush-red colour

6     *fairer . . . falser* none more fair but, on the negative side, none more false

14    *as soon as* as quickly as

15    *framed* caused
      *foiled* destroyed

17    *whether* which of the two

### VIII

'If Music and Sweet poetry Agree' by Richard Barnfield. From *Poems: In Divers Humors'*, added to *The Encomion of Lady Pecunia* (1598).

### IX

2     A line is missing in Octavo 1.

5     *steep-up* steep-sided

8     *pass those grounds* pass along the low-lying ground at the foot of the hill

12    *sore* wound

### X

1     *vaded* faded

3     *timely* early
      *shaded* dulled

8, 10    *For why* because

### XI

'Venus with Young Adonis Sitting by Her' by Bartholomew Griffin. From *Fidessa* (1596).

### XII

This attractive poem appeared as the first verse of a longer poem with the title 'A Maiden's Choice Betwixt Age and Youth' in Thomas Deloney's *Garland of Good Will* (earliest surviving edition, 1631), a ballad anthology probably of the 1590s. Thomas Nashe refers to the poem in 1596. Possibly by Deloney, but there is no positive evidence to this effect.

1    *Crabbed* crooked, bad-tempered
2    *pleasance* delight

The Octavo capitals for Age and Youth throughout, except in the first line, give the poem the flavour of a dramatic Interlude.

### XIII

2    *vadeth*. See *PP*, X, lines 1–2.
4    *presently* immediately
7    *seld* seldom
10   *cement* The accent is on the first syllable.
     *redress* repair

### XIV

3    *daffed* sent me away
     *cabin* lodge, a willow cabin, especially appropriate to lovers. See *Twelfth Night* (I, v, 254): 'Make me a willow cabin at your gate'.
4    *descant* a tune woven round and elaborating on the basic musical theme; hence, to think over and elaborate on, with a suggestion of the lover singing verses, such as this poem, about his woes
8    *nill I* I will not
     *conster whether* interpret which
11–2 *like myself . . . As take . . .* such as myself who
12   *pelf* reward, treasure
14   *charge the watch*. This could mean either 'enjoins the night-watch to hurry through his duties' (Malone) or 'accuse his watch [time-piece] for marking the time too slowly' (Maxwell).
15–6 Octavo 1 has a comma after 'rest' and stop after 'eyes'. Malone and others reverse the punctuation, correctly, I think. The poet watches for the dawn and waits for the sun to awaken all his senses; but, not trusting to his sight alone, he turns to hearing, and waits for the song of the nightingale to be replaced by that of the morning lark.
     *cite* summon
17   *Philomela* the nightingale

*sings*. Octavo 1 has 'sits and sings', carried over from 'I sit and mark'.

18 *lays* songs

19 *she* the lark

20 Two syllables appear to have been lost. Prince suggests 'And daylight drives . . .'

21 *packed* sent away, sent packing
   *post* hasten

24 *For why* because
   *sighed*. In Octavo 1, 'sight', an obsolete form of the past participle.

27 *moon* month. In Octavo 1, 'houre', emended by Steevens and quoted by Malone.

28 *Yet not for me* even if not for me

29 *Pack night*. Cf. 'Pack Clouds Away and Welcome Day' by Thomas Heywood.
   *peep*. Cf. *Macbeth* (I, v, 51): 'Nor heaven peep through the blanket of the dark'.
   *of night now borrow* borrow some time from the night

30 *Short night . . . length*. Maxwell interprets the line as 'Let us have a short night tonight', and relates 'length' (lengthen) to 'night': 'lengthen yourself tomorrow night in compensation for what you will lose tonight'. It seems more likely that both 'short' and 'length' are addressed to 'good day': 'Good day, borrow some time from night: shorten tonight and lengthen yourself tomorrow [since his mistress bade him come again tomorrow].'

## XV

This curious old-fashioned poem is perhaps a song from a play or a romance. Steevens placed it in a line of 'It was' ballads: 'It was a Blind Beggar', 'It was an Old Man and his Poor Wife', 'It was a Lady's Daughter', etc. The debate between the scholar and the knight is a traditional one. The fourth line of the stanza without a rhyme is common and can be found in the poems of Thomas Lodge, for example.

1 *lording's* a petty lord

2 *master* teacher

8 *silly* simple

9 *mickle* great

### XVI

A version of Dumaine's 'sonnet' in *Loves' Labour's Lost* (IV, iii, 96–115). It also appeared in *England's Helicon*. The texts of Octavos 1 and 2 are identical except for minor points of spelling and a misprint in Octavo 1, line 12: 'pruck' was corrected to 'pluck' in Octavo 2. There are slight variations between *The Passionate Pilgrim* and *Love's Labour's Lost*.

| | |
|---|---|
| 2 | *was*. 'is' (*LLL*). |
| 6 | *'gan*. 'can' (*LLL*). |
| 11 | *alas* 'alack' (*LLL*). |
| | *hath* 'is' (*LLL*). |
| 12 | *thorn* (*England's Helicon*). 'throne' (Octavos 1, 2 and *LLL*). Octavo 1 omits a couplet between lines 14–15 that is in *LLL*. |

### XVII

Text in Octavos 1 and 2. Also in Thomas Weelkes's *Madrigals to 3, 4, 5 and 6 Voyces* (1597), and a little earlier in Harleian MS 6910. A version exists in *England's Helicon*.

#### TEXTUAL VARIANTS

| | |
|---|---|
| 4 | *denying*. 'denieng' (Octavo 1 and Weelkes). 'nenying' (Octavo 2). 'renying' (*England's Helicon*). |
| 21 | *My sighs* (Weelkes). 'with sighs' (Octavo 2 and *England's Helicon*). 'My sights so deep, doth cause him . . .' (Harleian). |
| 28 | *back peeping* (*England's Helicon*). 'blacke peeping' (Octavo 1). 'back creeping' (Weelkes). |
| 33 | *lass* (Weelkes). 'love' (Octavo 1 and *England's Helicon*). |
| 34 | *moan* (*England's Helicon*). 'woe' (Octavo 1). |

| | |
|---|---|
| 2 | *speed* thrive |
| 4 | *denying* rejection |
| 5 | *jigs* dances |
| 8 | *a nay* a refusal |
| 9 | *cross* quarrel |
| 14 | *forlorn* made forlorn, abandoned |
| | *thrall* slavery |
| 16 | *speeding* fortune |
| | *fraughted* laden |
| | *gall* bitterness |

17   *no deal* not at all
19   *curtal* with its tail docked
22   *In howling wise* noisily
23   *heartless* without feeling
26   *dye* colours


## XVIII

In Octavos 1 and 2, Folger 1.112 and 2071.7. The stanzas in Octavo 2 are in the wrong order.

2    *stalled* rounded up, penned in
4    *fancy's partial might* (Furnivall). 'fancy partyall might' (Octavo 2) 'fancye parcyall like' (Folger 1.112) 'parciall fancie like' (Folger 2071.7). The line is clearly corrupt, and Furnivall's emendation is sensible: 'Let reason control and direct your behaviour as well as the biased power of fancy even in courses of action that are blame-worthy.'
10   *a halt* a lame person
12   *set thy person forth to sell* (Folger MSS and Maxwell) show off your person to advantage. 'And set her person forth to sell' (Octavos 1 and 2).
14   *Spare not to spend* don't hesitate to spend money
21   *unjust* false
24   *proffer* press your case, make advances
     *put thee back* resist you
32   *ban* curse, abuse
39   *toys* whims
43   *to strive with men* (Octavos 1 and 2). 'love to match' (Folger 1.112). 'seeke to match' (Folger 2071.7). Both Folger versions are clearer than Octavos 1 and 2, but the sense is plain if line 44 is taken to mean 'with the object of sinning but never of being holy'.
45   *be holy then* (Folger 2071.7). 'There is no heaven by holy then' (Octavo 2).
46   *attaint* sully, spoil
51   *stick* hesitate
     *round me on th'ear* take me to task. 'round me on th'are' (Octavo 1).
54   *bewrayed* betrayed

## XIX

'Live with Me, and be My Love' and 'Love's Answer' are usually attributed to Marlowe and Ralegh respectively.

## XX

'As It Fell upon a Day' by Richard Barnfield. From *Poems: In Divers Humors* added to *The Encomion of Lady Pecunia* (1598).

# 'SHALL I DIE?'

1   *die* suggesting the sexual *double entendre* that is normal in love poetry
3   *sorrow breeding* which breed sorrow
4   *sue* Rawlinson. 'shew' (Yale).
10  *joying* Rawlinson. The Yale version, 'joyninge', is equally valid, and the choice depends on whether one takes 'retire' or 'despair' as the key word.
13  *by my love conceiving*. Rawlinson has 'breeding', which breaks the rhyme scheme and may have been carried over from the previous verse. Yale has 'by my love bred', rhyming with 'all my hopes dead' at line 16. This keeps the rhyme but loses the rhythmical pattern. Oxford emends 'conceiving' to rhyme with 'deceiving' in line 16. The meaning would seem to be 'the pain that my love breeds'.
17  *O keep out* (Rawlinson). 'O suspicious doubt' (Yale).
19  *Fie, away* (Yale). 'Fly away' (Rawlinson). The latter, though repetitive and less dramatic, could well be the correct version.
21  *accuse* (Rawlinson). 'excuse' (Yale).
22  *prove* test
27  *howe'er* whatever the outcome. 'I will bear' (Rawlinson). 'I'le bear' (Yale).
28  *pleasure* (Rawlinson). 'pleasures' (Yale).
29  *will* (Yale). 'wit' (Rawlinson).
30  *doth* (Rawlinson) by wronging him who pays homage to her. 'to doe' (Yale).
31  *it* (Rawlinson). 'I' (Yale).
38  *for pleasure* (Yale). 'for our pleasure' (Rawlinson).
41  *sport did find* (Rawlinson). 'sport it fine (Yale).
49  *You* (Yale). 'then' (Rawlinson).
    *prove* find out by experience

50  *inflection* presumably in the sense of a bending towards, exerting pressure
    *force* (Rawlinson). 'forces' (Yale).

51  *Next her hair* next to her hair

52  *next doth lie* (Rawlinson and Yale). Oxford emends to 'neat doth lie', presumably to avoid the repetition of 'next' in line 51. The dream, however, contains a methodical description of the lady, beginning with her hair, then forehead, brows, eyes, cheeks, chin, neck, breasts. The change to 'neat' breaks the sequence.

55  *win* (Rawlinson). 'winns' (Yale).

59–  *O admiring desiring/Breeds* admiring breeds desire, though the
60  phrase suggests that it works the other way round as well

61  *Then* (Yale). 'Thin' (Rawlinson), which Oxford retains. I accept 'Then' because thin lips were not normally taken as a sign of beauty, and because 'Then' carries on the progress down the mistress's body: 'next . . . next . . . then . . .'
    *fancy's* (Rawlinson). 'fancys' (Yale). (The lover's fancy is fed with all it desires when he is allowed to kiss her, 'there to trade'.)

68  *Of all that's called commendation* (Rawlinson and Yale). Oxford emends to 'of all their culled commendations'. The line may be corrupt, but the MSS make sense. (Her chin wins from everybody what is accepted as commendation.)

70  *admiration* (Yale). 'admirations' (Rawlinson).

71  *Pretty bare* (Yale), echoing 'Pretty chin' in line 67. 'A pretty bare' (Rawlinson), the cleavage between her breasts, 'those plots' that excite men to madness even though they are separated by the 'Pretty bare'.

72  *which besots* (Rawlinson). 'witts besots' (Yale).

73  *asunder* (Rawlinson). 'sunder' (Yale).

74  *It is meet* it is fitting.

75  *that so rare* that which is so rare

77  *mishap* (Rawlinson and Yale). Oxford emends to 'mis-shape'. I retain the MSS reading, which pairs 'mishap' with 'scape' (transgression) and contrasts them with the more physical blemishes, 'No blot, no spot' in line 79.

80  *in election* by everybody's choice

82  *From* (Yale). 'For' (Rawlinson).

83  *pleasures plenty* (Yale). 'pleasures in plenty' (Rawlinson).

# THE EPITAPHS

### I 'UPON JOHN COMBE'

This epitaph exists in a variety of versions through the seventeenth century. It was not initially associated with Combe but was written about an unnamed usurer, and not attributed to Shakespeare until 1634. Shakespeare could have written it, since Combe was a wealthy townsman of Stratford with whom he had business dealings. Combe left Shakespeare £5 in his will, and Shakespeare left his sword as a keep-sake to Combe's nephew and heir. John Aubrey wrote that Shakespeare made the epitaph 'extemporary' in a tavern; and Nicholas Rowe elaborated and developed the anecdote extensively. I give Rowe's version of the verse. For full details see Chambers (II, Appendix A, pp. 138–40, also II, pp. 246, 268–9) and Schoenbaum, *Shakespeare's Lives* (pp. 79–80).

*Ten in the hundred* the percentage of interest charged by usurers

### 'Another Epitaph upon John Combe'

This is recorded in a commonplace book by Nicholas Burgh (*c*.1650), which also includes a shorter version of the first epitaph (Bodleian Library, MS Ashmole 38, p. 180). Transcript in Chambers (II, p. 246). See also Schoenbaum, *A Documentary Life* (p. 186).

### II 'ON ELIAS JAMES'

James was a brewer at Puddle Wharf near the Blackfriars Theatre. He was involved with Shakespeare in buying the Blackfriars Gate House. (See Honigmann, *Shakespeare: The Lost Years* (p. 79)). The epitaph is attributed to Shakespeare in the Rawlinson MS 160 f 41 in the Bodleian. It is transcribed by Chambers (I, p. 551) and Schoenbaum, *Shakespeare's Lives* (p. 77).

## COMMENTARY: THE EPITAPHS

### III 'ON BEN JONSON'

In Nicholas Burgh's commonplace book, quoted above. Transcribed
by Chambers (II, p. 246) and Schoenbaum, *Shakespeare's Lives*
(p. 76).

### 'A Later Variant'

In Thomas Plume, Plume M S in library at Maldon Essex, transcribed
by Chambers (II, p. 247) and Schoenbaum, *Shakespeare's Lives*
(p. 77).

### IV 'EPITAPHS ON THE STANLEYS IN TONG CHURCH, SHROPSHIRE'

These epitaphs were ascribed to Shakespeare by Sir William Dugdale
in his *Visitation of Shropshire* (1664). The two Stanleys commemorated
are probably Sir Thomas (d. 1576) and his son, Sir Edward (d. 1632).
For Shakespeare's connection with the Stanley family, see the Intro-
duction on 'The Phoenix and Turtle' (p. 52) and Honigmann,
*Shakespeare's Lost Years*. The dates of the two deaths have raised
questions about the ascription, since Sir Edward died sixteen years
after Shakespeare; but it was not uncommon for the epitaph to be
commissioned and written during the life-time of the person it
commemorated, and Shakespeare could have composed both
epitaphs for the family tomb in the early seventeenth century. See
Honigmann (pp. 79–81), Schoenbaum, *Shakespeare's Lives* (p. 78) and
Chambers (I, pp. 551–4).

### V 'ON HIMSELF'

In the church at Stratford–upon–Avon. First ascribed to Shakespeare
by Dowdall (1693). See Chambers (II, p. 259).

### VI 'UPON THE KING'

Attributed to Shakespeare in *The Oxford Shakespeare: The Complete
Works*. Printed at the foot of the effigy of King James I, forming the
frontispiece to his *Works* (1616).

# THE MAIN SOURCES OF *VENUS AND ADONIS* AND *THE RAPE OF LUCRECE*

## VENUS AND ADONIS

Ovid, *Metamorphoses*
  (Venus and Adonis: X, 519–59 and 708–39.
  Narcissus: III, 340–500.
  Salamacis and Hermaphroditus: IV, 287–390.

In Arthur Golding's translation of the *Metamorphoses* (which appears in *Shakespeare's Ovid*, edited by H. D. Rouse), the references are as follows:

  Venus and Adonis: X, 610–40 and 826–63.
  Narcissus: III, 427–42.
  Salmacis and Hermaphroditus: IV, 347–481

Most of these are included in Bullough, *Narrative and Dramatic Sources of Shakespeare*, vol. I; Prince, Appendix 1; and Rollins, pp. 401–4.

## THE RAPE OF LUCRECE

Ovid, *Fasti*, II, 721–852
Livy, *Historia*, I, 57–60.
William Painter, *The Pallace of Pleasure* (1566) and *The Second Novell* (a translation of Livy).
Chaucer, *The Legende of Goode Women*, 1680–1885.

See also Bullough, vol. I; Prince, Appendix 2; and Rollins, pp. 416–46.

# FURTHER READING

This is a short bibliography of the texts which I have found most useful, in editions which are generally accessible. For a comprehensive account of the texts, sources and criticism of the poems up to 1938, Hyder Edward Rollins's *The Poems: A New Variorum Edition of Shakespeare* should be consulted. There are useful bibliographical references in Lever (*Shakespeare Survey* 15), Hamilton, Hulse and Keach (see below). The most reliable modern text of the poems themselves is that of Maxwell, and the fullest, most useful commentary on them that of Prince (Arden).

### TEXTS OF THE POEMS

Adams, Joseph Quincy, *The Passionate Pilgrim*. The Folger Shakespeare Library Facsimile (Folger, 1939).

Kerrigan, J., *The Sonnets and A Lover's Complaint*. New Penguin Shakespeare (Penguin, 1986).

Lever, J. W., *The Rape of Lucrece*. New Penguin Shakespeare (Penguin, 1981).

Malone, E., *The Plays and Poems of William Shakespeare*. With the corrections and illustrations of various commentators. Vol. XX (London, 1821).

Maxwell, J. C., *The Poems*. The New Cambridge Shakespeare (Cambridge University Press, 1965).

Pooler, C. Knox, *Shakespeare's Poems*. The Arden Shakespeare (Methuen, 1911).

Prince, F. T., *The Poems*. The Arden Shakespeare (Methuen, 1960).

Rollins, Hyder Edward, *The Poems: A New Variorum Edition of Shakespeare* (Lippincott, Philadelphia, 1938).

*Shakespeare's Poems*. A facsimile published for the Elizabethan Club (Yale University Press, 1964).

Wells, Stanley, and Taylor, Gary, *The Oxford Shakespeare* (Oxford University Press, 1986).

## BACKGROUND MATERIAL

Alexander, N., *Elizabethan Narrative Verse*. Stratford-upon-Avon Library 3 (Arnold, 1967).

Baldwin, T. W., *On the Literary Genetics of Shakespeare's Poems and Sonnets* (University of Illinois Press, 1950).

Bullough, G., *Narrative and Dramatic Sources of Shakespeare*. Vol. I (Routledge & Kegan Paul, 1957).

Castiglione, Baldassare, *The Book of the Courtier* (Everyman, 1959).

Chambers, E. K., *William Shakespeare: A Study of Facts and Problems* (Oxford University Press, 1930).

Donno, E. S., *Elizabethan Minor Epics* (Routledge & Kegan Paul, 1963).

Marlowe, Christopher, *The Complete Poems and Translations*. Penguin English Poets (Penguin, 1971).

Onions, C. T., *A Shakespeare Glossary* (Oxford University Press, 1982).

Ovid, *Metamorphoses*. Loeb Classical Library and Penguin Classics (Loeb, 1977, and Penguin, 1970). Arthur Golding's translation has been published as *Shakespeare's Ovid*, edited by W. H. D. Rouse (Norton, 1966).

—*Amores*. Loeb Classical Library (Loeb, 1921).

Puttenham, George, *The Arte of English Poesie*. Edited by Gladys Doidge Willcock and Alice Walker (Cambridge University Press, 1936).

Schoenbaum, Samuel, *Shakespeare's Lives* (Oxford University Press, 1970).

—*William Shakespeare: A Documentary Life* (Oxford University Press, 1977).

*Shakespeare's England*. Vol. II (Clarendon Press, 1916).

Sidney, Sir Philip, *An Apology for Poetry*. Edited by Geoffrey Shepherd (Nelson, 1967).

—*The Countess of Pembroke's Arcadia*. Edited by Albert Feuillerat. The Prose Works of Sir Philip Sidney. Vol. IV (Cambridge University Press, 1970).

—*Astrophel and Stella* in *Selected Poems*. Edited by Katherine Duncan Jones (Oxford University Press, 1973).

Spenser, Edmund, *The Faerie Queene*. Edited by Thomas P. Roche (Penguin, 1978).

CRITICISM

## General

Bradbrook, M. C., *Shakespeare and Elizabethan Poetry*. Peregrine (Penguin, 1964).

Bush, Douglas, *Mythology and the Renaissance Tradition in English Poetry* (Norton, 1963).

Hulse, C., *Metamorphic Verse: The Elizabethan Minor Epic* (Princeton University Press, 1981).

Keach, William, *Elizabethan Erotic Narratives* (Harvester, 1977).

Lever, J. W., 'Shakespeare's Narrative Poems' in *The New Companion to Shakespeare Studies*. Edited by Kenneth Muir and Samuel Schoenbaum (Cambridge University Press, 1976).

Lewis, C. S., *English Literature in the Sixteenth Century* (Oxford University Press, 1954).

Rollins, Hyder Edward, *The Poems: A New Variorum Edition of Shakespeare* (see Texts of the Poems).

*Shakespeare Survey 15* (Cambridge University Press, 1962). Includes essays by J. W. Lever, D. C. Allen, M. C. Bradbrook and Robert Ellrodt.

## Individual Poems

*Venus and Adonis*

Akrigg, G. P. V., *Shakespeare and the Earl of Southampton*. (Hamish Hamilton, 1968).

Allen, D. C., 'On Venus and Adonis' in *Elizabethan and Jacobean Studies*. Presented to F. P. Wilson (Oxford University Press, 1959).

Beauregard, D. N., '*Venus and Adonis*: Shakespeare's Representation of the Passions' in *Shakespeare Studies* 8 (1975).

Bowers, A. Robin, '"Hard Armour" and "Delicate Amours" in Shakespeare's *Venus and Adonis*' in *Shakespeare Studies* 12 (1979).

Bradbrook, M. C., 'Beasts and Gods: The Social Purpose of *Venus and Adonis*' in *Shakespeare Survey* 15 (1962) and *The Artist and Society in Shakespeare's England*. Vol. I (Harvester, 1982).

Butler, C., and Fowler, A., 'Time Beguiling Sport: Number Symbolism in Shakespeare's *Venus and Adonis*' in *Shakespeare: 1564–1964*. Edited by Harold Bloom (Brown University Press, 1964).

Dickey, Franklin M., *Not Wisely But Too Well* (San Marino, 1957).

Hamilton, A. C., *The Early Shakespeare* (Huntington Library Publications, 1967).

Hatto, A. J., 'Venus and Adonis and the Boar' in *Modern Language Review* 41 (1946).

Hulse, C., *Metamorphic Verse: The Elizabethan Minor Epic* (see General Criticism).

Keach, William, *Elizabethan Erotic Narratives* (see General Criticism).

Lever, J. W., 'The Poems' and 'Venus and the Second Chance' in *Shakespeare Survey* 15 (1962).

Maxwell, J. C., 'Introduction' in *The Poems*. The New Cambridge Shakespeare (see Texts of the Poems).

Miller, Robert P., 'Venus, Adonis and the Horses' in *Journal of English Literary History* 19 (1952).

Muir, Kenneth, *Shakespeare the Professional* (Heinemann, 1973).

Muir, Kenneth, and O'Loughlin, S., *The Voyage to Illyria* (Methuen, 1937).

Price, Hereward T., 'The Function of Imagery in *Venus and Adonis*' in *Papers of the Michigan Academy of Science, Arts and Letters* 35 (1945).

Prince, F. T., 'Introduction' in *The Poems*. The Arden Shakespeare (see Texts of the Poems).

Putney, R., '*Venus and Adonis*: Armour with Humour' in *Philological Quarterly* 20 (1941).

—'Venus Agonistes' in *University of Colorado Studies* 4 (1953).

Rollins, Hyder Edward, *The Poems: A New Variorum Edition of Shakespeare* (see Texts of the Poems).

Watson, D. G., 'The Contrarieties of *Venus and Adonis*' in *Studies in Philology* 75 (1978).

*The Rape of Lucrece*

Allen, D. C., 'Some Observations on *The Rape of Lucrece*' in *Shakespeare Survey* 15 (1962).

Bowers, A. Robin, 'Iconography and Rhetoric in Shakespeare's *Lucrece*' in *Shakespeare Studies* 14 (1981).

Bradbrook, M. C., *Shakespeare and Elizabethan Poetry* (see General Criticism).

Donaldson, I., *The Rapes of Lucrece* (Oxford University Press, 1982).

Hamilton, A. C., *The Early Shakespeare* (see *Venus and Adonis*).

Hulse, J. C., 'A Piece of Skilful Painting in Shakespeare's *Lucrece*' in *Shakespeare Survey* 31 (1981).

Kahn, Coppelia, 'The Rape of Shakespeare's Lucrece' in *Shakespeare Studies* 9 (1976).

Keach, William, *Elizabethan Erotic Narrative* (see General Criticism).

Lever, J. W., 'Introduction' in *The Rape of Lucrece*. New Penguin Shakespeare (see Texts of the Poems).

—'The Poems' in *Shakespeare Survey* 15 (1962).

Levin, R., 'The Ironic Reading of *The Rape of Lucrece* and the Problem of External Evidence' in *Shakespeare Survey* 31 (1981).

Maxwell, J. C., 'Introduction' to *The Poems*. The New Cambridge Shakespeare (see Texts of the Poems).

Muir, Kenneth, *Shakespeare the Professional* (see *Venus and Adonis*).

Prince, F. T., 'Introduction' in *The Poems*. The Arden Shakespeare (see Texts of the Poems).

Rollins, Hyder Edward, *The Poems: A New Variorum Edition of Shakespeare* (see Texts of the Poems).

## 'The Phoenix and Turtle'

Alvarez, A., '"The Phoenix and the Turtle"' in *Interpretations*. Edited by John Wain (Routledge & Kegan Paul, 1972).

Buxton, J., 'Two Dead Birds' in *English Renaissance Studies*. Presented to Helen Gardner (Oxford University Press, 1980).

Carleton Brown (editor), *Poems of Sir John Salusbury and Robert Chester* (Early English Text Society, 1914).

Chester, Robert, *Loves Martyr, or Rosalins Complaint* (Grosart, 1878).

Copland, M., 'The Dead Phoenix' in *Essays in Criticism* 15 (1965).

Cunningham, J. V., 'Essence in the "Phoenix and the Turtle"' in *Journal of English Literary History* 19 (1952).

Dronke, P., '"The Phoenix and the Turtle"' in *Orbis Litterarum* 23 (1968).

Ellrodt, Robert, 'An Anatomy of "The Phoenix and the Turtle"' in *Shakespeare Survey* 15 (1962).

Fairchild, A. H. R., '"The Phoenix and the Turtle": A Critical and Historical Interpretation' in *Englische Studien* 33 (1904).

Honigmann, E. A. J., *Shakespeare: The Lost Years* (Manchester University Press, 1985).

Matchett, W. H., *'The Phoenix and the Turtle': Shakespeare's Poem and Chester's Loves Martyr* (Moulton, The Hague, 1965).

Maxwell, J. C., 'Introduction' in *The Poems*. The New Cambridge Shakespeare (see Texts of the Poems).

Petronella, V., 'Shakespeare's "The Phoenix and the Turtle" and the Defunctive Music of Ecstasy' in *Shakespeare Studies* 8 (1975).

Prince, F. T., 'Introduction' to *The Poems*. The Arden Shakespeare (see Texts of the Poems).

Rollins, Hyder Edward, *The Poems: A New Variorum Edition of Shakespeare* (see Texts of the Poems).

Underwood, R. A., 'Shakespeare's "The Phoenix and the Turtle": A Survey of Scholarship' in *Salzburg Studies in English Literature* 15 (1974).

## The Passionate Pilgrim

Adams, Joseph Quincy, 'Introduction' to *The Passionate Pilgrim*. The Folger Shakespeare Library Facsimile (see Texts of the Poems).

## 'Shall I Die?'

See the discussion of letters to *The Times Literary Supplement* in the Introduction, pp. 63–5.

## The Epitaphs

Chambers, E. K., *William Shakespeare: A Study of Facts and Problems* (see Background Material).

Honigmann, E. A. J., *Shakespeare: The Lost Years* (see 'The Phoenix and Turtle').

Schoenbaum, Samuel, *Shakespeare's Lives* and *A Documentary Life* (see Background Material).

# READ MORE IN PENGUIN

In every corner of the world, on every subject under the sun, Penguin represents quality and variety – the very best in publishing today.

For complete information about books available from Penguin – including Puffins, Penguin Classics and Arkana – and how to order them, write to us at the appropriate address below. Please note that for copyright reasons the selection of books varies from country to country.

**In the United Kingdom**: Please write to *Dept. EP, Penguin Books Ltd, Bath Road, Harmondsworth, West Drayton, Middlesex UB7 ODA*

**In the United States**: Please write to *Consumer Sales, Penguin Putnam Inc., P.O. Box 999, Dept. 17109, Bergenfield, New Jersey 07621-0120.* VISA and MasterCard holders call 1-800-253-6476 to order Penguin titles

**In Canada**: Please write to *Penguin Books Canada Ltd, 10 Alcorn Avenue, Suite 300, Toronto, Ontario M4V 3B2*

**In Australia**: Please write to *Penguin Books Australia Ltd, P.O. Box 257, Ringwood, Victoria 3134*

**In New Zealand**: Please write to *Penguin Books (NZ) Ltd, Private Bag 102902, North Shore Mail Centre, Auckland 10*

**In India**: Please write to *Penguin Books India Pvt Ltd, 210 Chiranjiv Tower, 43 Nehru Place, New Delhi 110 019*

**In the Netherlands**: Please write to *Penguin Books Netherlands bv, Postbus 3507, NL-1001 AH Amsterdam*

**In Germany**: Please write to *Penguin Books Deutschland GmbH, Metzlerstrasse 26, 60594 Frankfurt am Main*

**In Spain**: Please write to *Penguin Books S. A., Bravo Murillo 19, 1° B, 28015 Madrid*

**In Italy**: Please write to *Penguin Italia s.r.l., Via Benedetto Croce 2, 20094 Corsico, Milano*

**In France**: Please write to *Penguin France, Le Carré Wilson, 62 rue Benjamin Baillaud, 31500 Toulouse*

**In Japan**: Please write to *Penguin Books Japan Ltd, Kaneko Building, 2-3-25 Koraku, Bunkyo-Ku, Tokyo 112*

**In South Africa**: Please write to *Penguin Books South Africa (Pty) Ltd, Private Bag X14, Parkview, 2122 Johannesburg*